Advance Praise for

Adolescents on the Autism Spectrum

"Parents raising a teenager on the spectrum will find this clearly written and carefully documented guidebook to be full of important information and practical advice. Helping adolescents transition from the pre-teen years through puberty and on to young adulthood is a difficult task. This book will provide invaluable help and guidance to both parents and professionals. It is highly recommended."

—Bernard Rimland, Ph. D., Director of the Autism Research
Institute, Founder of the Autism Society of America, and Editor
of *Autism Research Review International*

"Earlier this year, I had the honor of reading Chantal Sicile-Kira's first book *Autism Spectrum Disorders*. With *Adolescents on the Autism Spectrum,* she has once again written a book that should be read by every parent of a child on the autism spectrum. Chantal provides useful, practical, and insightful guidance on topics ranging from transition to sexuality. These are tough topics and she handles them with tremendous wisdom, frankness, and grace. Any parent who opens this book will find a wealth of incredibly helpful information."

—Dr. Cathy Pratt, Director, Indiana Resource Center for Autism
Chair, National Autism Society of America (ASA)

Praise for
Autism Spectrum Disorders

"An essential source of information and advice in plain everyday language that can help anyone who is affected by autism today."

> —Portia Iversen, cofounder and scientific liaison, Cure Autism
> Now Foundation (CAN)

"Chantal Sicile-Kira has written an encyclopedia book with care and concern for those persons who must deal with autism. I recommend it most highly."

> —Joseph E. Morrow, Ph.D.,
> professor of psychology, California State University, Sacramento,
> and president, Applied Behavior Consultants

Adolescents
on the
Autism Spectrum

*A Parent's Guide to the
Cognitive, Social, Physical, and Transition Needs
of Teenagers with Autism Spectrum Disorders*

Chantal Sicile-Kira

A PERIGEE BOOK

THE BERKLEY PUBLISHING GROUP
Published by the Penguin Group
Penguin Group (USA) Inc.
375 Hudson Street, New York, New York 10014, USA
Penguin Group (Canada), 90 Eglinton Avenue East, Suite 700, Toronto, Ontario M4P 2Y3, Canada
(a division of Pearson Penguin Canada Inc.)
Penguin Books Ltd., 80 Strand, London WC2R 0RL, England
Penguin Group Ireland, 25 St. Stephen's Green, Dublin 2, Ireland (a division of Penguin Books Ltd.)
Penguin Group (Australia), 250 Camberwell Road, Camberwell, Victoria 3124, Australia
(a division of Pearson Australia Group Pty. Ltd.)
Penguin Books India Pvt. Ltd., 11 Community Centre, Panchsheel Park, New Delhi—110 017, India
Penguin Group (NZ), Cnr. Airborne and Rosedale Roads, Albany, Auckland 1310, New Zealand
(a division of Pearson New Zealand Ltd.)
Penguin Books (South Africa) (Pty.) Ltd., 24 Sturdee Avenue, Rosebank, Johannesburg 2196,
South Africa

Penguin Books Ltd., Registered Offices: 80 Strand, London WC2R 0RL, England

This book is an original publication of The Berkley Publishing Group.

Copyright © 2006 by Chantal Sicile-Kira.
Cover design by Dorothy Wachtenheim
Cover photo by Superstock

ISBN: 0-399-53236-3

PRINTING HISTORY
Perigee trade paperback edition / March 2006

PERIGEE is a registered trademark of Penguin Group (USA) Inc.
The "P" design is a trademark belonging to Penguin Group (USA) Inc.

This book has been cataloged by the Library of Congress

PRINTED IN THE UNITED STATES OF AMERICA

10   9   8   7   6   5   4   3   2   1

For Jeremy, Rebecca, and Daniel
and all our fellow travelers on this journey

You must be the change you wish to see in the world.

—Mahatma Gandhi

The responsibility to help current and future generations of children with autism and Asperger's syndrome develop their strengths in order to lead meaningful lives in our society belongs to all of us. That includes people on or near the spectrum, family members, teachers and anyone who comes in contact with people with autism and Asperger's syndrome.

—Stephen Shore, *Beyond the Wall*

CONTENTS

ACKNOWLEDGMENTS

ALTHOUGH the author is the one who sits down and does the writing day in and day out, a book such as this could not exist without the help, support, encouragement and expertise of many people.

Thanks go to Marian Lizzi, my editor, for convincing me to write this book in the first place. Thanks to Jim Levine, my agent, for his continual support and mentoring, and Debra Ginsberg and Douglas Kennedy (fellow authors) for their pearls of wisdom.

Once again, I am indebted to Temple Grandin, Ph.D., associate professor of Animal Science at Colorado State University and author of *Thinking in Pictures, Developing Talents*, and *Animals in Translation*, as well as Bernard Rimland, Ph.D., founder and director of the Autism Research Institute for being generous with their time and expertise. Thanks as well goes to Dr. Cathy Pratt, Director of the Indiana Resource Center for Autism, and chair of the National Autism Society of America.

Many thanks to The Schafer Report and Autism One Radio for being places where parents and professionals, no matter where they are, can daily access the latest information about autism spectrum disorders and all its complexities. Knowledge is empowerment.

No man is an island, and if wealth were judged by the number of true friends a person had, I would be considered very rich indeed. I thank all my friends on both sides of the Atlantic and on both coasts for their enduring friendship over many years. They know who they are, and I do not want to list them all for fear of inadvertently leaving someone out. However (at the risk of stirring the pot), a particular merci beaucoup goes to Rich Ellis, my oldest friend. Thanks also to my numerous siblings, parents, nieces, nephews, extended family members, in-laws, and other relatives spread out all over the globe.

Raising a child like Jeremy cannot be done alone. Thanks to the San Diego autism community for being there. Special thanks to the San Diego Chapter of the Autism Society of America, La Casa Center for Autism, San Diego Regional Center, Dr. Sylvia Mende, Dr. Schirin Sherkat, Phylinda Clark-Graham, Dr. Josh Feder and Caron Feder, and Valerie Dodd-Saraf. For your help in teaching Jeremy and believing in him, thanks to Allan Gustufson, Maureen Shull, Monique, Mark, Dana, Janine, Mary Jane Palmer, John Hooker, APE Joy, Carissa Deniell and Joe Medrano.

Last but not least, thanks to Jeremy, Rebecca, and Daniel for their patience and understanding while I was in "book mode." It was much appreciated.

FOREWORD

TEENAGE years were the worst years of my life. When my hormones turned on I began to have unrelenting panic attacks. As if this was not bad enough, then the teasing started. I was called "retard" and "tape recorder" because I always kept talking about the same thing. Walking back from class another girl called me a retard, so I hurled a book at her. This got me kicked out of school.

In my new school I had a great science teacher who motivated me to study by taking my obsessive interests and directing them into scientific projects. The right people can make all the difference for a troubled teenager. Mr. Carlock's science lab was a refuge from teasing, where the other geeky students like me found intellectual companionship. For teenagers on the high-functioning end of the autism/Asperger continuum, adults who can serve as mentors can help bring about success. A mentor could be a retired telephone engineer who teaches a teenager electronics, or the choirmaster at church who develops a teen's musical talent. Parents and teachers always need to be on the lookout for people who can be mentors.

Autism Variability

One of the difficulties in working with individuals on the autism spectrum is that they are so variable. We can vary from a high-functioning genius like Einstein to a person who has epilepsy and no speech. There are some things that are the same for all types, and other things that are very different. Problems with overly sensitive hearing, touch, or vision may occur at all functioning levels. When my hormones hit at puberty, my touch sensitivity problems worsened. Loud noise was like a dentist's drill hitting a nerve and scratchy clothes were like coarse sandpaper against my skin.

Other problems are much more variable, such as the ability to learn basic living skills. Teaching a teenager who is fully verbal and can read is totally different from teaching a teen who is nonverbal.

Chantal Sicile-Kira is the mother of a seventeen-year-old who is on the less able end of the spectrum, with very limited speech. She deals frankly with adolescent issues that many people do not want to discuss, such as sexuality. She deals with these issues in a practical, straightforward manner.

Clues from Brain Research

Brain research provides information that helps to explain why the autism/Asperger spectrum is so variable. Dr. Eric Courchesne in San Diego and Dr. Nancy Minshew in Pittsburgh both explain that autism is a disorder of the connections between different brain systems. I like to visualize the brain as a big corporate office building with many different departments such as the CEO's office (frontal cortex), finance department, sales department, information technology department, and so on. The local departments may be working fine, but some connections *between* departments may be missing. The connections that are hooked up are highly variable. This may explain why one autistic person is a math savant and another remains nonverbal.

I cannot emphasize enough the importance of working with an individual's strengths and preferred way of learning. Some are visual learners, while others are auditory learners. People with severe visual processing challenges who see distorted colors and shapes may learn better with their ears. Individuals like me will learn better visually. (I still have problems hearing hard consonant sounds.) Some nonverbal individuals will learn best by touch because their vision is scrambled and their ears are like a bad mobile phone connection that fades in and out.

The Need for
Specific Information

Teens of all levels of functioning on the spectrum do not handle vague information well. Dr. Minshew discovered that the normal brain tends to leave out the details, whereas the autistic brain processes all the details but fails to comprehend a concept. This is true at all levels of functioning. The statement "Get ready for school" is too vague. Instead it's much better to say, "Make sure you have your lunch, books, and homework in your backpack before the school bus arrives." Chantal provides the same level of detail for all of the new things a teen has to learn at puberty.

This book provides a wealth of sources of information on just about everything a parent or teacher will need. It provides a balanced approach to different types of treatments. Parents sometimes make the mistake of being too single-minded on one form of treatment. If one method does not work, you should try something else.

The book also contains a great section on sibling and family issues. Both the family and the siblings need to have some time away from autism to pursue their own interests. The respite will help you to be a better parent. My mother had her theater group, which she acted with. This helped her keep going.

—Temple Grandin, Ph.D.
    Author of *Thinking in Pictures, Developing Talents*
    and *Animals in Translation*
    Associate professor at Colorado State University
    Founder and president of Grandin Livestock
    Handling Systems, Inc.

AUTHOR'S NOTE

I have used the terms "the autism spectrum," "the spectrum," and "autism spectrum disorders" (ASDs) throughout this book to mean autism, pervasive developmental disorder (PDD), and Asperger's Syndrome. When speaking specifically about people with Asperger's Syndrome I have used the term Asperger's or AS.

I've used the term "tween" to refer to children in the preteen years, more specifically between the ages of nine and twelve. As three out of four people with an ASD are male, I have most often used the pronoun "he." I would ask the reader not to be put off by the third-person construction as in "the individual" or "the person."

For more information about the author visit her website:
www.chantalsicile-kira.com

INTRODUCTION

TWO years ago, my son Jeremy was fifteen, attending a class for the severely handicapped and the annual review of his Individualized Education Program (IEP) had just taken place. Jeremy's classroom teacher, aide, and speech therapist had just started using the Rapid Prompting Method (RPM) to teach my son. The IEP meeting notes read, "Jeremy's ability to recognize letters has been sporadic," and went on to document my request that Jeremy participate in a mainstream core class at his high school, an idea that was not supported by the district-paid autism behavior specialist. Nonetheless, the team agreed to do so for a trial period. As we were all getting ready to leave at the end of the meeting, the autism behavior specialist turned to me and said, "You never give up, do you?" My reply to her was, "Give up? I'm his mother. Why would I give up on my own child?"

*   *   *

As our children grow and change, so do our expectations, hopes, and dreams. For some, who had hoped for a "recovery" or a "cure" comes the slow realization that for their child, there may be none. For others, there may be the realization that although their child is growing and changing, their expectations and treatment of their child has not. For all parents, there is the realization that they must somehow balance acceptance of their child for who he or she is, while continuing to provide as much support as they can at home and at school to provide them with the skills they need to live as independent and fulfilling a life as possible.

Adolescence is a difficult time of life for everyone. Bodies are changing, hormones are raging, moods are swinging. Both teenagers and parents are in a state of flux. The adolescents on the less able end of the autism spectrum are dealing with their changing bodies and feelings they may not understand. For the more able teens, there is the added difficulty of trying to navigate in a social world where their peers are at a different emotional level. For parents, there is much worry and concern, and there is the need to inform their teenagers and to arm them with the skills they need in an environment that is not always supportive of their differences.

Most parents will find it hard, after so many years of advocating for their child in the educational system, to continue to do so. Our children are older, and so are we, and we are tired. The battles are harder at the middle school and high school level because the powers that be often do not have the same expectations for learning as when our children were younger. Often, the view is if he hasn't "gotten it" by now, he never will, so they are less willing to put resources into this age group. However, it's vital for you to keep in mind that the human brain is pliable, and it is never too late to teach someone new skills or try biomedical interventions or traditional medications that may be helpful in certain cases. Don't allow anyone to tell you to lose hope or write off your teen's potential to learn, cope and progress.

In the year following the publication of my first book, *Autism Spectrum Disorders* (recipient of the 2005 Autism Society of America's Outstanding Literary Work of the Year Award), I was invited to different parts of the country to speak about adolescent issues, including the transition from school to work. Temple Grandin and Stephen Shore, both successful professionals who themselves are on the spectrum, talked to me on numerous occasions about their concern that not enough was being done to prepare the more able teenagers for a successful and independent adulthood. At the same time, my son Jeremy was attending high school, and I realized that although legally he should be preparing for transition, there seemed to be a lack of knowledge and follow through about how to go about doing that for someone as impacted by autism as he is. This led to much research and soul searching, and the realization that adolescence is a unique and crucial stage in a person's development, as important as the early intervention years—yet not enough practical information was readily available to parents (or to educators) on how to teach these teens of all functioning levels or academic abilities—in all the areas important to all adolescents.

The most important thing a parent can do is to become empowered with the knowledge that can help their teenager. For this reason, this book covers areas such as puberty and hygiene as well as the more difficult topic of sexuality. The middle and high school years are discussed, as well as transition planning, with an overview of the various options currently available for adults after high school. Family life is greatly impacted by autism, and those concerns are also addressed. Although our teenagers are no longer little, there are still many effective treatments, therapies, and strategies that can be useful to them. I've provided an analysis of what is currently known and available.

Not every idea suggested in these pages will be right for every family or individual, as every situation is unique, and there is such a wide variability among the functioning and academic levels of teens on the different ends of the spectrum and in between. Yet with every topic discussed, I have included suggested books, websites and other resources to help you in your quest for useful information for your particular need. As in my first book, *Autism Spectrum Disorders,* I have included "Food for Thought" pieces written by authors on the spectrum as well as other experts.

This book is written not only as a guidebook but also as a call to action, in the hopes of inspiring parents, professionals, and people on the autism spectrum to join together and create options for transition to real life for everyone on the spectrum. They are counting on us.

*   *   *

Last year, Jeremy's annual review included a WAIT II assessment by his special education teacher that read: "Jeremy was tested in two sections in English. . . . It was not until he reached the high school level did he have trouble answering questions. Words such as negotiate, treacherous, and poise were missed on the test. However, these sections showed us something very important: Jeremy's ability to understand courses at the high school level. With the help of a staff member attending, the case manager believes that Jeremy can learn and will improve his knowledge through courses offered to the general education students. . . . Jeremy can handle language at a high school level and if Jeremy does not know he can be easily taught."

How could one short year show such a difference? The answer is that I never gave up on Jeremy. I never stopped believing in him and searching for new ways to help him. I found a way, then worked hard to teach Jeremy. After that, it was my son who convinced everyone else that he had potential, that he could learn. The people who work with him and teach him saw his capability and believed in him.

It takes a village to raise a child, and as parents we need a village of individuals—teachers, instructional assistants, speech therapists, occupational therapists, community members, and those able individuals on the spectrum—to believe in our children and help them grow and prepare for a future of interesting possibilities.

But as a parent, you need to take the first step—no matter how small—and never give up.

1

Autism Spectrum Disorders and How They Affect Adolescents

Puberty arrived when I was fourteen, and nerve attacks accompanied it. I started living in a constant state of stage fright, the way you feel before your first big job interview or public speaking engagement. But in my case, anxiety seized me for no good reason. Many people with autism find that the symptoms worsen at puberty. When my anxiety went away, it was replaced with bouts of colitis or terrible headaches. My nervous system was constantly under stress. I was like a frightened animal, and every little thing triggered a fear reaction.
—TEMPLE GRANDIN, *Thinking in Pictures*

WHEN my son Jeremy hit puberty, he started emptying all the bookcases in our house. "He's redecorating again," my husband would say. I called it "doing a Martha Stewart." Every day for two years he did this. Behavioral intervention didn't help. What he learned was to empty the bookshelves when we were not in the same room. Each day, we were spending one or two hours prompting and supervising him while he put the books back. He didn't seem to mind doing it. As soon as the Afternoon Angel would leave and he had "free time," he would go at emptying the bookshelves all over again. We couldn't supervise him constantly, and it was frustrating for his sister as well as for us. Finally, we packed away all our books, except for one bookshelf downstairs and one in his room. He kept emptying these, over and over. We couldn't constantly redirect him. We were so desperate, we even tried medication, yet it only made it worse. He became more compulsive about getting to those bookshelves.

Then one day, it just stopped. Nothing had changed in our family routine; Jeremy just stopped emptying the bookcase and went back to his usual favorite activities. Was it his hormones? Was he going through some physiological change that he and we couldn't understand? Did he finally find what he was looking for? We'll never know. All I know is that we were happy to have our old Jeremy back and to be able to put our books back in the house, within our reach. And we were glad Jeremy had weathered whatever that storm was.

Autism Spectrum Disorders: A Brief Overview

Like adolescence itself, the conditions that make up the autism spectrum is a fascinating phenomenon like no other, with unique challenges, setbacks, and steps forward, and with great variability between individuals. Together, adolescence and autism can form a volatile mix. For a parent, it is hard to comprehend that the growing person with the adult body odor who is sprouting both hair and pimples was once the sweet-smelling baby you held in your arms. Now, as a teenager your child is going through what all adolescents go through, and he needs some space. On one hand you want to protect him from the dangers of the world, yet you know you must allow him the freedom to experience life, give him choices and decisions to make, be less controlling yet always supportive. Sometimes, it will seem as if your child is now much more noncompliant—welcome to adolescence!

This first chapter is dedicated to explaining how adolescence and puberty affect those on the autism spectrum. The strategies for addressing the challenges faced by our growing children of various functioning levels will be discussed in the following chapters. As some children with Asperger's Syndrome (AS) are not diagnosed until they are nine or ten years old, or even older, some parents reading this book may be new to the spectrum. For their benefit, as well as for new educators and professionals to the field, this chapter will begin with a simple review of some facts about autism spectrum disorders (ASDs) in general. Knowledgeable readers may wish to skip to the next section, Challenges Faced by Adolescents on the Spectrum, on page 12.

THE FACTS ABOUT AUTISM

Autism spectrum disorders are considered to be the result of a neurological disorder that affects the functioning of the brain and are some of the most common developmental disabilities. It is generally accepted in the scientific community that ASDs are the result of an environmental influence (pre-and/or postnatal) on a genetic predisposition. Currently, there is no medical test to diagnose ASDs. A diagnosis is based on behavioral characteristics after other causes have been ruled out. Though the different ASDs may vary in the number and intensity of the behavioral symptoms they share, currently a diagnosis is still based on impairments in these three characteristics: social relationships, social communication, and imaginative thought.

These characteristics can be present in a wide variety of combinations. Two people diagnosed with the same label can have varying skills, deficits, and aptitudes. It is important to note that there is a huge variability between those on one end of the spectrum to the other. One of them could be severely incapacitated, nonverbal and needing help in all areas of daily living, while the other might appear only to be a bit odd and lacking in social graces while being intellectually gifted and verbally astute. There is no standard type or typical person with an ASD, just as there is no standard type of nonautistic or neurotypical individual. Thus, people with ASDs present a wide spectrum of abilities. Autism is considered a spectrum, meaning that symptoms can vary from very severe (Kanner type) to mild (Asperger type).

THE HISTORY OF AUTISM

In the early 1940s both Leo Kanner and Hans Asperger, pioneers in the field of autism, used these terms in their publications (independently of each other), describing children with the characteristics we recognize today as being autistic; hence the label autism was born. Both professionals described children who developed special interests, but also had deficits in the areas of communication and social interaction. Kanner's description was of children with severe autism, with the conclusion that it was a disastrous condition to have. Asperger's description was of more able children, and he felt that there might be some positive features to autism that could lead to great achievements as an adult. For thirty years, Kanner's description became the most widely recognized.

THE STATISTICS

ASDs are four times more prevalent in males than females and typically appear during the first three years of life. At time of writing, it is estimated by the Centers for Disease Control and Prevention that autism affects 1 in 166 individuals. According to data complied by the Autism Research Institute, regressive or late-onset autism cases (in which babies develop normally and regress between the ages of eighteen months and two years) currently outnumber early-onset cases by about five to one (early-onset refers to babies who never developed at a normal pace). This is in contrast to the 1950s, 1960s, and 1970s where late-onset cases were almost unheard of.

THE THREE SYMPTOM AREAS THAT CHARACTERIZE AUTISM SPECTRUM DISORDERS

As mentioned earlier, there are three basic areas of observable symptoms that characterize ASDs. Some of the symptoms may be mild, others more obvious. It is the number and severity of these symptoms that leads to concerns on the part of the parent or the professional. These areas are:

- **Difficulties with social relationships:** An individual may not use or understand nonverbal behavior or develop peer relationships that are appropriate to his developmental level or age group. The person may not understand body language or facial expressions, or may appear aloof and indifferent to other people.

- **Difficulties in communication:** There may be a total lack of or delay in the development of speech (with no attempts to communicate by gestures). The individual does not sustain or initiate conversation, or uses language in a stereotyped and repetitive manner. Those who are verbal may have difficulties understanding colloquial language and may understand only the literal meaning of language.

- **Obsessive or inappropriate attachment to objects or rituals:** An individual may have an all-encompassing, intense preoccupation with one interest or topic or have inflexible, nonfunctional rituals or routines. Repetitive motor mannerisms such as hand flapping or spinning of objects may be observed. Often there is a lack of make-believe or social imitative play when little.

Diagnostic and Statistical Manual of Mental Disorders (DSM-IV)

This medical diagnostic handbook, currently in its fourth edition, is internationally used and recognized. When the *DSM* was revised in 1994, some changes were made. Previously, the category of pervasive developmental disorders (PDD), which includes autism, was coded or classified with other long-term stable disorders that have a poor prognosis. Now PDD has been classified with more transient, temporary, and episodic clinical disorders. This is a positive move that reflects what current research is now showing: that there is a possibility of improvement with intervention, and that symptoms can vary in intensity. Interestingly, although difficulties in sensory processing are not considered a diagnostic criteria for ASD's, individuals on the spectrum who write about their life experiences discuss at length the challenges they face in this area.

GETTING DIAGNOSED AS A PRETEEN OR ADOLESCENT

Teenagers on the less able end of the spectrum will most likely have been diagnosed before reaching the preteen or adolescent years. However, often those with Asperger's are not diagnosed until they get to second grade, or even around the age of nine or ten in fourth grade. This is because until then, they are managing with the schoolwork and perhaps their social skills do not appear to be much different from their peers. When schoolwork starts getting more complex, they may continue to do well academically on a day-to-day basis. However, it may become apparent, when they are given longer projects to complete at home, that they are having a rough time with organizing their work on a timeline, note taking, organizing, and other skills needed as they progress through the school system. Also, as the nature of social relationships and communication change as a neurotypical child progresses, the AS child does not mature at the same rate socially and emotionally, which raises concerns.

There are cases of individuals who do not get diagnosed until the teen years or even as young adults. According to Tony Attwood, a leading authority on Asperger's Syndrome, many young adults with AS report intense feelings of anxiety, and sometimes the person may develop panic attacks or compulsive behaviors. When a person seeks treatment for those issues, the medical professional involved may be the first one to diagnose AS.

For more information on the diagnostic criteria for Asperger's Syndrome, read *Asperger's Syndrome: A Guide for Parents and Professionals,* by Tony Attwood.

THE IMPORTANCE OF AN ACCURATE
DIAGNOSIS

If your teen or tween does not have a diagnosis of an autism spectrum disorder and yet you have concerns, it is important that you consult with a medical professional who is experienced in diagnosing ASDs, including Asperger's Syndrome. To find the right professionals in your area, contact your local chapter of the Autism Society of America (ASA). They will be able to give you the names of professionals in your area and put you in contact with parents of children with similar ability levels.

Some parents feel that a diagnosis is not important. If the tween or teen is doing well in all areas of life, is happy, and does not appear to need any extra support, then that may be the case. However, a diagnosis is extremely helpful for adolescents who are falling between the cracks, who are doing well in some areas, but not in others. The diagnosis in and of itself will not change anything, but will help parents and educators know what supports or strategies can help in the areas that the teen appears to be having difficulties. Without the diagnosis, it may be harder to access the services and supports the student needs, whether it be from school or other agencies who can offer services to help.

Another important consideration is that if your child has a diagnosis before the age of eighteen, he may qualify for services—if and when needed—from various government agencies. After the age of eighteen, it may be harder to qualify for some services and supports. It is important to keep in mind that many on the more able end of the spectrum may do well at school, then find themselves with no options when high school ends, fall into depression, and enter the mental health system. With the diagnosis of an ASD, such a person may have access to services that could help prevent this type of outcome, including help and support finding employment or getting into college.

In the past, parents were often hesitant about applying a label because they felt that the label of autism was permanent and signified that there was no hope for that person. This should no longer be the case. As mentioned earlier, since 1994, ASDs are classified as pervasive developmental disorders, reflecting the medical profession's belief that intervention can lead to improvement and, in some cases, recovery.

Be aware also that over time, the diagnostic criteria change, and the opinion of the experts as to what those criteria should be changes as well. So although a diagnosis is helpful and necessary to access services, as a parent you would do better to focus on the *behavioral characteristics,* which tell you more about the child and how to help him, than to get hung up on the diagnosis and what it means.

Sometimes it may take a long while for a formal diagnosis to be reached. You may need the diagnosis to access services from government agencies; however, as a parent there are things you can be doing to help your teen while you are waiting. This is also a good time to be researching your options.

Keep in mind that each person is unique, whether he or she has an ASD or not, as Jerry Newport (an adult with Asperger's) reminds us with the title of his book: *Your Life Is Not a Label.*

For more information about ASDs in general as well as the possible causes, I refer readers to my first book, *Autism Spectrum Disorders: The Complete Guide to Understanding Autism, Asperger's Syndrome, Pervasive Developmental Disorder, and Other ASDs.*

Challenges Faced by Adolescents on the Autism Spectrum

Some of the challenges faced by tweens and teens with autism or Asperger's are the same ones they faced when they were younger. Some are worse or different—some because of a change in environment and expectations, or because of the adolescent's changing body, and others because neurotypical teenage behavior changes so much from elementary school that it widens the gap between those that are on the spectrum and those that are not. In this section, the challenges these tweens and teens on the spectrum face will be described in some detail.

FOOD FOR THOUGHT

On Remembering They're Not Little Anymore

Living with your child, you don't see the changes bit by bit as they happen, especially when it is your firstborn. One day, I looked at my son Jeremy and realized he was up to my shoulder, and the following week, practically up to my chin. It just didn't seem possible. I bent down to brush something off his shoe, and noticed the hair on his legs was thicker. When he talked and sang, his voice was cracking.

Jeremy's behavior started to change, too. He had always been a very compliant child; his noncompliance was basically limited to going floppy. We spent years trying to teach him to say "no" and to mean it. So I was actually thrilled when at about fourteen he started to get a bit uppity with us. He didn't want to do what we wanted him to do anymore. He didn't comply as usual; he would refuse to turn off the TV or to go to bed. He would refuse to sit down to eat dinner with us, and then sneak downstairs to get into the refrigerator and cupboard when he knew we were occupied elsewhere in the house.

Then he took down all the surfing and skateboarding posters in his room that his sister Rebecca had helped pick out and that he had approved of to decorate his room. So we got all the posters together that we had from different sporting events and asked him to choose what he wanted to put up. He chose only one—a big poster of the San Diego Chargers cheerleaders in bathing suits. He is, first and foremost, a male teenager.

We realized he was changing, and we had to change, too. When your teenager has little spontaneous communication, it is hard to remember to ask his opinion and to give him choices as often as possible. We realized that although he still needed a routine, he also needed to have more say over his schedule; he needed to choose when he would do what. We needed to remember to give him more control over his life.

It is important to note that for each behavior or symptom observed, there could be a few possible causes, leading to different treatment strategies. If a teen throws off his clothes, is it because the texture is bothering his skin (a sensory integration problem) or because he is angry about something (an emotional issue)? Take careful and detailed notes of these situations when they occur and look for patterns (for example, does he remove his clothes whenever there are clothing tags attached, or is it whenever he has been told he cannot do something?). Is a teen crying because he is in pain from intestinal problems or is he having a temper tantrum? All the behaviors exhibited need to be analyzed carefully, and for tweens or teens, especially those unable to communicate effectively about their bodies and themselves, it is particularly important to remember that behavior is a form of communication. It is also important to keep in mind the wide range from one end of the spectrum to another. Sensory processing and social communication are areas that are difficult for all on the spectrum, whereas some are academically challenged and others are intellectually gifted. Although they may share the same overall condition, their strengths and weaknesses will vary and this must be taken into account when individualizing strategies to help them thrive.

Health Concerns

Our bodies are our engines that keep us going and feed our brains. If our bodies aren't running properly, we are not going to get where we need to be. For this reason, your teen's physical health should be every parent's first area of focus.

THE BRAIN/GUT CONNECTION:
WE ARE WHAT WE DIGEST

Many children diagnosed with autism spectrum disorders over the past decade also have compromised immune systems or digestive challenges and food or other types of allergies. However, there are also adults such as Donna Williams and teenagers such as Luke Jackson who describe a difference in how they feel and cope when on particular diets. If their bodies cannot handle certain foods (such as gluten, casein) or their bodies are not absorbing nutrients properly, then we end up with, as author Jaquelyn McCandless, M.D., so aptly put it in the title of her book, *Children with Starving Brains*.

We are what we eat and this is not particular just to people on the spectrum. Every day in the media we hear about the importance of good diets and healthy eating habits, and why certain cultures with certain diets have less of a specific health problem related to what they eat. Eating a diet of processed food with additives such as food dyes, perservatives, added sugars, and artificial coloring does affect the behaviors of some individuals.

Observing your tween or teen's eating patterns and their subsequent behaviors can give you a clue as to whether or not diet is a factor. Is your teen eating only certain foods because of sensory issues with textures, or has he associated certain foods with a particular pain or upset in his body? Does your daughter have abnormal bowel movements, such as chronic constipation or diarrhea? Does your tween or teen look sickly and pale? Is he allergy prone or illness prone? Does your noncommunicative son have tantrums for no apparent reason? Perhaps he is having stomach or digestive pain that he is unable to communicate to you. Perhaps you have had testing done by a regular doctor and a regular lab, but unless they knew what to look for, they might not find anything.

With teens on the autism spectrum with good communication skills, a parent can usually find out more about what is going on in this area. For those less communicative, charting behaviors and eating patterns can tell you much about whether or not this is an area to investigate. Whether your teen is just a picky eater or there are more serious digestive concerns, his absorption of proper nutrients needs to be looked at.

SEIZURES

During puberty, about one out of every four autistic individuals will experience seizures. Although the exact reason is not known, this seizure activity may be due to hormonal changes in the body. Sometimes the seizures are noticeable. For many the seizures are small and subclinical and are typically not detected by casual observation. Some signs that a teen or tween may be experiencing subclinical seizures include:

• making little or no academic gains after doing well during childhood and preteen years

• losing some behavioral and/or cognitive gains

• exhibiting behavior problems such as self-injury, aggression, and severe tantruming

An EEG may show seizure activity. However, if the EEG does not detect abnormal brain wave activity during the testing, this does not necessarily mean that the person is not having seizures. To increase the likelihood of detecting subclinical seizures, it is best to have the person assessed with an EEG for twenty-four to forty-eight hours. The majority of autistic individuals do not have seizures during puberty. However, parents need to be aware of the fact that if left untreated, seizures may be harmful.

DEPRESSION

Depression can be hard to identify in individuals on the autism spectrum who are noncommunicative. Behaviors may escalate, or individuals may "shut down," requiring us to rely on our interpretation of their behaviors and the environment around them to try to decipher what they mean. A high proportion of individuals with Asperger's Syndrome are diagnosed with depression during the teen years, and some are on antidepressants. It is during the teen years that many of them realize how different they are from their peers and experience difficulty trying to fit in. Also, some AS teens tend to blame themselves if something negative happens and feel that they are doomed to repeat that same failure again.

The risk of depression should be taken seriously, as research has shown that there is a higher incidence of depression or manic depression in families with a child on the autism spectrum, perhaps due to a biological predisposition. It is important that a person who is depressed be treated by a professional who is knowledgeable about the condition. It is important for parents to do their homework and research all available options for treatment, including nontraditional approaches. Different possible treatments are discussed in chapter 6.

HYGIENE PROBLEMS

Good hygiene is also a precursor to good health, and our teens on the spectrum need assistance in this area. Some tweens and teens have a difficult time dealing with the usual body changes (growth of body hair, growing body) associated with normal puberty. This may be due to a dislike of change in general and the unpredictability of these transformations. Many do not understand what is happening to their bodies, and why they feel different when the hormones start kicking in.

Many teens on the spectrum have sensitivity issues that can affect developing good hygiene. Some may not tolerate the smell or textures of certain soaps and shampoos. Others may have sensitive scalps and therefore may not want to wash their hair. Others may have difficulty with brushing teeth, another sensitive area. Hygiene and grooming needs will be explored further in chapter 3.

PRECOCIOUS PUBERTY

A little known but intriguing fact is that precocious puberty—where children enter into puberty at an earlier age than their peers—has been estimated to be twenty times higher in children with neurodevelopment disabilities. It has been found that families of children with autism have higher testosterone than family member controls of nonautistic children. The testosterone is prenatal and can be considered a risk factor. The signs a parent might see in precocious development include: pubic hair growth; more hair growth on back, under arms, on the face; genital development, breast development, increased touching and rubbing of genitals, and more aggressive behavior. Children may have increased height and advanced bone plate growth. If a parent has any concerns in this area, they should discuss this with the trusted medical professional who is treating their child and share the above statistic with him or her.

TOILETING ISSUES

This may still be a concern for a few autistic teens, particularly those with motor-control issues, those supersensitive to the environment around them (too bright, too noisy), and those who get lost in their own world and don't "feel" the urge to go until it is too late. Others may not have mastered the art of wiping themselves when needed. A few individuals may still be into "feces art" at this age.

Toileting issues have nothing to do with intelligence. Donna Williams, a very intelligent, articulate, and creative woman with autism, describes how when she is unwell due to food reactions, she will be unable to move or remember to walk to the bathroom to use it.

MASTURBATION

Your child may have discovered masturbation long before the teen or tween years. However, this is an area that can become problematic during adolescence. Masturbation in and of itself is a normal activity enjoyed by many on and off the autism spectrum; it becomes a problem only when it is not practiced in private, or when it turns into an obsession. For some teens on the spectrum, there may be a lack of inhibition and a lack of understanding or caring about the fact that the behavior is socially inappropriate when around others. Also, many children with autism spend (let's face it) time they may consider tedious and dull sitting in special education classrooms and at home. They may find that masturbation is a good way to pass a boring moment if they are not otherwise occupied. For others who suffer from obsessive-compulsive behaviors, masturbation may become a new obsession. We'll look at ways of handling this awkward problem in chapter 3.

SEXUALITY

Again, this is an area that is of normal human interest for teenagers, yet can be problematic if the teen does not understand about the birds and the bees, sexual feelings and why we have them, appropriate and inappropriate touching, as well as all the religious, ethical, philosophical, and even legal questions involved in this area. We'll look at this in more detail in chapter 3.

Sensory and Motor Skill Issues

We know from research as well as anecdotal accounts that everyone on the autism spectrum experiences some form of sensory issue, regardless of the apparent ability level of the individual. I cannot overstate the importance of our senses in how we learn and how we interpret our environment. This, in turn affects our behaviors, which are also a form of communication. It is therefore important when analyzing a person's behavior to take careful note of environmental factors that may be affecting that behavior (such as noise, light, strong smells).

Sensory integration difficulties and sensory processing challenges are not required symptoms for a diagnosis of an autism spectrum disorder yet every book written by a person on the spectrum contains passages, if not chapters, that describe at length their challenges in this area. Temple Grandin, Donna Williams, Stephen Shore, Luke

Jackson, Tito Mukhopadhyay, and Liane Willey have all described, in their books, how much they are affected by these issues. In *Aquamarine Blue: Personal Stories of College Students with Autism*, edited by Dawn Prince-Hughes, sensory processing difficulties are discussed by the various authors as part of their college experience.

Many parents will attest to how their children on the spectrum are challenged by some or all of their senses. Research shows us that sensory issues are common to everyone on the autism spectrum, no matter what their functioning level, but in different ways. These challenges range from mere discomfort to very painful situations, and can result in a sensory overload and total shutdown. This is very important for parents to know, because often in early intervention we are addressing the behaviors of the children without looking at the underlying causes. Sometimes simply addressing the sensory issues by removing the sensations that are creating the overload, and desensitizing the children over time to their sensitivities, can make a world of difference in their comfort level and ability to sit still, listen, and learn.

On another note, some of the sensory differences between a person on the autism spectrum and someone who is neurotypical can be seen as positive attributes. Temple Grandin, in the book she wrote with Catherine Johnson, *Animals in Translation*, describes how people with autism tend to see the details in everything, whereas neurotypicals see the big picture. Temple describes how a teenager with autism will notice every single screw on a wall that he is passing and will stop to look at each one. This kind of attention to detail can be a positive attribute for certain careers.

Donna Williams, a talented and highly intelligent autistic woman who has written memoirs about her life, describes the sensory challenges and perceptual difficulties that challenge many autistic people and the strategies for tackling them. In *Autism: An Inside-Out Approach*, Williams says that parents and professionals need an understanding of how they might be able to identify different types of underlying problems so they can work with the causes and not just the symptoms. Williams discusses how the three recognized traits of

FOOD FOR THOUGHT

What Does Autism Mean?

I am diagnosed as having "autism." If you asked me what that word means, I would tell you that for me it is about having trouble with connections. I would tell you that having trouble with CONNECTIONS also causes me to have trouble with TOLERANCE and trouble with CONTROL. The word "autism" doesn't tell anyone this, any more so than the labels of some of its "cousins." People with difficulties like mine are not meant to be capable of being so intentionally self-expressive, so insightful, so aware and certainly, throughout large chunks of my life, I, too, appeared to be none of these things. Yet, when I write I am all of these things. This is because my writing, unlike speaking, is (both fortunately and unfortunately) a largely automatic skill so I don't have to be aware of what I'm unknowingly aware of. If it is in there, it just comes out. . . . Some people call these automatic, almost unconscious, skills, "savant" skills. I call them useful.

—Donna Williams, *Autism: An Inside-Out Approach*

autism—impairment in social interaction, communication disorder, and what Williams calls bizarre behaviors—are a result of three basic types of problems:

• Problems of control: compulsion, obsession, and acute anxiety. These are about being **able to respond with intention** to the world and/or oneself.

• Problems of tolerance: sensory hypersensitivity, emotional hypersensitivity. These are about being **able to stand the world** and/or oneself.

• Problems of connection: attention problems, perceptual problems, systems integration problems, and left-right-hemisphere integration problems. These are about being **able to make sense of the world** and/or oneself.

SENSORY PROCESSING DISORDER

There are different types of sensory issues, but all of them are related in one way or another to sensory integration dysfunction. According to Carol Stock Kranowitz, M.A., author of *The Out-of-Sync Child: Recognizing and Coping with Sensory Processing Disorder,* sensory processing disorder (or sensory integration disorder) is the inability to process information received through the senses. It can mean that a person is oversensitive or undersensitive to a stimulation in one or more of his senses and will seek out more or less stimulation in that sense to compensate.

Although sensory issues are a common characteristic of people on the autism spectrum, they are not considered a defining criterion for diagnosis. Over the past decade more attention has been paid to sensory issues in children. However, less is mentioned about the sensory challenges faced by adolescents on the spectrum. This is in part because many of the sensory issues disappear or decrease in some individuals after proper treatment, and in part because in many school districts, these issues are not given serious consideration when a child reaches junior high school.

It is important that parents have a clear understanding of how sensory issues may be affecting their child and take this into consideration when making plans for the student's educational program and employment opportunities, as well as when providing a relaxing home environment. As the parent or caretaker, you have a better idea of your youth's sensory challenges, and it will most likely be up to you to inform the school of your concerns and how it could affect him at school and impact his learning.

Sensory processing disorder can affect any, if not all, of seven sensory areas.

Vestibular: The vestibular system provides us with information about where our heads and bodies are in relation to the surface of the earth. This sense has to do with balance. The receptors for vestibular sensations are in the inner ear, and they register sensory messages about balance and movement from the neck, eyes and body. The receptors are stimulated by movement and gravity and tell us about direction, speed of movement, and whether or not it is us or our surroundings that are moving. What goes on in the vestibular system provides the framework for the other aspects of our experience, and the other types of sensation are processed in reference to this.

A person with vestibular dysfunction has difficulties in integrating information about movement, balance, space, and gravity. This can cause a person to be oversensitive or undersensitive to movement, or a combination of both. Someone with vestibular hypersensitivity cannot regulate movement sensations, making the person intolerant of movement. A person may appear uncoordinated and awkward, bumping into furniture, losing her balance easily. A person with vestibular hyposensitivity may have an increased tolerance of movement and needs a lot of vigorous activity or may seek to resist gravity by hanging their head over the edge of the bed.

Proprioceptive: The proprioceptive system tells us about our body position, where a certain body part is, and how it is moving. This is the "position sense," and its function is to increase body awareness and to contribute to motor control and motor planning. Receptors for this sense are in the muscles, joints, ligaments, tendons, and connective tissue and are stimulated by movement and gravity.

A person with a proprioceptive dysfunction lacks instinctive knowledge of subconscious sensations about the position and movement of his head and limbs. Usually proprioceptive dysfunction is accompanied by problems with the vestibular and/or tactile senses. The person has difficulties with controlling or monitoring his fine and/or gross motor skills so motor planning is very difficult, leading to clumsiness and frustration.

Touch: The tactile system is a vast sensory system that plays a major role in determining physical, mental, and emotional mental health. It gives us information needed for motor planning, body awareness, and visual perception, and also for academic learning, emotional security, and social skills. Receptors for this sense are in our skin from head to toe and are activated by touch sensations of pressure, movement, temperature, vibration, and pain. We are always passively being touched by something (clothes, the air around us) or actively touching something (objects we are using, other people).

The tactile sense is made up of two components: the protective system (that alerts us to potential harmful stimuli) and the discriminative system (that tells us about the qualities of the objects around us, (such as sharp, dull, hot, cold, smooth, rough). As a baby grows and children mature, the discriminative role should take more precedent over the protective or defensive role.

Tactile dysfunction is the inefficient processing in the central nervous system of sensations perceived through the skin, and a person may be defensive to touch, underresponsive to touch, or have poor tactile discrimination.

Sight: Vision is a complex process and should not be confused with eyesight. Healthy eyes and good eyesight (the basic ability to see the big letters on the wall chart at the optometrist's office) are a prerequisite for vision. Eyesight contributes to our basic visual skills called ocular motor (eye movement) skills. Vision enables us to identify sights, to anticipate what is coming at us, and to prepare for a response. Vision provides us information about the objects and persons around us and helps us define the boundaries as we move around. The vestibular system has a huge impact on ocular motor skills, which include fixation, tracking, focusing, and binocular vision. The vestibular system also has a profound effect on visual processing, including spatial awareness.

A person with vestibular dysfunction usually has problems with visual-spatial processing as well as basic eye motor skills. Because the brain is not effectively integrating sensations from the eyes and the body, reading, writing, and arithmetic may be challenging. Activities involving eye-hand coordination may be a real challenge, and the person may be overwhelmed by people and objects moving around him.

Hearing: The auditory system works with the vestibular system to process sensations of sound and movement. They are closely entwined because they both begin to be processed in the receptors of the ear. The receptors located in the inner ear for the auditory system are stimulated by both air and sound waves. Hearing is the ability to receive sounds, and people are either born being able to hear or not; you can't learn it. Comprehension—understanding the sounds we hear—is an acquired skill. This skill requires that we integrate vestibular sensations and learn to interact purposefully in the environment. This enables us to develop sophisticated auditory processing skills that include auditory discrimination between sounds and auditory discrimination between sounds in the foreground and in the background. Most important, with sophisticated auditory processing skills comes the understanding of language.

A person with poor auditory language processing may have difficulty detecting likenesses and differences in words and may have trouble attending to someone's voice without being distracted by background noise. She may have trouble talking or talking well.

Smell: The olfactory system provides information about different types of smell through receptors located in the nasal structure and is closely intertwined with the taste (gustatory) system. A person who is oversensitive to smells may smell odors strongly that others can barely detect and will avoid foods, objects, persons, or places with odors that they object to that may seem innocuous to others. Someone who is undersensitive may not notice or ignore odors that are unpleasant to others, such as dirty diapers, and may sniff food, objects, and people.

Taste: The gustatory system gives information about the different types of taste through receptors located on the tongue and is closely associated with the smell (olfactory) system. An individual with an oversensitive taste system may strongly object to certain textures and temperatures of food and may gag when he eats. The person who is undersensitive may lick or taste inedible objects and may prefer foods that are very spicy or very hot.

For more information on sensory processing disorder, read *The Out-of-Sync Child: Recognizing and Coping with Sensory Processing Disorder,* by Carol Stock Kranowitz.

Specific Challenges in Sensory Issues for Teenagers

Individuals may have intense and often painful physical reactions to certain sensory experiences, and may have emotional difficulties related to their sensory processing. This is true for all on the autism spectrum, no matter their functioning or academic level. Most neurotypicals are able to regulate their reactions by paying attention to the sensory messages that are important to them and ignoring the others. Those on the spectrum are unable to do so naturally. This becomes more of a challenge as they reach the tween and teen years because of the change in their environment at school.

In elementary school, children usually stay in the same class all day or move from one classroom to another in a group, and only a few times a day. In middle school and high school, students change classes many more times a day, and all the students are going off in different directions at the same time. This means that when walking down the hallway to his class, a student may be brushed up against by many people. To a person on the autism spectrum who is fully included and is sensitive to touch, this may be very painful. At the beginning of the day, he may tolerate this painful (to him) sensation, but near the end of the day he may be heading toward a meltdown, because of changing classes and getting touched so many times on top of other stresses.

In addition, by the end of the day he will have experienced lunchtime in the cafeteria and taken a physical education class, which includes spending time in the locker room. These are all environments that not only assault the senses of touch, sight, and hearing, but requires the student to use a great deal of his vestibular and proprioceptive senses, which in and of itself is challenging.

For students who spend most of their time in special education classes, including classrooms for the severely handicapped, one would think that the sensory challenges would not be such an issue because of the students being in a more controlled environment. However, most of these classrooms have fluorescent lighting, as well as fire alarm bells and intercom announcements that are extremely loud. Many times the students are all on different schedules, which means that there is a steady parade of aides, speech and occupational therapists, and students coming and going, which is very distracting to the visual as well as auditory senses. Add to that the new students who are transferred in the middle of the school year with behavior problems, aggression, or constant noisy verbalizations and it's safe to say that students with sensory problems face a challenging environment in which to learn when they head off to school in the morning.

SENSORY PROCESSING CHALLENGES

As previously described, a dysfunction in any of the senses affects how we process information about the environment. In addition, some individuals with autism cannot process information from different sensory sources at the same time and therefore "choose" which sense they will focus on. For example, author Tito Rajarshi Mukhopadhyay, who is severely autistic, consented to perception testing under the auspices of Dr. Michael Merzenich, a neuroscientist at the University of California, San Francisco Medical School. In perception testing, where lights are flashed on a computer screen at the same time as the sound of beeps is issued, most people can sense the beep and the light at the same time. However, Tito cannot see the light on a computer screen unless it appears a full three seconds after the beeps. Tito explains that he can only use one sense at a time, and he has chosen to use his ears.

This is in marked contrast to Dr. Temple Grandin, a professor at Colorado State University who holds a doctorate in animal science

FOOD FOR THOUGHT

Scrambled Sensory Problems

Autistic children seem "wild" for a lot of different reasons, not all of which relate to animals. A huge problem for autistic children, but not for animals, is scrambled sensory processing. The world isn't coming in right. So young autistic children end up looking wild for the same reason Helen Keller looked wild: parents and teachers can't get through to them. In some ways it's almost like they have to raise themselves. A lot of them do a good job at it, because over the years they seemed to start piecing things together. One mother told me she felt as if her son had to "learn to see," and I bet there's a lot of truth to that.

—Temple Grandin and Catherine Johnson,
*Animals in Translation: Using the Mysteries of Autism
to Decode Animal Behavior*

and has autism. Grandin explains that she thinks totally in pictures, that thinking in language and words is incomprehensible to her, and that she has difficulty with her ultrasensitive hearing because she cannot tune out unwanted noise the way most of us can.

This inability to process information from different sources at the same time could explain why some people with autism appear to have a delayed reaction time, and it is important for those living with, caring for, and teaching teens on the spectrum to remember. It is also important to remember that, contrary to popular assumption, not all autistic individuals are visual learners. There are many individuals who appear to be visual learners because they are often looking at books or moving images, but many are looking at these items for visual stimulation, they are not always processing the information. It is important to keep this in mind and to figure out for each person what their learning channel is—auditory, visual, or tactile.

Individuals may have intense and often painful physical reactions to certain sensory experiences and may have emotional difficulties related to their sensory processing. This is true for everyone on the autism spectrum, no matter their functioning level.

In addition to the commonly known motor awkwardness discussed above, there are also reports from people who appear more functionally disabled and severely impacted by their inability to control their movements or make their body parts move, even as they wanted to, somewhat like patients who have suffered strokes. This area requires more research, but it throws a different light on current assumptions about a lack of intelligence or understanding in those who are unable to communicate independently in a consistent fashion.

Motor Skills

During the adolescent years, most teenagers are intensely aware of themselves and their bodies, yet most students on the autism spectrum are still grappling with sensory motor challenges irregardless of where they fall on the spectrum. Not only are they getting used to the bodies they have always had, they are also dealing with all the physical and hormonal changes affecting their teenage bodies. As men-

---

FOOD FOR THOUGHT

Listening and Looking at the Same Time

Sometimes it is too hard to concentrate on listening and looking at the same time. People are hard enough to understand as their words are often so very cryptic, but when their faces are moving around, their eyebrows rising and falling and their eyes getting wider, then squinting, I cannot fathom all that out in one go, so to be honest I don't even try.

—Luke Jackson, *Freaks, Geeks & Asperger Syndrome:*
A User Guide to Adolescence

tioned above, sensory challenges affect fine and gross motor skills as well as where one's body is in space. This impacts how a person moves. Tasks that appear simple, such as sitting down or moving around desks, require motor planning, which is often not instinctive to students with sensory challenges. Handwriting and taking notes from a blackboard or filling out a test may take longer than for other students, and so may not reflect on a teenager's true understanding of the material or his knowledge of the subject.

Students with ASDs may appear clumsy and will have difficulty with team sports. The students on the spectrum who are fully included may be the last ones picked to be on a team during PE. Changing into PE clothes may take longer than others, causing more stress. In today's culture, how you move and look is more and more important in the tween and teen years, and so any physical awkwardness can be a source of stress and emotional discomfort.

Behavior Problems

Many teenagers on the autism spectrum have behavior problems of one sort or another, for a variety of reasons. Behavior is a form of communication. The hard part is figuring out what the behavior is telling us. A student may not be able to communicate what is going on because they only have basic functional communication skills, or he may have good communication skills but cannot use them at that moment because he is overwhelmed. This leads to behaviors from intense rocking and self-stimulatory behavior, to rages and meltdowns.

Along with ASD-specific behavioral problems, tweens and teens on the autism spectrum also face the usual noncompliance issues that go along with being an adolescent. Also affecting behavior is the inability of the teen to understand or deal with the hormonal and physical growth changes his body is going through.

For those on the less able end of the spectrum who do not normally have good communication skills, it will be harder to piece together what is causing the behavior, as they will not be able to tell you once they have calmed down. However, a student with Asperger's Syndrome will most likely be able to tell you the sequences of his day, once he has calmed down, which can help you to piece together the cause of his problem behavior.

Generally, we can usually figure out a person's behavior by analyzing the environment or what happened before the behavior took place that might have set it off. A student with autism will increase his rocking and self-stimulatory behavior or have an outburst or meltdown for various reasons, including:

- stress related to dealing with overwhelming sensory input, as previously discussed

- anxiety related to coping with everyday changes in the environment and routine

- interruption from being engrossed with favorite object or special interest, or interruption from self-stimulatory behavior

- inability to communicate his needs, wishes, and feelings

- boredom

In her book *Asperger Syndrome and Adolescence: Practical Solutions for School Success,* Brenda Smith Myles identifies five areas of difficulty for adolescents with AS that could lead to a tantrum, rage, or meltdown:

- the inability to understand rules and routines

- the longing for friendships paired with few skills to fulfill this desire

- disruptions in pursuing an engrossing special interest

- the stress related to dealing with the everyday challenges of change and overwhelming sensory input

- the inability to protect oneself from teasing and bullying

Parents need to be aware of these tantrum triggers, in order to help ASD tweens and teens avoid and cope with them as effectively as possible.

FIGHT-OR-FLIGHT RESPONSE

As humans, we all have the same mechanism of responding instinctively to potentially dangerous situations by activating our nervous systems. This fight-or-flight response releases adrenaline into the body, pumps blood into our muscles, and increases heart and breathing rates in order to prepare us to either run away from the danger or fight it off. Most neurotypical individuals, with fairly efficient regulatory systems, are able to ponder the accuracy of this primitive response before they actually react. However, for people on the autism spectrum, the actual fight-or-flight reaction (that is, hitting the perceived "predator" or bolting away) has often already occurred before they have time to think about it. Obviously, this can create potentially dangerous—or at the very least, uncomfortable—situations.

Cognitive Challenges

INTELLIGENCE

Intelligence has always been a difficult area to measure or ascertain for students on the autism spectrum. Since many are unable to follow through on test directions or do not respond to questions, it is often assumed they are mentally retarded.

On the other end of the spectrum, students with Asperger's typically have average to above-average IQs, and many have IQs that are considered superior to what is seen in the general population. However, a high IQ is not the best determinant of school ability and functioning, for the various reasons discussed below as well as others touched upon in the last sections on sensory issues and behavior problems.

GENERALIZATION

Individuals with ASDs often have problems applying learned skills and information across environments and people. They often have problems integrating learned material and experiences, or applying information in a functional context. For example, a person on the less able end of the autism spectrum might have been taught and tested that he understood that a quarter equals twenty-five cents, and that two dimes and a nickel equals a quarter, but will be unable to pick out the correct coins to use at the store to pay for an item. A person with Asperger's might memorize a set of procedures to follow in a given situation, but be unable to apply them when needed.

PROBLEM SOLVING

The problem-solving skills of students on the autism spectrum are often inconsistent. A person with Asperger's might learn one problem-solving strategy and use it for all situations, regardless of whether or not it is an effective strategy for the situation. Or, the student may have learned many different strategies, but cannot access or recall the information while under stress, creating even more frustration that can lead to a meltdown. For the less functionally able, it is hard to know how much they have taken in, but they have the same issues with dealing with situations under stress. For all on the autism spectrum, they may show well-developed problem-solving skills when investigating an area of special interest to them, but be unable to demonstrate those skills in day-to-day tasks.

MEMORY

Rote memory: People with Asperger's tend to have few problems recalling factual information or data stored in rote memory, such as what movie they saw at their favorite local movie theater on a specific date several years ago, or what towns the Amtrak train stops at on its

Pacific Coast line, if they are interested in trains. Those on the less able end of the autism spectrum will show their memory in some way. For example, my son was born in Paris, and we lived there until he was four. To this day, whenever we go back to Paris and visit our old neighborhood, he will insist we go into certain buildings so he can look and follow once again specific mosaic floor tile patterns he remembers seeing from when we lived there more than a decade ago. Rote memory can be an asset, and students with AS often excel at geography and spelling bees and other contests where a huge amount of information on one topic can come in handy. Rote memory can also be misleading, because being able to memorize and use phrases may give the impression that someone has well-developed higher-level comprehension skills, whereas the student is comprehending only at the factual level.

Working memory: This is the short-term memory that allows us to hold on to bits of information while performing mental operations on that information, and it can be a challenge for people with ASDs. This is the kind of memory you need while doing mental arithmetic, for example. Middle and high school Asperger's students might need to perform experiments in biology and chemistry lab, and at the same time remember the safety precautions necessary for handling chemicals. A student with autism might be making his way from his special education classroom to the cafeteria (with an aide following behind), and while remembering to look for landmarks in order to know when to turn left or right, he might get caught up in the details of the landmarks and forget where he is headed.

Remembering to remember: Students with Asperger's might forget that they have information, strategies, or skills that can be helpful when faced with a problem. They don't always make connections between the current situation and similar ones in the past. Perhaps their memories are stored in separate compartments, and there are not connecting ties between these separate memories. They may have problems in retrieving information because although they may know they have relevant information about the situation, they are missing the conceptual links linking it all together, they can't pull it out when they need it. Students with classic autism may have the same challenges, although it may be hard to discern if it is about "remembering to remember" or whether it is prompt dependency developed over time.

EXECUTIVE FUNCTIONS

In a corporation, executives must be able to analyze situations and put strategies into place to move the company forward in a productive manner toward a predetermined goal, and they rely on executive secretaries or assistants to perform the follow-through. Executive functions are all about multitasking, shifting attention, organizing resources, planning timelines, analyzing information, and shifting strategies when necessary. These are the same functions that teenage students need to use, on a smaller scale, more and more as they get into middle school and then high school.

Executive functions are used by all of us in organizing our daily lives, be it at home or at work, and therefore it is important that each student—no matter their ability level—learn these executive functions. They should be taught starting on a small scale, as in reality school is a preparation for adult life, and these are the skills people need to organize their lives and work in whatever field they find employment.

For the tween or teen at home, organizing and planning are part of what is needed to carry out each self-help skill or household chore, or for planning social outings. Adolescents with autism do not naturally pick up on organizing and planning; they need to be systematically taught.

For Asperger's students following a mainstream curriculum, many homework assignments are long term and can include projects that involve lots of reading, preparing a model, and then writing a concluding paper. This creates much stress and worry because the student with Asperger's does not know how to approach such a complex task and does not naturally think about creating a timeline to break the project into manageable parts. The problem-solving challenges come into play here because a student may waste hours attempting to find information in the same unproductive manner without thinking to change the strategy (for example, using the same word in an Internet search engine over and over, although none of the results are helpful). Organizational challenges plague students with Asperger's and more severe autism. A student with Asperger's usually does not have a system figured out to keep his textbooks and papers together, and may not be able to tell which papers should be kept and which he can discard. He may do his homework, but cannot find it when it is time to hand it in. On another level, a student with autism may not be able to organize all the materials he needs in order to complete a simple homework assignment or a functional skill such as cooking a simple dish.

Shifting attention is also an area of difficulty with individuals with ASDs. As discussed earlier, some individuals with autism have difficulties tuning into more than one sensory channel at a time and need time to take it all in. Shifting attention from listening to the teacher to writing a response in a notebook is not easy, and the student may not be able to write until the teacher has stopped speaking. And of course, if a student has challenges with shifting attention, multitasking will be quite difficult.

Another concern, described by Teresa Bolick, Ph.D., in her book *Asperger Syndrome and Adolescence: Helping Preteens and Teens Get Ready for the Real World,* is the "Why does it matter?" phenomenon. Usually teens can understand that they should make their bed or hang up their jacket—even if it doesn't matter overall in the big picture—because they know they should try to please their parents. A teen with Asperger's does not usually understand the idea of doing something "just because." This is also true of teens more impacted by autism. They often don't understand why we do things for the sake of politeness (for example, saying hello when meeting someone, or not coming down the stairs totally naked). In school, this can create difficulties in the classroom as well as the social world inherent to school life.

SPECIAL INTERESTS AND OBSESSIONS

The special interests that students with ASDs tend to have can be useful in teaching academic subjects as well as functional skills and can lead to career opportunities, but they can also be a challenge. As Brenda Smith Myles mentions in her book *Asperger Syndrome and Adolescence: Practical Solutions for School Success,* it is difficult to determine whether or not a particular special interest will turn out to be a "primary obsession" that will prevent the teen from engaging in other activities, or if it will be a secondary interest and a useful motivator. At home, a special interest can be used as a motivator to get chores and homework done, but if it is a primary obsession, the parent will likely be spending a lot of time trying to get the teen to do anything else. It is very difficult on family life when teens have pervasive obsessions, as they interfere with everyday activities. This is true regardless of whether or not the obsession is a favorite book, video, or object the teen likes to "stim" with, or whether it is looking up information or talking about a particular topic such as the stock market or weather patterns. At school, when working one-on-one with a student, it is possible to work the special interest into the curriculum to help with teaching. However, if a student is fully included in a mainstream classroom, it can be difficult at the middle and high school level for teachers, who see hundreds of students a day, to alter their curriculum to encompass a special interest for one child, especially if they have a few ASD students, each with their own particular interests.

Theory of Mind Challenges

Many people with Asperger's have a difficult time with understanding the mental state of others. How they view the world and interpret what is happening around them is different from the way others do. For one thing, they have difficulty understanding that others around them have thoughts that are separate and different from their own.

For another, they don't understand that a comment they make could embarrass or offend another person, and that an apology would help to make the person feel better. Neurotypical teens have their cool words and body language, and it is often basically understood by the other teens what that word means in a particular context; it doesn't have to be spelled out. They often act subtly cool and nonchalant. Teens with Asperger's and more severely impaired autistic teens, on the other hand, have a difficult time picking up on body language and subtle cues and do not understand about "acting cool." This makes it very difficult for those who are fully included to fit in socially at school. Another issue is that teachers often require students to understand unspoken expectations. For example, Luke Jackson, in his book *Freaks, Geeks & Asperger Syndrome,* gives an example of sitting in a classroom and being told by his teacher to open his book to page eleven, which he did. Then the teacher reprimanded him for just sitting and waiting. Her expectation was that the students would get to work on that page, which all his fellow students did, while Luke awaited further instructions.

Emotions and Emotional Maturity

Teens on the autism spectrum are often much less mature than their typical peers. Many of the adolescents severely impacted by autism may still have obsessions or special interests in subjects or objects that are not appropriate for their age group, such as *Sesame Street* or Disney movies.

Those on the more able end of the spectrum may be obsessed and monopolize conversations talking about a particular topic that is of much less interest to their peers.

Individuals with autism do not naturally understand facial expressions and the emotions they represent. They have a hard time recognizing the emotional state of others—and even, in many cases, their own emotional states. They may realize they are feeling something, their body is feeling different, but they don't necessarily recognize what it is. Since they have difficulty reading nonverbal clues, they do not instinctively "read" the expressions of emotions on other people's faces—that is, which expression means angry, or surprised, or frustrated.

Many teens with Asperger's appear naive because of their difficulty with picking up on social clues and body language, and therefore do not conform to the behavioral and social expectations of their peers.

ANXIETY AND STRESS

Many times increased stress in adolescents is due to the sensory issues or the five areas of difficulty listed previously in the Behavior section. Sometimes it is due to the hormonal and physical changes going on during puberty. Temple Grandin has often written and spoken about how during puberty she started feeling very nervous. Sometimes the way an adolescent with Asperger's shows stress is not how a neurotypical teen would. As a parent, you may have noticed small signs that your teen exhibits before escalating into a meltdown. For example, your teen may start with a slight rocking, then faster rocking, then flicking his fingers before reaching out and hitting people.

Communication, Language, and Social Communication Challenges

On the autism spectrum, communication challenges can range from a person who is nonverbal and has only functional communication skills via a picture system, or a dynavox, to a person who is very verbal with few discrete difficulties.

COMMUNICATION AND LANGUAGE

Communication is one of the most basic human needs, and for people who are unable to take care of themselves independently, it is even more necessary. Imagine the frustration of those who know what they want but can't reach for it and can't ask for it. In addition, if a person is unable to communicate, then most people assume the person does not understand language and what is going on around him. Speech is a complicated process involving much motor control. Handwriting can also be difficult for those with motor and/or visual processing issues.

Some adolescents with ASDs may be strong on receptive language, yet weak on expressive language. For example, they might be able to follow through on simple requests and can get items that are asked for, yet may not be able to verbally express themselves and may rely on another method of communication to do so. There are some individuals, rarer still, who have some expressive skills, but appear to have little or no receptive skills. For example, when he was seven, my son Jeremy had more than 100 items mastered expressively—he could correctly verbally label 100 items and pictures, and generalize to different representations of the same object. Yet if you asked him to give you the correct item or picture out of three or four placed on the table in front of him (chosen from the ones he could verbally label), he could not consistently select the right item.

SOCIAL COMMUNICATION CHALLENGES

Unfortunately, the social and language skills of tweens and teens with ASDs often seem to deteriorate as the environment becomes more complex—that is, when there are more people to interact with, there are more challenging tasks to master, and there's more noise and other stimuli to confront—regardless of whether the person is less able or more able.

By the time they reach the age of five, children with High Functioning Autism (HFA) usually do not have general delays in language. However, they do have impairments in specific language skills, the most important being the use of language in a social context, as do those with Asperger's Syndrome. This is particularly a problem during the teen years, when socialization with peers is often the primary motivator at this age.

In her book *Asperger Syndrome and Adolescence: Practical Solutions for School Success,* Brenda Smith Myles identifies six areas of difficulty for adolescents with Asperger's:

• **Lack of understanding that nonverbal cues express meaning and attitudes.** Teens miss out on many social opportunities because they don't understand that a smile and glances from another person could mean they like him, or that teachers give a "look" that is a warning and should be interpreted as meaning to calm down and get to work.

• **Problems with using language to initiate or maintain a conversation.** AS teens will often start a conversation with a comment that seems irrelevant, or may walk up to a group of teens and want to join in, but does not because he doesn't know how or when to join in.

• **Tendency to interpret words or phrases concretely.** AS teens often only understand the literal meanings of words and phrases and not expressions such as "You're pulling my leg" and "Pull yourself together." Or, as in the example from Luke Jackson's book quoted earlier, they will do exactly as told and will not understand the implied statement, which leads teachers to think the teen is a smart aleck.

• **Difficulty understanding that other people's perspective in conversation need to be considered.** This can lead to one-sided monologues, because the AS student is talking about his area of interest and is not monitoring whether or not the listener is interested.

• **Failure to understand the unspoken rules of the hidden curriculum or a set of rules everyone knows, but that has not been specifically taught.** Things that are important to teens, such as how to dress, what to say to whom, how to act, and how to know the difference between gentle teasing and bullying.

• **Lack of awareness that what you say to a person in one conversation may influence how that individual relates to you in the future.** A teen may make a candid remark to another teen, not realizing it was hurtful, and may be puzzled by the person's lack of response later that day.

Some of these may be a problem for the less able as well. But as they are not usually as intellectually achieving as their Asperger peers, there is usually not the expectation that they will possess the same social skills as the rest of the adolescent student population.

In chapter 3, 4 and 6, we'll look at different teaching strategies as well as treatments, and therapies for helping your adolescent address these challenges. In the next chapter, we'll look at the home life of tweens and teens on the autism spectrum.

FOOD FOR THOUGHT

Adolescence and Me

by Tito Rajarshi Mukhopadhyay

It came all quiet, like the nascent evening
It came to me like a silent thought
It stayed all along with or without my shadow
And left all its footprints on my heart.

Thus came my adolescence . . .

My voice started to change when I was eleven. It goes by the belief that I am mute although I do talk my words aloud ever since I "found my voice" (quoted in my book, *The Mind Tree*).

I never paid much attention to how my voice sounded anyway. That is because I am used to concentrating on the content of my words. It makes me ignore my quality of sound production, to the utter frustration of my speech therapists.

I remember my equal frustration when in one of the laboratories in San Francisco in the year 2001, I got a delayed feedback of my voice. My voice sounded terrible. I remember being in such a shock hearing myself speak for the first time, that I ran out of the room. "Tito, your voice is changing!" my speech therapist in India told me. Mother showed her concerns. I think mothers prefer us younger because we are easier to manage.

And Kaki (quoted about her in *The Mind Tree*) told me my voice was changing.

That is how I knew my voice changed when I was eleven.

I started to grow strong.
And I started to grow obsessive.

"Obsession . . .
Thou art beyond
My conscious reasons!"

There was a growing anxiety within me.

"I must get a magazine." My mind started to talk to me. I started to talk it aloud. "I must get a magazine" and again "I must get a magazine" it continued.

Mother started to explain that it could get too expensive if I had so many magazines together in one week.

"I know it is expensive, Mother, but I must have it. Otherwise I will not survive. . . ."

I do not remember what went after that. Perhaps it is too painful to remember any of that. All I can do now is confess to you, Mother, that I never meant to hurt you like that. Not then, not again.

I became paranoid to every extent.

I was all alone waiting to be judged by the world.

The reality of autism was too naked out there teasing me.

I started to take Risperidal, to keep my stress under my control.

And I continue to do so even now at sixteen.

She was singing in my heart
She was swinging all my dreams

She was all around my thoughts
She was all in betweens . . .

I knew I would never be loved back by women.
And then I heard that Deepa had become a mother of a baby boy.

How old was I then?
Perhaps twelve. But didn't I write my best poems on her?

Wish my heart was one of those
That bloomed your garden all
Wish that I was named a rose
And by it you would call.
Wish the hands with what you cared
And touched those petals pure
Could touch my heart with tenderness
I would want no more.
And wish that at the end of day
When on the garden you tread
I would wither on your way
And on your feet fall dead.

Mother explained that she was twenty-five and I was twelve. "And maybe realistic hopes would work better for me."
My thoughts got Mutilated.
My world got Mutilated.
I became the Mutilated Spirit. . . .

Mutilated spirit . . .
Dark from the claws of death
Has come to love its own lost breath.
A longing look at mankind,
Which has grown to love its own mutilated spirit.
And Mutilated Spirit, with tender pain,
Gives a blind look toward heaven.

I will touch my seventeenth birthday this 30th July 2005, and plan to write the blessings and curses of adolescence more from my mutilated sights.
Till then,

Let me hang up in the sky
Let me swallow up the dark
Let me travel round the stars
With the chisel on my heart. . . .

Tito Rajarshi Mukhopadhyay is the author of *The Mind Tree: A Miraculous Child Breaks the Silence of Autism.* Tito's mother, Soma, who taught her son and developed the Rapid Prompting Method, is the educational director of HALO. For more information go to www.halo-soma.org. Tito prefers to write rather than type and recently published *The Gold of the Sunbeams,* a collection of stories.

2

Family Life: The Teenager at Home

Autism is a condition that affects every family member of the person on the autism spectrum. The rigors of raising a child on the autism spectrum to a fulfilling adulthood are daunting for a very good reason: autism affects every aspect of life.
—TEMPLE GRANDIN AND KATE DUFFY, *Developing Talents: Careers for Individuals with Asperger Syndrome and High-Functioning Autism*

FINDING it particularly difficult to teach my son Jeremy in a self-care area that I had put off dealing with for way too long, I asked a behavior specialist who knew the family well to meet with my husband and me in our home. Jeremy has a difficult time with his motor planning and muscle control, and so learning self-help skills takes a lot of work on his part as well as on the part of those who teach him. As my husband and I sat at the dining room table listening to the specialist, I felt guilty about having put this off for so long. I had tried sporadically to teach Jeremy in this area, but I'd been so exhausted from working and everyday life with an autistic son that I had not been consistent enough with this particular issue.

I knew what we should be doing to get a grip on this particular issue, but I needed to hear someone *tell* me what to do, I needed to hear someone tell me I was *capable* of doing it and that I had to take care of this issue *now*. I also needed buy in from my husband. I needed someone to explain to him that we *both* needed to take responsibility for getting this under control. I didn't want to tell him what we were supposed to be doing; he needed to hear it from someone else, and I needed him to *share* in this responsibility. I couldn't do it alone.

Having the behavior specialist come over and meet with us together was a good way of handling this situation. It gave me the support I needed to do what had to be done. It put some of the responsibility on my husband, and he heard what he needed to hear. It also made me realize we can't always be perfect, sometimes we let things slide, and that's okay for a little while, but then you still have to face the music. And when you do, there are people there to help you and your family tackle the challenges together.

Family Life

Adolescence adds a whole new perspective and flavor to family life. For parents, there is the realization that there is no going back, their child is growing up, and if they haven't accepted the child for who he is by now, it's time to do so. Along with the need for facing and embracing their situation, they must also continue to advocate for services at school and elsewhere.

Families living with autism experience greater stress than neurotypical families. When the children are small, many families are hoping for a cure or recovery, or to teach them as much as possible while their brains are still growing. When the children are teenagers, the stress may change form, but it is still there. One day you wake up and realize your child is not a kid anymore, and then you start focusing on the life skills they need to learn in order to have the most productive, independent, and fulfilling life possible.

There are the usual concerns of teaching a preteenager all about his changing body, about sexuality. There is the reality that as teenagers, our kids develop their own opinions and want more and more control. As well, there is the need for constant supervision for many less able teens, and the worry about the safety of the more able teens out alone in the community, and the threat of bullying at school.

Then there is the fact that as parents, we receive less support and help from available services because the trend is toward early intervention, and our child is now too old; supposedly his "window of opportunity" has closed. Add to this the incessant and growing worry about what will happen as the teenager becomes an adult and ages out of the educational system, and it is easy to understand how families with adolescents on the autism spectrum can easily become overwhelmed and dysfunctional. Our plates are full, but we must not despair, and we must learn to take it one step at a time. In reality, there is more acceptance and understanding than ever before, and it is possible to work toward creating options for our children's future happiness.

Autism is 24/7. Siblings, the marriage or partnership, the family dynamics—all are involved and affected by the autism spectrum disorder, not just the teenager on the spectrum. What is important is to do whatever can be done to support the family home life and make it as healthy and enjoyable an environment as possible for everyone. More important than *what* we are dealing with is *how* we approach the challenges and our attitude toward the situations we face.

Some parents, after having tried many treatments and therapies, may still be faced with a child whose aggressive or self-injurious behaviors escalates during puberty, or a teen who needs constant supervision. In these situations, it may be necessary to look at available options in terms of in-home support services or, even possibly residential placement. Obviously, this is a difficult cross in the road to be standing at, especially after having tried so hard to help and teach your child.

Balancing the needs of each family member can be a challenge, but it is an essential one. Now that your child on the autism spectrum is a teenager, as a parent you need to accept the inevitable—your child may learn new skills and improve in many ways, but he will probably not be "cured," no matter how many hours of therapy you give him. (We'll look at the therapies and treatments available in chapter 6, but the hopes you might have had for a "total recovery" should by now seem like a fading memory.)

However, your teen on the autism spectrum still needs to learn many skills. These may be taught either in school or at home or both, depending upon the functional level of the adolescent as well as the focus of his educational program at school. Regardless, all skills need to be reinforced and generalized in all environments. Even if domestic skills are taught at school, each teenager should have chores they are responsible for, just like any other teenager. Not only are chores a way for the teenager to contribute to family life and the home environment like everyone else, but they also teach him about the bigger picture of living in the real world, where as citizens we must all contribute to society in one way or another.

Ensuring some quality time for everyone is necessary to a healthy family life. If there are other children in the family, they need your support as well. Perhaps there are other teens in the household. All these growing people in your home make demands on you, and dealing with their emotions when you are still dealing with your own is not easy, yet it is a necessary part of being a parent.

As a parent, you will also be responsible for ensuring that your child learns self-esteem and self-advocacy, which begin at home. These skills are vital to the person's makeup, will affect his future happiness, and are dependent on the parents' attitude toward autism and their child. How parents talk about ASDs and their child, what messages they give off in the family environment, are of the utmost importance.

Behavior management and sensory processing issues are also areas that need to be looked at in all environments. As the child gets older it is important to try to get him in charge, when possible, of his own behavior management. Parents need to analyze what is causing any problem behaviors at home, and sensory processing issues can be resolved with some practical strategies.

The skills that should be taught primarily at home (other than hygiene, personal care, modesty, and sexuality, which are covered in the next chapter) will be addressed in this chapter. Practical strategies for keeping the family environment healthy for all who live there while providing the supports needed for the tween or teen on the spectrum will be discussed as well.

FOOD FOR THOUGHT

You Never Get Over It, You Just Learn to Deal with It

When my daughter Rebecca was graduating from sixth grade, I dropped her off at her first dance, organized by some parents at a local community center. It was wonderful to see all these young boys and girls having a great time, dancing away.

A few hours later when I returned to pick up my daughter, the dancing sixth-graders were still at it. I was thrilled to see how much fun Rebecca was having with her classmates and thinking about this rite of passage from being preteens to attending middle school. She was growing up.

As we were leaving I bumped into one of Rebecca's classmates and his older brother Ryan, who had come to take him home. Ryan was about my son's age. I had not seen this teenager in so long that I almost didn't recognize him, and I couldn't believe he was now old enough to drive. And then that all-too-familiar ache came back, the reminder that my son would never do those ordinary things: he would never drive a car, pick up his sister, or go for a ride with his friends. And I thought once again about all the rites of passage Jeremy never had experienced and would never take part in.

The feeling of emotional pain was so acute I could barely breathe. It came so unexpectedly and so uninvited—as they usually do—the feeling again of being apart, of having a child and life so unlike my neighbors and the other parents in this perfect-seeming suburb, and this sadness for my son that he would never experience much of what most teenagers do. I thought I was "over" it, but I wasn't, and I knew I never would be.

As I drove Rebecca home, she was so thrilled with her evening, so bubbly and happy, yet I was feeling so despondent. Obviously I submerged my feelings until she was in bed and I could be alone with my pain. Eventually after a not-so-good night's sleep, I was "over" it again, back to feeling good about our life and our family and grateful that we are who we are. The heartbreaking feelings of the night before were gone with the darkness, but the memory of Rebecca's joyous evening remained with me.

For Parents—the Importance of Taking Care of Yourself

Parents, if you are going to make it through the teen years with all your marbles intact, you need to take care of yourselves. When the children are little, many parents get by on little sleep and may, for a few years, be able to function with few breaks. There is that rush of adrenaline, that hopeful push when we might believe that these are the years our children are going to "recover" or at least greatly improve—that we need to get it all done while the window of opportunity is still open.

However, just like every marathon runner needs to stop and let her body recuperate, parents cannot keep going at that mad pace for the long run. For one thing, as our children get older, so do our own bodies, and we realize that we only have so much energy. At some point we need to focus on the whole picture, on our own lives and the rest of the families' lives, and not just on the child we are trying so desperately to help. If your tween or teen on the spectrum requires constant supervision, you will need to enlist other responsible individuals to help you. Every state is different, but most offer respite or in-home support to some extent. If you have funding but need to hire your own support team, read *A "Stranger" Among Us: Hiring In-Home Support for a Child with Autism Spectrum Disorders or Other Neurological Differences* by Lisa Lieberman, MSW, LCSW.

Parents, you need to take care of yourselves. As a parent, the family unit depends on you. No discussion of a healthy family unit can take place without considering the well-being of the parent or parents. Flight attendants tell the adult passengers during take off that in the event of an emergency, they must put their oxygen masks on themselves before putting them on their children. The idea is if you don't take care of yourself, you will be unable to take care of those for whom you are responsible. In family life, parental self-care is the oxygen mask that can make or break a family. For this reason, the first topic in this chapter is the importance of taking care of yourself. Below are some strategies to keep in mind.

DEAL WITH YOUR LOSS OF EXPECTATION: PRACTICE ACCEPTANCE

If you are still feeling the loss of expectation of the child you wish you had, now is the time to let that go. Don't let this mourning for the child you never had (but wish you did) ruin any more of your life or color your relationship with your child. Being comfortable and happy with your life has to do with acceptance. Acceptance of the reality of your lot in life, acceptance of the fact that your teen in not neurotypical and never will be. You will never appreciate the child you *do* have, or your life, if you are still wishing things were different. It is what it is, and you have no control over the hand you have been dealt, so free yourself from thinking about the "what-ifs" and "if onlys" and enjoy your teen. We have a lot to learn from our quirky teens, and the

---

FOOD FOR THOUGHT
The World Makes No Promises

I now look at Ben, whom I have finally found. And I forgive myself. I love and accept him because I see him as he is—beautiful in his unique brilliance, courageous in his struggle to live in a world that could not appreciate him, and inspiring in his capacity to be grateful for all that he is and all that he has.

At last, I understand, I was only a mother suffering from a disappointment I had refused to come to terms with. And sometimes, from a century ago, I hear the echo of John Oliver Hobbes: "Disillusion," all comes from within, "from the failure of some dear and secret hope. But the world makes no promises," he tells us, "we only dream it does and when we wake, we cry."

—Barbara LaSalle, *Finding Ben: A Mother's Journey Through the Maze of Asperger's*

---

sooner you open your eyes to this fact, the more you can learn—and the more our teens will learn their own self-acceptance.

Acceptance of the reality of your child's ASD does not mean, however, that you stop trying to support him in every way that you can, or that you give up trying to secure the best services to assist him, or to teach him the skills he needs to learn to be a functionally independent and happy person. It means that you accept him for who he is, autism and all. It's not about changing your teen, it's about teaching him how to adapt and live in this world.

BAN THE NEGATIVE

You may not have control over everything you would like to in your life, but you *can* control your thoughts. Life is hard enough as it is, and if you are constantly thinking negatively, life will seem even more impossible. Everything ever done in this world, good or bad, originated as a thought before it was put into action. At first it may seem impossible to find anything positive in a given situation, but there is always a positive aspect, even if you have to dig for it. When you find that aspect, focus on it. You will find that you will feel over time that you can see the cup is half full, not half empty. Things could be better, but they could always be worse, as well!

Another important step is to distance yourself from the naysayers. Naysayers are those who are pessimistic and constantly see the sky falling in. They are the ones who know all the reasons why something will not work out or is too difficult to pull off. You cannot afford to surround yourself with negative energy. Even if these are family members that you cannot avoid forever, you can limit these energy sappers by screening your calls and limiting the amount of time you give them. Don't feel guilty about this; your well-being, and your children's, come first, and for that you need to save your energy.

Surround yourself with uplifting music, art, colors, and other influences. If you listen to depressing music and watch sad movies, you will feel depressed. Watch something invigorating and listen to sounds that make you happy, that make you feel good.

DEVELOP A SENSE OF HUMOR

Research shows that humor has a beneficial impact on our health. Laughter activates the immune system and decreases the stress hormones. Admittedly, not everything about autism is funny, but everyone can remember situations that at the time were difficult, but in the retelling afterward you could see the funny side. Maybe it's only "humor noir" but whatever gets you through the day that doesn't hurt anyone is fair game, as far as I'm concerned.

If you don't train yourself to see the humorous side of situations, you will undoubtedly feel depressed and overwhelmed by how autism has impacted your life. It is better to extend energy by laughing than to stay angry, frustrated, and stuck.

PHYSICAL EXERCISE—THE NATURAL ANTIDEPRESSANT

With autism in your life, you are at risk for depression and may soon find yourself reaching for those antidepressants or extra martinis. Exercise is a healthier alternative to fighting mild to moderate depression. Research shows that it only takes thirty minutes of aerobic exercise three times a week to reduce depressive symptoms. The brain chemical PEA is a natural stimulant produced by the body, and people with depression tend to have low levels of PEA. Exercise raises those levels of PEA, thus creating a natural antidepressant action in the brain. Exercise also alters the levels of serotonin, a neurotransmitter that has been linked to depression. Other neurotransmitters such as dopamine and norepinephrine seem to be altered by exercise.

Endorphins have been linked to "runner's high," the feeling runners experience after thirty to sixty minutes of running. However, not everyone has to go to the extreme of Ironman athletes. Exercise can be defined as any physical activity that is more than what is done on a typical day. So if you spend most of the day in front of the TV or sitting at a computer, doing fifteen minutes of deep-breathing exercises would be considered a good place to start, then working your way up to a fifteen-minute walk and so on. If you do not exercise on a regular basis, check with your doctor before starting any exercise routine.

There are other positive reasons why exercise should be the antidepressant of choice. First of all you do not risk the possible side effects from taking medication. Second, exercise is good for your heart and keeping your blood pressure stable. And finally, studies have shown that the effects of exercise on depression kick in faster than the effects of antidepressants, and continue for about five months after you stop exercising. A Duke University Medical Center study found that a quick ten-minute walk may be enough to make clinically depressed people feel better. The study involved a group of inactive, depressed people who were fifty and older. After just eight minutes of walking, 82 percent of them said they felt less tense, tired, and angry.

EAT HEALTHY: YOU ARE WHAT YOU EAT

Making healthy choices about food will help you feel better—more positive and energetic and more equipped to ward off those bugs that all kids tend to bring home. Eating healthy is not about going on a strict diet that is impossible to stick to. It's about eating moderate portions of a variety of foods including plenty of vegetables, fruits, whole-grain products, low-fat dairy products, lean meats, poultry, fish, and legumes. Drink a lot of water and a glass of red wine once in a while, and you will be keeping your body happy.

TIME OUT FOR YOURSELF: THE LITTLE PAUSES THAT REFRESH

If you are like most parents, you don't have the financial resources, the live-in help, or the time to go off on mini-vacations for a break from real life. However, it is important that you take the time to give yourself little pauses that refresh every day, even if they are only for five to ten minutes.

Make an "indulgence" list of moments or treats that you really en-

FOOD FOR THOUGHT

When the Night Demons Come to Visit

It's past midnight and the night demons are visiting. The "How am I going to get everything done this week?" demon sneaks up around my pillow, quickly joined by the "I've got to find someone to help me with my son" demon. I try visualization techniques, imagining peaceful, tranquil beaches. Nothing doing, so I get up and pop a few Melatonins, a natural relaxer, hoping that will help.

I'm almost there, and the heavy-duty demons start to prey on my mind: "What if mediation doesn't work and we have to go to due process," "How are we going to pay for all this?" Now the real torture starts: "Is all this autism stuff negatively impacting his sister?" This sleepless night hits its climatic peak when the grandmaster of all demons arrives, the "What will happen when we are no longer here to look after him?" demon. Another sleepless night, but demons are like Dracula—they don't like daylight so they disappear in the morning mist. I am exhausted, but I have to get up and start on my parental duties and work deadlines. I stumble down to the kitchen and swallow my necessary jolt of caffeine. As the caffeine hits my brain cells, the night demons don't seem so bad. After the kids are off to school and before I get to work, I go for my obligatory run, and I feel so much better. Somehow, exercise makes me feel invincible—those night demons may visit, but they won't stay.

joy and that you can do in a short period of time. It could be ten minutes of *American Idol*, reading the paper, taking a catnap, having a cup of coffee and reading a book, playing a video game, or doing your nails. The important thing is that it be a real break, and a short period of time so you can fit one treat in every day. Then, make a point of scheduling one into each day. Perhaps once a week you can schedule a longer break: maybe a beer with the guys, or a movie with your gal pals, a pedicure, or window-shopping. Or how about a date with your life partner?

KEEP BALANCE IN YOUR LIFE

Don't get swallowed up totally by your family life and autism. What is important to you and what do you want out of life? What were you planning to do before autism hit your life? Set some goals for yourself if there are things you have wanted to do or learn but have never had the chance to do so. Have you always wanted to learn painting? Is there a class at the local community college? Perhaps you've always wanted to improve on your computer skills or learn to salsa. There are inexpensive classes available in all communities for adult learners. Is there a museum exhibit nearby you have wanted to visit and haven't gotten to yet? Never lose sight of *you*.

The Adolescent at Home

Your child is now a teenager. His needs are changing as he is getting older. The changes between the tween or teen and his peers appears more and more apparent to everyone, including him. His home is his refuge, and he needs to feel safe, feel good about himself, know he is accepted as he is, and be loved unconditionally.

SELF-ESTEEM—IT BEGINS WITH PARENTS

Even for neurotypicals, self-esteem is an essential characteristic for a successful life. People must believe in themselves in order to ask for what they need or want and to feel that they are just as valid as any other human being, that their life has meaning. Learning self-esteem, and truly owning it, begins early on at home, and is first shaped by how your parents and siblings respond to you. Eventually, that circle is widened, but the family unit is where it all begins. When children reach the tween years, their peers start taking a more important role in how they view themselves and their self-esteem, which is why self-esteem needs to be addressed at school as well. However, home is where the first and continual influences come from.

FOOD FOR THOUGHT

On Acceptance

Ben hadn't accepted himself any more than I'd accepted him. But at least he knew it. At least he was doing something about it. I could see it. I could feel it. He was beginning to say yes to the person he was, because he was telling the truth; he was telling *me* the truth. "It's just how it is, Mom. This is reality, and both of us—you and I—have to accept it."

—Barbara LaSalle, *Finding Ben: A Mother's Journey
Through the Maze of Asperger's*

In order for a parent to instill feelings of self-esteem and self-worth in his child, the parent must believe in the value and merit of the child. Before expecting your child to accept himself, warts and all, you have to accept him yourself. How we feel about our child is mirrored back to him. If you focus on your child's deficits or challenges every time you look at him, then he will always be thinking of his deficits as well. If you feel sorry for your child and often speak in front of him about autism as if it were a nasty disease, he will grow up feeling sorry for himself and using the autism as an excuse for his behaviors and his lot in life. In this way, our children are no different from all others.

Raising Your Teenager's Self-Esteem

Listen to the messages your teen is hearing and experiencing at home about his autism spectrum disorder. Videotaping or having a notebook and noting down what is said and done in the house around your teen and the interactions with and reactions of your teen over a few days will give you an idea of the kind of environment your tween or teen is growing up in. We all have behaviors and habits of saying and doing things, sometimes without even realizing it. For example, when meeting the Aspie son of an acquaintance for the first time, the acquaintance immediately identified him as having Asperger's and started to talk about all the difficulties this created for him. This is not conducive to thinking positively about oneself. How parents talk about their children sets the stage for how they think of themselves.

If your notes or video show that your remarks seem not very supportive or positive for your child, or puts the "label" before the person, you need to work on replacing them with more positive behavior patterns and language. In the example above, it would have been much better for the woman to simply introduce her son by name and let the conversation flow from there. If he wanted to share the fact of his Asperger's with me, she could have followed up with a comment about the positive attributes this has brought him (for example, that he's a whiz at math, can fix any broken computer, etc.). Once you've set the stage for a more positive and accepting environment, your teen's self-esteem will improve.

All the above is true even for parents of the less functionally able. You may not know how much your teen is hearing and understanding, especially if his communication skills are low. Always assume that your teen understand everything and speak respectfully to him and about him, as you would with any child.

Start emphasizing the positive behaviors you see in your child, instead of focusing solely on the negative ones. Let him know how much you appreciate having him as your son. Stop treating him like a problem, and start treating him as a positive part of your life. Teens on the more able end of the spectrum may find it useful to read *Asperger's and Self Esteem: Insight and Hope Through Famous Role Models*, by Norm Ledgin.

TEACHING SELF-CARE

Self-care has been given its own section in chapter 3.

TEACHING CHORES AND OTHER HOME-CARE SKILLS

Learning to contribute to home life is an important part of growing up, and all teenagers need to have some responsibilities in this area. Whether the teen eventually lives on his own or with others, he will need to do his share of the chores to keep a home. Learning to do chores will help the teen become responsible and will add to his self-esteem when he sees he is a contributing member of the household. He will also earn the respect of his siblings when they see that he carries out his chores ably, just as they do.

No matter the functioning level of any teen or tween with an ASD, there is much he can learn to do around the house. To begin with, create a list of all the chores and tasks that you can think of that are involved with taking care of a home. A great resource for teaching home care skills is *Steps to Independence: Teaching Everyday Skills to Children With Special Needs* by Bruce L. Baker and Alan J. Brightman. There is a useful chart that lists all the homecare items you could ever think of as necessary for the upkeep of a home.

List all you can think of (you may wish to jot them down on a piece of paper over a few days when you remember something) under the main headings of Cleaning (for example, puts things away, sweeps, cleans sink), Laundry (separates light from darks, measures soap, uses dryer), Food Preparation (sets a table, makes sandwiches, uses oven), Replacing Used Items (toilet paper roll, burned-out lightbulb), Tool Use (stepladder, wrench), Routine Adjustments and Maintenance (adjusts shades, temperature control, weeds and trims garden, changes sheets on the bed), and Nonroutine Repairs (resets a circuit breaker, hangs a picture). Not all teens on the spectrum will learn to do all these tasks, but some may be able to eventually learn them all as they get older and prepare to be on their own, if that is what they choose to do. If your son or daughter only learns a portion of these over the years left until he or she is a young adult, you will know what she has left to learn and what he or she might have to ask, pay, or barter someone else to do.

Baker and Brightman suggest that you perform a home-care assessment by making a chart of all the skills under each heading, and checking off for each skill in the following level of mastery:

- **Basic steps not mastered**—The teen cannot do all the basic steps on his own; he still needs to learn some (or all) of the steps involved.

- **Needs assistance with decisions**—The teen has mastered the basic steps needed for a skill, but he needs help in the decision-making process. In other words, he may still need to be told when to perform the task, what materials are needed, when to begin, or whether the skill has been done well or not. (Many neurotypical teens may have challenges in this area as well!)

- **Can do well and independently**—These are the skills your teen can do all the necessary steps and make all the necessary decisions for, and you do not need to be there at all.

It's also a good idea to analyze each skill in terms of the teen's motivation in two other columns:

- **Motivation is a problem**—The teen is not motivated to perform this chore; he needs constant reminding, and you will need to find a way to get him motivated to do this.

- **Motivation is not a problem**—The teen will perform these tasks on a regular basis without needing encouragement or the promise of a reward.

TEACHING A NEW SKILL AROUND THE HOUSE

For those parents familiar with applied behavior analysis and task analysis, you may find this section a bit redundant. However, many parents of older teens may not have had the benefit of a behaviorally based program to teach their child and may find this information useful.

To teach your tween or teen a new skill, begin by assessing his mastery of some of the chores or home care you would like him to learn as outlined above. Then do the following:

- Pick two or three tasks at the "basic steps not mastered" level (as described above), and teach the steps that are needed. Do this by analyzing each step necessary and teaching that step until it is mastered.

- Pick two or three tasks at the "needs assistance with decisions" level. Do this by teaching your child to think about *when* he needs to do the skill; *what* materials he needs; *which* step is first and what comes next; *when* has he finished and done a good job? This can be done through social stories. (For more about social stories, see pages 232–233.

- Develop a routine using skills that the teen can do well independently, coupled with some from that needs assistance with decision making. Make a chart in a convenient place such as the refrigerator or the bedroom or bathroom door, depending on the routine (that is, getting ready for school, getting ready for bed).

- Motivate performance for those skills the teen is having a motivation problem with. This can be tied into the chart with tokens being earned for each skill performed, and another chart with the number of tokens needed to buy a favorite activity.

More ideas on teaching skills are offered in the next chapter under hygiene. *1001 Great Ideas for Teaching and Raising Children with Autism Spectrum Disorders,* by Ellen Notbohm and Veronica

Zysk, is another wonderful book full or great tips and ideas for all aspects of raising a child on the spectrum, including great tips for helping with self-care skills.

TAKING RESPONSIBILITY FOR BEHAVIOR—SELF-REGULATION

As discussed in chapter 1, behaviors are a form of communication, and we can usually figure out a person's behavior by analyzing the environment or what happened before the behavior took place that might have set it off. Remember that behaviors can be a result of different factors, such as:

- stress related to dealing with overwhelming sensory input

- anxiety related to coping with everyday changes in the environment and routine

- interruption from being engrossed with a favorite object or special interest, or engaging in self-stimulatory behavior

- inability to communicate needs, wishes, and feelings

- boredom

Since the home is an environment we can control, it's a good idea to make your home, and particularly your teen's room, as stress-free as possible. If the teenager is having an outburst or meltdown for a particular reason, he needs to learn how to recognize that he is being overwhelmed by something before the situation gets out of control. He can then learn some calming techniques. Many people on the spectrum use rocking and self-stimulatory behavior when stressed; they often find it soothing, and they should be free to do so in the privacy of his own home. (Hopefully the teen will learn other coping strategies. Some of these are discussed in chapters 4 and 6).

When dealing with meltdowns, temper tantrums, or noncompliance in the home, here are a few constructive steps to take:

• **Analyze the behavior and see if there is a pattern as to what sets it off—and if the teen is being inadvertently rewarded as a result of the behavior.** Whenever the behavior occurs, make a written record, detailing what it looks like. It is important that you also note what happened immediately preceding the onset of the behavior and immediately following. Then, look at the data and see if there is pattern in the ABC of the behavior: the Antecedent (what happened before the behavior), the Behavior (what the teen did), the Consequence (what was the result of the behavior—did he get out of completing a chore or doing his homework, or did he have a privilege taken away). Try to remove the antecedent, and see if the behavior persists. If you discover a hidden reward, do everything you can to take it out of the picture. This should help the behavior trail off.

• **Look at where these behaviors are happening and in what context.** Do the behaviors take place in environments that share some characteristics (such as too bright, noisy, crowded)? Do they take place on days when there has been an unannounced change in the schedule? See what can be changed in order to support the teenager in helping him be more in control of himself.

  ○ Is this behavior occurring every time the music or TV has been blaring for a while (overwhelming sensory input)? If so, make sure he has a quiet place to go to get away from the noise, and teach others to lower the volume.
  ○ Is this behavior occurring whenever there is a change in the routine? Whenever possible, give your teen warning about changes in routine. In structured teaching situations, you can use social stories and teach him about how sometimes there are changes, and what we can do when they occur.
  ○ Is this behavior occurring when the teen is interrupted from

taking part in a favorite activity? Giving the teen advanced warning with a timer is helpful in helping him transition to another activity.

o Is he unable to communicate his needs at that time? Even very able individuals with autism have written about how under stress they are unable to communicate, so you need to set up a system for these moments. For example, sometimes my son is feeling sensory overload and needs deep pressure or another type of sensory activity to help him calm down. At those times he is usually not able to verbalize it or spell it out (his two methods of communicating). So we have the words written on icons he can pull out of his notebook or easily available at home to give us when necessary.

o Is he bored with what he is doing? Making sure your teen has access to interesting activities in between the real-life stuff we all have to do is important for his well-being.

• **Recognize the signs that the teen is getting overloaded.** A teen may start with slight rocking, then faster rocking, then flicking his fingers, before actually reaching out and hitting people and objects. By observing and noting in different environments you can recognize the signs, and you can also recognize if they are occurring particularly in a certain type of environment or not (for example, crowded, noisy, very bright), or in a particular context (someone is sitting in "his" spot). The signs might last a few minutes, they may last a long time.

• **Teach the teenager to recognize the signs in himself that he is heading toward a meltdown.** Teach your teen to recognize the signs you have noticed that show he is getting to the point of no return. Have him realize that it is good that he has his own "warning system" that he can recognize. Then teach him what strategies he can use to avoid the meltdown and to manage his anxiety or stress. Even the less able can learn this, but need an easy way to communicate to others when they are getting to that level.

• **Teach him a few appropriate strategies to avoid the meldtown.** These strategies should be ones that has been worked out by him and all of you that know him well (for example, leave the room and go to his quiet private place). Find strategies that can help him avoid getting close to the meltdown, such as, does chewing gum or squeezing a rubber ball during the weekend help him feel calmer? Does he need to have his time structured at home? Does he need periodic sensory or exercise breaks scheduled in? For those who need more help with structuring, you can gauge what it needs to be and explain to your teen that you would like him to try this out to see if it helps him.

• **Give him a safe, quiet place all his own where he can be alone and quiet when he wants to.** Every teen needs privacy, but teens on the spectrum need even more quiet and time away from it all. Having a place all their own that is quiet and comforting, even if it is a tent in a shared bedroom or a hiding place under the stairs, a comfort zone, will help.

WHEN MORE HELP IS NEEDED

Often, the parent may have tried various strategies at home but will still need help from another source. For ideas on more strategies, biomedical and traditional medical interventions see chapter 6. Behavioral specialists and other professionals who are experienced with autism spectrum disorders and how they effect adolescence should be able to help you. Check with the local chapter of the Autism Society of America if you are unsure who can help in your area.

For parents of children who are acutely impacted by autism, it may become apparent that, although your child may need adult supervision at all times, you are unable to provide this 24/7. The services available vary from state to state, but in-home-support services of some kind exist in each state under the Medical Waiver Programs, where a parent's income is not taken into account. For more information, contact the Developmental Disabilities Council in your state.

In some cases, a child's aggressive or self-injurious behaviors may increase with the arrival of puberty. Parents may attempt all the different behavioral, biomedical, and traditional medical treatments available with the help of knowledgeable professionals.

Sometimes, the parent realizes that they cannot provide the necessary care at home, or that their teenager would benefit from a 24-hour program in one environment. This realization and ensuing decision to move ahead and look for residential placement is difficult and emotional. Once this decision is reached, parents should know that it is not easy to find appropriate placements for individuals on the spectrum. For more information about what may be available in your area, check with:

• The Autism Society of America www.autism-society.org/

• National Association of Resident Providers for Adults with Autism http://www.narpaa.org/ They may be able to indicate residential facilities for teenagers.

• Developmental Disabilities Council in your state

• The ARC—This organization is not autism specific but does have information about residential placement possibilities. http://www.thearc.org/

DATING

This is a tough topic for most parents to think about, even regarding neurotypical teens. For our teens on the autism spectrum, it's an even tougher topic. Many teenagers on the more able end of the spectrum are not very interested in dating until they are in their early twenties as they mature emotionally at a slower rate that the average teen. However, they are hearing about it all the time at school.

As a child on the spectrum approaches puberty, parents should know that there are safety issues to consider. For girls there is the risk of putting themselves in compromising situations because of their inability to read social cues and body language, and because of their gullibility. They may not realize that others may wish to take advantage of them. For teen boys, they may be egged on to take part in inappropriate behavior, not knowing they are doing anything wrong.

On the positive side, it could be wonderful for your teen to have a romantic friendship with someone else. Again, there are risks involved in not knowing proper conduct. For both the positive and the negative reasons, it is important that the teen on the spectrum be taught about body cues, hidden meaning, and hidden agendas as well as what is and is not appropriate behavior, on their part and on the part of others. They need to know how to act, and what to do if someone acts inappropriately toward them. These are the social communication challenges typically faced by the more able on the spectrum, and in chapter 4, these areas will be covered and resources suggested. As for the specific topic of dating, there are a couple of good books to help you understand what an adolescent on the spectrum is going through:

Freaks, Geeks & Asperger Syndrome: A User Guide to Adolescence, by Luke Jackson. This book is useful for both the parents and teenagers to read. Luke Jackson is a teen on the spectrum, and this book offers an honest, inside view of his experiences.

Autism-Asperger's & Sexuality: Puberty and Beyond, by Jerry and Mary Newport. Jerry and Mary Newport are a married couple who both have Asperger's. In this book, they share their experience and advice about puberty and sexuality.

Sexuality is covered in chapter 3.

Sibling Issues

Siblings react differently, depending on their personality, as well as where they fall in the family pecking order, how old they are, and how many of them there are. Some are very helpful and involved with their sibling on the spectrum, while others barely interact with them. Keep in mind that many of these issues are sibling issues, not autism-related ones. Siblings will complain, compete, and experience some tension, no matter what. That's just part of family life.

It's not always easy to be a sibling of a teenager, but having a teenage sibling on the autism spectrum can add another dimension. These challenges can have both positive and negative effects on a sibling, and much depends on how the parents act and talk about autism spectrum disorders and what kind of attitude they have toward their teen and living with autism in the house. Parents need to be aware of the attitude they are portraying as well as the sibling's feelings in order to develop strategies of support to help him adjust.

Birth order and the number of siblings in a family affects the sibling experience. An older sibling has spent time with the parents before the birth of the younger one and so has developed communication patterns with the parents and created his own social network. Younger siblings usually accept life as it is, because it is all they know. If they have no other siblings, they may miss out on the social skills and "give and take" that brothers and sisters usually learn from one another.

Siblings who are the only other child seem to have a harder time coping. They may wish they had another sibling to relate to and have a "normal" relationship with. They may also feel that all their parents' hopes and dreams lie on them, and as a result they may strive to be perfect. In a way, being an only sibling is like being an only child, with many of the same pressures, expectations, and dynamics.

Siblings from a larger family will have other brothers and sisters to relate to and share the experiences, and they will realize that others have mixed emotion about the situation as well. There may be less pressure to help and others to be with when the parents are busy caring for the teen with autism. However, not all siblings relate the same way, and not all provide support. Their may be division caused by some taking the caretaker role and others refusing to take any responsibility.

Many siblings feel resentment at the extra attention the teenager with autism may require, and some feel guilt over their own good health. They may also feel saddled with what they perceive as parental expectations for them to be high achievers. If the sibling is a teenager as well, they may have difficulty in developing their own identity, either because they feel guilt about developing independence or they overidentify with their brother or sister. They may show embarrassment at having the brother or sister that they do and may not want to be seen with him or her in public. As they get older, siblings are more and more concerned about the reactions of their friends. They may be concerned about not being "cool." Often there is a feeling of resentment at having to take on extra household chores, coupled with restrictions in social activities.

On the positive side, many siblings develop a maturity and sense of responsibility greater than that of their peers, take pride in the accomplishments of their brother or sister, and develop a strong sense of loyalty. Siblings of ASD children are usually more tolerant of the differences in people and show compassion for others with special needs. Teenage siblings will be trying to make sense of their own values and feelings, and the "meaning of life" like all teenagers, and having the teen brother or sister on the spectrum can have a positive influence on their developing their own value system.

In all of this, it is important to remember that even without autism in a family, siblings have issues with their brothers and sisters. Most siblings can remember wishing they had a different brother or sister at one time or another, even when there was nothing wrong with him or her. Sibling rivalry is rampant, and there is no reason for it to abate during the teen years of the teen with an ASD. And most teen siblings feel embarrassed even by neurotypical brothers or sisters!

LIVING WITH A BROTHER OR SISTER WITH AN ASD

By the time the brother or sister on the spectrum is a teenager, the sibling has most often grown somewhat accustomed to his quirks and other behavioral characteristics inherent to autism. However, it is still hard to foster a relationship with a sibling who does not show much interest in you, needs strict adherence to routine, or is extremely sensitive to any noise in the house, which can be a problem if the sibling likes to have friends over. How can a sibling feel comfortable inviting friends over, knowing her older teen brother with an ASD may come running down the stairs with no clothes on at any moment? Although you may have taught your teen modesty, sometimes these things still can happen. Some of the behaviors exhibited by an adolescent on the spectrum would be typical of a younger child's behavior, but it can be hard for a neurotypical sibling to accept that they are still occurring. As time goes on and the behaviors continue (or are replaced with other more interesting ones) it can be hard for the sibling to feel anything but frustration and resentment.

FACTORS CONTRIBUTING TO HOW A SIBLING ADJUSTS

There are a number of factors that affect how a sibling adjusts, including the family size, the severity of the brother or sister's impairment, the age of the sibling at the time of the diagnosis, as well as the gender and age of the sibling and their place in the birth order. All in all, the parents' attitudes and expectations have a strong bearing on how a sibling adjusts.

HOW PARENTS CAN HELP

Even though the sibling by now has most likely had many years to adjust while their brother or sister on the autism spectrum was growing up to be a teenager, the siblings still need help and support from the parents. Here are some tips:

• Keep the lines of communication open. Knowing that they can discuss their feelings and ask questions is the most important thing for siblings. Let them know their feelings are normal.

• Remind siblings that if you need to give more of your time and attention to the tween or teen on the spectrum, it does not mean that you also give him more of your love. Let them know you love them just as much, and that they are just as important. They need to hear it.

• Make sure that siblings have a private, autism-free zone to call their own. Install locks to make sure they have a secure place to keep their precious objects. Siblings need to feel they are safe and have privacy.

• Set up consequences for the child with an ASD if he wrecks or ruins siblings' belongings.

• Explain to the sibling what it is like for the tween or teen on the spectrum to be going through puberty. If they are older and have experienced becoming a teenager, they will understand. If they are younger, they will need more information about how this can be a time of turmoil.

• Make time to spend alone with the siblings on a regular basis. It doesn't have to be a long period of time. Even a quick breakfast alone together or fifteen minutes before bedtime with you can help them feel important and let them know they can talk to you privately. Schedule a special outing every once in a while.

• Do what you can to try to get the behaviors, obsessions, and oversensitivities of the teenager on the spectrum under control. See "Taking Responsibility for Behavior–Self-Regulation" in this chapter, as well as chapter 6 on ideas on how to do this.

• Make sure the teenager has learned to do some chores and has some household responsibilities. This will ensure that he is contributing to the household (which he should) and also make the sibling feel that your household rules are fair.

• Make sure siblings have some time when they can have friends over and spend time with them without having to always include their brother or sister and without having to worry about problem behaviors from the teen on the spectrum.

• If the sibling doesn't understand how autism affects the teen brother or sister, make more information available to her. Perhaps having someone outside the family unit explain it to her would be useful.

• It may be helpful for siblings to meet or talk to children in the same situation. Check with your local organizations to see if a support group for siblings exists in your area. If not, see if there is any interest, read the book *Sibshops: Workshops for Siblings of Children with Special Needs,* by Donald Meyer and Patricia Vadasy, and start your own workshop with other families.

• There are books out there about having a sibling with autism or with special needs. Some are geared toward the parents and others toward the sibling. A good one for parents is *Being the Other One: Growing Up with a Brother or Sister Who Has Special Needs,* by Kate Strohm.

Marriage, Spouses, and Partners

It's a well-known fact that the divorce rate of parents of special-needs children is higher than the national average. Many couples look forward to having children, and each person has his idea of what the expected child will be like. When the child does not match the expectation, or becomes seriously ill or regresses, there is a loss and anguish felt by the parent not unlike the stages of grief that people who are grieving the loss of a loved one experience.

Autism permeates the very core of family life the way water seeps into a sponge. Every pore is affected. Family life is all about communication and relationships: relationships between two adult lovers, relationships between parents and children, relationships between siblings. Yet, autism is all about communication challenges, misunderstanding of social cues, and lack of emotional understanding, thus affecting every relationship in the family.

Every couple that decides to start a family goes through a transition—from being two people in love, focused solely on each other, to adding a baby to the mix. Most couples with neurotypical children adjust, even if the road isn't always a smooth one. For parents of children with autism, adjusting is difficult for a myriad of reasons, the first being the loss of expectation, the loss of the child you thought you were having. For those whose child developed normally and then regressed around eighteen to twenty-four months, there is the added loss of the child they knew slipping away. And for those couples who have a child who never connected in the usual way—not much eye contact, no reaching out for or giving of affection, no reaching out for comfort when hurt, no asking for attention—it is hard for the parents not to feel rejected or unimportant to the child.

Keeping any marriage happy and healthy is hard work. It takes good communication, patience, understanding, and forgiveness. It requires emotional support from one to the other. It takes time—time to share intimate moments, time to enjoy a social life together, and time for relaxing moments. All too often, these necessary and important moments get swallowed up by our autistic children's needs. The problems and tensions that existed before children came into the picture get exacerbated, and new tensions arise as well. In many cases, one parent is more accepting, while the other is more in denial. One parent becomes the super healer, while the other takes a backseat or, worse, sticks his or her head in the sand. One becomes emotional, the other stoic.

One spouse may believe in being proactive, doing all they can to help the child; the other may listen to the traditional professional's outlook of "no hope" and feel the professionals know best. How much time, energy, and money is to be spent on helping the child is based on personal philosophy, and in this the couple may clash.

Sometimes there can be a reaching out to one other, and the couple becomes closer than ever, bonded in their shared circumstances and challenges. Unfortunately, more often than not the stress of dealing with autism and all it entails—the constant and necessary advocacy at school, the fighting for services and supports, the added financial burden, trying to handle behaviors and meltdowns at home—becomes a wedge pushing the spouses further and further apart. Overwhelmed, stressed, and exhausted, the couple's communication becomes impaired and even autistic-like, lacking emotion and reciprocity, making it hard for one to feel empathy and understanding for the other spouse. (This resembles the lack of theory of mind autistic individuals often display, as explained in chapter 1.)

Avoiding becoming a dysfunctional marriage requires a commitment from both spouses. It means agreeing on what lengths to go to in treating the child or teaching him skills. It means work at scheduling time alone together, work at communicating in a positive and empathetic manner, work at splitting up the household and family responsibilities so that neither partner is overload. Remembering and focusing on why the two came together out of love for one another, and started a family in the first place, may help in getting through the rough patches. Couples' retreats, away from the children, where parents can learn to reconnect and be together can be helpful as well.

KEEPING YOUR MARRIAGE OR SIGNIFICANT RELATIONSHIP INTACT—A FEW SUGGESTIONS

- **Accept the fact that your partner may react to autism differently from you.** Every person reacts differently to the diagnosis, and as the child becomes a teenager there are other issues that come into play and bring up different beliefs and reactions in the spouses. You may not always agree, but you need to be able to understand that everyone reacts differently.

- **Keep the lines of communication open.** Both partners need to feel comfortable sharing concerns, emotions, beliefs, and desires. The ability to discuss what to do, and each person's feelings and opinions, is important to any couple's relationship.

• **Reexamine your personal beliefs in regard to disability and sickness.** Both partners will need to think about their personal belief system. Both may have differing philosophies in regard to disabilities, and when your child is not "cured" and your teenager will obviously be facing challenges, the parents will need to reassess their personal beliefs. Sometimes the parents have differing philosophies that add another point of dissension to a troubled marriage. For others, a difference of belief is not a concern. Every couple is different.

• **Arrange for scheduled time alone together on a regular basis.** This is an important part of any relationship, and with a teen on the autism spectrum, it's easy to let this essential time fall by the wayside. Don't let it.

• **Decide together what the division of labor will be.** There is a lot more to be done when you have a child with an ASD. It is rare to find a partnership that naturally absorbs the extra work and stress without one of the partners feeling as if the burden has been placed on them. Usually, one person jumps right in and takes over (often this is the mother). This leads to burnout and even more disengagement on the part of the other partner. Sometimes, when one parent is working to support the family and the other is the homemaker, the extra burden falls on the homemaker, while the breadwinner tends to be around less and less, as the workplace starts to seem more comfortable than the home environment at the moment.

• **Find someone to talk to.** Talking to other parents in the same situation can be helpful. Just being with another couple who know what the two of you are living every day can make you feel better. Perhaps you can help each other out by sharing information or tips, or just meet up to relax among understanding grown-ups. You can meet other parents ASD teens and teens through local support groups.

• **Go to couples' counseling.** If you are having a difficult time and feel that your relationship is severely suffering and heading the wrong way, couples' counseling can be helpful. Don't wait until things are so bad that you are thinking of splitting up. And if your partner refuses to go, go alone. Contact your physician for a referral. Try to find a therapist who has experience with ASDs. Ask your local support group for the names of any professionals they may know.

Listed below are some additional resources parents might find helpful:

Book: *A "Stranger" Among Us: Hiring In-Home Support for a Child with Autism Spectrum Disorders or Other Neurological Differences*, by Lisa Lieberman, MSW, LCSW.

Educational directory: www.autismtutors.com. This is a great nonprofit website where parents can find tutors and other professionals to help them in their geographical area.

Books about the parent experience:

Elijah's Cup: A Family's Journey into the Community and Culture of High-Functioning Autism and Asperger's Syndrome, by Valerie Paradiz.

Finding Ben: A Mother's Journey Through the Maze of Asperger's, by Barbara LaSalle.

Books that give tips for helping your teen on the spectrum at home:

Incentives for Change: Motivating People with Autism Spectrum Disorders to Learn and Gain Independence, by Lara Delmolino, Ph.D, and Sandra L. Harris, Ph.D.

1001 Great Ideas for Teaching and Raising Children with Autism Spectrum Disorders, by Ellen Notbohm and Veronica Zysk.

Parenting a Child with Asperger Syndrome: 200 Tips and Strategies, by Brenda Boyd.

FOOD FOR THOUGHT

A Couples Retreat Can Help

by Delores Fraser McFadden

A weekend retreat designed to strengthen and support couples parenting children on the autism spectrum with extremely challenging behaviors was created in Orange County, New York, last fall by the county's Department of Mental Health/Developmental Disabilities Division. The retreat was designed to help couples destress, reconnect, learn communication and coping strategies, with a special emphasis on getting through the holiday season.

Fifteen couples stayed in a bed-and-breakfast type facility at the Warwick Conference Center where they dined by candlelight, participated in workshops that focused on communication and coping strategies, learned massage and aromatherapy techniques, participated in concurrent mom and dad groups and enjoyed a mini-spa experience with giveaways. Key to the weekend's success was the provision of respite; families were given the choice between three options.

By all accounts the retreat was successful; four indicators of success are highlighted below.

- Fathers were actively engaged in discussions, socializing, and networking. This was a unique opportunity for dads to meet other dads with similar issues and experiences. The presence of autism in the family can result in fathers either having a very limited or no social circle or a very active social life that does not include the wife and child with a disability.

- The contrast between how parents looked on Friday and Sunday afternoons was remarkable. Physically, they looked more alert, healthier, and relaxed on Sunday.
- The families have become a resource for each other. One of the parents created an online group for retreat participants to vent, to set up play dates, organize moms' night out and dads-only social activities. Some have initiated a baby-sitter exchange, watching each other's children.
- For most, it was the first time away overnight from their children. They now have the confidence to do it again.

Delores Fraser McFadden is director of Developmental Disabilities Services, Orange County Department of Mental Health. For more information, contact McFadden at dmcfadden@co.orange.ny.us.

3

What Every Teenager Needs to Know About Puberty and Hygiene, Grooming and Dressing, and Sexuality

My parents dropped the ball on this one. I needed information on sex. I also needed to know that it could be a healthy part of my life despite my teenage insecurity. I didn't get a shred of that. Judging from what I have heard at many conferences, I fear that Mother and Dad have lots of company. . . .

In many families, parents seem to hope that sex will be something they can avoid. That may be true in your family. However, there is a lot more to being a good parent than writing checks to all of the vendors. Some things you have to just do yourself and talking about sex is one of them.

—JERRY NEWPORT, *Autism-Asperger's & Sexuality: Puberty and Beyond*

PUBERTY and hygiene are areas I had never given much thought to as a parent. Then, gradually, it dawned on me that I was going to have to teach my son Jeremy all about these matters. When Jeremy started to grow and change, I was surprised by all the things I hadn't thought about that a parent needs to teach their preteen male. Coming from a family of five girls and one boy, the male teenage growth experience was not in my frame of reference. Having been raised with all those sisters and only one bathroom, I was never directly taught about changing bodies in puberty and about hygiene. I learned it all by osmosis, having to share the bathroom with my sisters—and we didn't include my brother.

Jeremy has a very difficult time with motor initiation, motor planning, sequencing, and has sensitivity issues. All this makes it hard for him to follow through on self-care routines, and makes it very hard for me to teach him independence in all areas. It's easier to have discussions with him about delicate matters you can't talk about in public than to get him to follow through independently on self-care such as brushing his teeth. And I'm not quite sure how motivated he is to learn any faster. It's so hard for him to get all his sensory processing and body parts working together that he needs to believe that the payback from learning all this will be worth it in the end. I know he needs to be independent, and if I don't teach him certain things, who will? Sometimes I feel badly that I haven't yet gotten him to be more independent, but I won't give up. When I look back over the years I see how much he has learned and how much we have managed to teach him, and I focus on that. That progress gives me the energy to move forward, one small step at a time.

Puberty: A Special Note for Parents

Life as a parent gets even more interesting as children grow and become teenagers, whether they are on the autism spectrum or not. The purpose of the tween years is to serve as a buffer between childhood and the real teenage years, not only for the child getting used to his or her changing body and emotions, but for us as parents to get used to them growing up. Whatever happened to that sweet smell of childhood? you wonder as you get a whiff of your twelve-year-old walking down the hallway, and you realize the discussion about deodorant is suddenly long overdue.

Puberty is an awkward time, even for neurotypical kids. Bodies are changing, hormones are raging, moods are swinging. All children nearing adolescence need to have an understanding of what is going on in their bodies and how to take care of themselves. Children with ASDs need even more information and input from parents at this time, and need to be taught specifically about puberty and all it entails. Those who are in a special education class for part of the day may have some of these areas covered in their program and addressed in the IEP. For those on the spectrum who are fully included in school, being part of the "in" crowd and being popular with the peers has a lot to do with hygiene, presentation, and clothes. This is very important in order for the student to fit in and to be less at risk for bullying. Fitting in is a necessary skill that is important for self-esteem as well as important for future success in the world of neurotypicals. For safety reasons, all need to have an understanding of appropriate public behavior versus private behavior, appropriate and inappropriate touching. Learning about sex and intimacy is important as well, since adulthood is fast approaching.

Remember that *how* you teach your child about these areas is as important as *what* you teach him. Having a calm, nonemotional, but "need-to-know" attitude will go a long way toward helping your child now and in the future.

What Teens on the Spectrum Have to Say

As always, books written by people with an autism spectrum disorder are very informative and can give you a peek as to what your teen might be feeling or experiencing. Some of the difficulties they encounter in terms of information and sensory processing as well as sensory overstimulation can help us understand teens who are more severely impacted by autism. Often, suggested strategies in these areas can be modified to help them as well. Although these authors have their own personal viewpoints, reading about their experiences with puberty, dating, and sexuality can give us insight on how to approach these personal subjects with our tweens and teens. Some of these books may have sections that are appropriate for your teen to read, with your approval. Some suggested books are:

- *Freaks, Geeks & Asperger Syndrome,* by Luke Jackson

- *Autism-Asperger's & Sexuality,* by Jerry and Mary Newport

- *Your Life Is Not a Label,* by Jerry Newport

- *Pretending to be Normal: Living with Asperger's Syndrome,* by Liane Holliday Willey

- *Asperger Syndrome in the Family: Redefining Normal,* by Liane Holliday Willey

- *Beyond the Wall: Personal Experiences with Autism and Asperger Syndrome,* by Stephen Shore

DECIDING WHEN TO TEACH WHAT

Every child, whether or not they have an ASD, will need to learn practical skills related to puberty and body changes: hygiene, grooming and dressing, different types of relationships, modesty and appropriate public behaviors, masturbation and sexuality. For teenagers on the spectrum, it is important that assumptions not be made about what they know or will pick up instinctively, or about their level of comprehension of what they are hearing and seeing. A teenager with Asperger's does not just "know" these things and learn them by imitating his mainstream peers, as another teenager might; he needs to be taught. Each aspect of health and hygiene, and why we are doing self-care, needs to be explained to the tween and teen in a way that he or she can understand.

In the sections below, suggestions have been made for explaining different aspects of puberty. For each child, you can elaborate or simplify, depending on your child's needs and abilities. As discussed earlier, even if your child is severely impaired and you are unsure of his level of comprehension, it is important that you explain and teach these areas to him, because he may be picking up a lot more than you think.

Here are some general guidelines regarding what, where, how, and when to teach your child.

• **Your child's chronological age.** The focus will be on different areas depending on whether or not your child is a tween (nine to twelve years old), a young teen (thirteen to sixteen) or an older teen (seventeen to nineteen).

• **What he has already been taught.** Perhaps in late elementary school your child sat through a film about hygiene or sex education, and then you verified that he understood the information, and you have added to it already. Perhaps your child doesn't have a clue. Some children at this age are fairly independent when it comes to self-help skills; others are less able and may still be dependent on others. Because of the high risk of sexual abuse in special-needs population, it is important that the less functionally able be taught how to take care of their bathing and hygiene needs themselves. As parents you will need to determine what your child knows and where to go from here.

• **The child's physical maturity level.** Your child may go through puberty at an early age, or he may be a physically late bloomer. It is important to teach your tween about puberty before his or her body starts developing. Otherwise, a girl may think she is bleeding to death when she first menstruates, and a boy may think there is something wrong when he first ejaculates.

• **The child's emotional maturity level.** Usually, teens with ASDs are emotionally less mature than their chronological peers, even if they are intellectually more mature. They may not be ready for some information about intimacy and sexuality, but they will need to have some sex education so as to not be at risk of behaving inappropriately or being sexually abused. Also, students who are fully integrated will be hearing their peers discuss the subject and need to be aware of what it all means.

• **Whether or not your child is fully integrated at school.** All teenagers need to know about grooming and dressing, but if your child is fully included in school, you will need to teach him much more about grooming, dressing, styles, dating, and why this area is so important to his neurotypical peers.

• **The level of understanding your teen demonstrates as well as his functional abilities.** How you decide to teach these different topics will depend on how much understanding your child has. My own philosophy is to explain to a person as if he understands, then back it up with visual and auditory input in the form of social stories and if necessary do a task analysis and put up a word or picture schedule. Also, motor planning and functional abilities need to be taken into consideration. All can learn, even if it takes a long time. It's finding out *how* to teach them that is the key.

• **His or her method of communication and learning style.** Your child may be a visual learner or an auditory learner; he may read words or understand pictures. Perhaps your child uses a voice output device. There are ways of teaching and verifying understanding of concepts at all levels.

• **Your philosophical and religious beliefs.** As discussed in chapter 2, every parent has his or her own beliefs about how much to teach about subjects such as masturbation, intimacy, and sex education. Keep in mind that a minimum needs to be taught to keep your child safe and healthy. Another important consideration is that when your child becomes an adult, and when he lives outside the home, he will have the right to choose for himself about being sexually active or not. As a parent, you are a trusted and important person in your child's life, and information coming from you could be very helpful in keeping your teenager safe, and in helping him when he is an adult to make informed decisions about this important part of his life.

• **Whether or not these areas will be addressed at home, at school, or both.** If your tween or teen is fully included in general education classes, chances are you will have to teach them about all these ar-eas at home. Even if during PE they have a lesson on hygiene and a sex education presentation, you will need to make sure that they have "understood" or taken away the most important messages from the class. For teens who spend part of their day in a special education classroom, there may be areas here that are taught or covered at school. Many middle schools and high schools have life-skill programs and access to curriculum for teaching these concepts. You may wish to ask your child's teacher about these ar-eas, and you may wish to have some covered in the IEP. Your teacher may be able to give you some suggestions for at home. If you have access to a behavioral expert, you may wish to ask them for some advice as well on how to teach some of these concepts.

Taking Care of Myself: A Hygiene, Puberty and Personal Cur-riculum for Young People with Autism, by Mary Wrobel, is an excel-lent resource for parents as well as educators. In this book, Wrobel has outlined stories and activities designed for students of different ability levels. These ideas can be adapted to your child's individual needs. She covers everything from teaching why and how you wash your body, to why we do not touch our private areas in public.

1001 Great Ideas for Teaching and Raising Children with Autism Spectrum Disorders, by Ellen Notbohm and Veronica Zysk, is another wonderful book full of great tips and ideas for all aspects of raising a child on the spectrum, including great tips for helping with self-care skills.

Growth and Development

WHAT PARENTS NEED TO KNOW

People on the autism spectrum usually like predictability and rou-tine and dislike change. Some teenagers have a hard time with the idea that their bodies are changing and growing and that they are getting bigger and growing out of their clothes. For this reason, it is important to prepare students for the changes to their bodies before they begin puberty.

Parents need to be aware of the following facts:

• Hygiene is an area that needs to be addressed or readdressed at this time. Puberty brings the onset of sweat, and some teenagers will develop acne as a result of intensified amounts of oil in their glands. Good habits need to be developed and emphasized. Daily face washing and the application of deodorant are good places to start. Boys need to be told about shaving facial hair. Girls will need to learn how to use feminine hygiene products.

• Seizure activity begins during puberty for one in four individuals with ASDs, possibly due to the increase of hormonal changes in the body. Sometimes the seizures are associated with convulsions and are noticeable, but for others they are very minor and may not be detected by simple observation. You may wish to keep an eye out for the signs that indicate seizure activity discussed in chapter 1 and contact a knowledgeable medical professional.

• Boys usually start puberty around age eleven or twelve and continue to develop until they are around twenty years old. They start producing testosterone, which leads to changes in the body such as hair growth on the face, thickening of the hair on their legs, and the growth of pubic hair. They begin to sweat more and excrete body odors that they did not have before. They have growth spurts and developing muscles as well as deepening of the voice, the growth of penis and testicles, and development of an Adam's apple.

• Girls generally start puberty before boys, beginning sometimes as young as eight or nine years old, and continue to grow in height, weight, and breast size until the age of sixteen. In girls, overall body shape starts to change as breasts and hips begin to develop. Often they have pubic hair by the time they are ten or eleven and many have their first period between the ages of eleven and twelve. However, girls develop at different rates, so it is difficult to predict when menstruation will occur.

• It is important that girls are told about the menstrual cycle before their first period, so they are not confused and upset and think there is something physically wrong. They will also need to be told who are the appropriate people to discuss this with (parents, a teacher, a girlfriend) and that it is not necessarily a lunchtime conversation topic in a mixed group. Also, specific instruction about how to use sanitary pads is necessary.

• Boys need to be told about how their bodies are changing, about erections and "wet dreams" that can happen while they are sleeping, and that ejaculation can happen when their penis is rubbed. Otherwise, they may be perplexed and wonder what is wrong with them. This area will be discussed in the masturbation section later on in this chapter.

• The child on the autism spectrum who has difficulty with meltdowns and aggression may calm down at puberty. However, the teenage years are often a time when tantrums appear or reappear. Usually these are due to frustration, because like all teens, autistic teens want to have their way and not always have to follow the rules that educators and parents set for them. Perhaps the teen is bored with being taught the same thing he didn't get in his special education class last year. Or perhaps the Asperger's teen doesn't understand the social cues and changes in his non-AS peers.

• As mentioned in chapter 1, precocious puberty has been estimated to be twenty times higher in children with neurodevelopment disabilities, which includes ASDs. Parents should watch their children and preteens for some of these signs: pubic hair growth; more hair growth on back, under arms, on the face; genital development; breast development; increased touching and rubbing of genitals; and more aggressive behavior. Children may have increased height and advanced bone plate growth. If you have any concerns in this area, discuss this with the medical professional who is treating your child.

• As mentioned in chapter 1, teenagers with ASDs may be physically maturing at the same rate as their teenage peers, but emotionally they tend to mature much later. Early adolescence is when most young people seek more independence from their parents, seek even more approval from their peers, and try to fit in with the crowd. Teenagers start showing an interest in romance, start dating, and perhaps getting physical with members of the opposite sex. This is usually in marked contrast with the ASD teenager, who may continue to stick to the rules and value high grades, while his peers are interested in romance and start testing the system.

• There is a risk of depression during these years as it becomes apparent to the teenager with an ASD how different he is from his peers. As he becomes more interested in socializing, he may be teased and scorned by others due to his lack of required skills. Your child may be experiencing feelings of anxiety, depression, or the "blues" that will go unrecognized if he is not encouraged to talk about his thoughts with you. Your child needs to know that these feelings are normal and how to recognize and identify the different feelings he is having. For those less able, picture icons or simple drawings of happy and sad faces can initially help the nonverbal person to communicate how they feel.

The risk of depression should be taken seriously as research has shown that there is a higher incidence of depression or manic depression in families with a child on the autism spectrum, perhaps due to a biological predisposition. It is important that a parent investigate all the traditional and nontraditional methods for treating depression, if the condition persists and if talking about it is impossible or not helping to alleviate the problem. In his book *Asperger's Syndrome: A Guide for Parents and Professionals,* Tony Attwood outlines some strategies for communicating about emotions. See chapter 6 for more information on possible treatments.

WHAT TEENAGERS NEED TO KNOW ABOUT PUBERTY

Although each teenager needs gender-specific information to learn about his or her body, both girls and boys need to learn general characteristics about the other sex. This is necessary for discussions about sex education, sexuality, and safety issues including appropriate and inappropriate touching. Parents can look at the other gender's section for ideas on what their child should know.

WHAT TO TELL YOUR SON, SIMPLY

His body will grow and change. This is okay, everyone's body changes, some more than others. Someday he will look like his dad and other adult men. Sometimes men grow heavier, sometimes men grow taller. His body will start to change in other ways. His chest will get bigger and his arms and legs will be muscular. His feet will grow and so will his nose. He will grow hair on his body, under his arms, and on his private areas. One day he will start to grow hair on his face, and he will learn to shave it. He will begin to sweat more, especially under the armpits, and he will excrete body odors that he did not have before. He will need to learn to use deodorant. Some weeks he will have growth spurts, meaning it will seem like his body is growing every day, and other weeks he will stay the same. His voice will get deeper, his penis and testicles will get bigger. He will develop an Adam's apple on his neck. His body will probably keep changing and growing every year until he is around twenty years old. It's okay to grow and change. It's okay to become a man.

WHAT TO TELL YOUR DAUGHTER, SIMPLY

Her body will grow and change. This is okay, everyone's body changes, some more than others. Someday she will look like her mom and other adult women. Sometimes women grow heavier, sometimes women grow taller. Her body will start to change in other ways. She will begin to grow breasts and she will need to wear a bra. She will grow hair on her body, under her arms, and on her private areas. Soon, she will start her period. Blood will come out of her vagina— her privates. Blood will come out every month for about five days and then stop until the following month. This is called her "period." During her period, she will need to wear pads in her panties to catch the blood. Her mom will show her how to use them. Her body is growing into a woman's body. This is okay, it is part of becoming an adult woman like Mom. She will begin to perspire more, especially under the armpits, and she will excrete body odors that she did not have before. She will need to learn to start using deodorant. Some weeks she will have growth spurts, meaning it will seem like her body is growing every day, and other weeks she will stay the same. Her body will probably keep changing and growing every year until she is around sixteen years old. It's okay to grow and change. It's okay to become a woman.

Hygiene and Health

Hygiene and health are also areas that need to be emphasized. Cleanliness is a contributing factor to self-esteem and health. Most tweens and teens on the autism spectrum do not independently learn what they need to know about hygiene and self-care. Although it is best to start teaching about hygiene, health, and self-care before puberty, it is never too late. The goal is to teach teens to be as independent as possible in these areas. For many, this will be an important, ongoing lifelong goal. Teaching your teen about independent hygiene skills also teaches them about modesty and responsibility.

Perhaps your child has already mastered some of the self-care areas discussed in this section. That's great; you can move on to another area. Perhaps you have been trying to get your child to be independent or take responsibility for these areas of his self-care and have not been successful. If that's the case, I hope you will find some helpful tips below.

FOOD FOR THOUGHT

From Their Perspective

Parents, don't scream at them to tidy their bedroom if you haven't explained exactly what tidy up means. . . . If the instructions are clear—first pick up the dirty clothes, then put them in the linen bin, and all that kind of stuff—then at least the child has something specific to do. . . .

I often wander around my room wondering where to start. Checklists and charts are good for that kind of stuff. The same goes for washing and personal hygiene: explain exactly how to wash their hair and their body and exactly how many times they have to change their underwear. Now this certainly doesn't mean that they will then be clean and tidy. Ha! . . . Without these explanations though, there will be no chance at all. I have to admit that even with specific instructions, washing and stuff like that are not a top priority in my life. I always feel as if I am doing it for the benefit of others because personally I don't care whether I am clean or dirty and don't care what other people think about me either. This is something I am trying to change, purely and simply because I have read my own dating chapter!!

—Luke Jackson, *Freaks, Geeks & Asperger Syndrome:*
A User Guide to Adolescence

TEACHING HEALTH AND HYGIENE SKILLS

Sometimes the lack of learning or implementing health and hygiene routines has to do with remembering the different steps, remembering which routines to do when, or not having the motor planning to follow through. Here are some basic strategies to teach basic self-help skills that may be helpful to your adolescent:

• **Make a schedule.** Place the self-care schedule, as a reminder, near where it should take place. For example, perhaps in the bathroom or his bedroom there is the schedule for taking a shower, putting on clean clothes, brushing his teeth, brushing his hair, putting away his things. Perhaps a teen prefers a daily planner that he likes to consult instead of reminders on the wall. Some prefer words, some need pictures. Whatever works is what you should use.

• **Use picture icons.** For visual learners who may not be reading, visual supports with picture icons are great tools for teaching them about all the area covered in this chapter, and also for visual reminders on the schedule. For those who are nonverbal, they can learn to communicate using these icons if the icons are in their communication book and the tweens and teens are taught what they represent.

• **Write up a task analysis.** Perform the task a few times yourself and analyze and note each and every step necessary to perform the task. Have your child do it and see if it's the best way for him to do it. Once you have written it up, watch your child and note for each step if he does it independently or with prompts, and what kind of prompts he needs. This is the baseline. You will see a pattern emerge of what steps you will need to focus on teaching him.

• **Use backward chaining.** If you need to teach all the steps of a self-care routine, start with the last step and when that is mastered add the next-to-last step, until it is learned, and so on. By starting with the last step, and working backwards, the teen always ends with completing the routine, which is rewarding as well as teaches the importance of completion. For example, if drying his hands on the towel is the last step of washing his hands, start with that. Then add the next to the last step, turning the faucet off, and when that is mastered, add the step of rinsing his hands under the water, and so on.

• **Teach "motor memory."** Some people on the autism spectrum have trouble getting their muscles or limbs to move to do what needs to be done and have described this in much the way stroke patients do—they try to "order" their limbs to move but they don't. However, by hand-over-hand physically moving and motoring your child through the self-care task one step at a time, it can create a "motor memory" for that skill. (See Food for Thought, page 96.)

• **Use music or songs as a mnemonic.** Rhythm, repetition, melody, and rhyme can all aid memory. Many individuals with autism can learn sequences to self-care by hearing the steps sung to familiar tunes (such as "Twinkle, Twinkle, Little Star" or "Here We Go 'Round the Mulberry Bush"). You can sing the memory tune as the task is performed, and then tape them so the teen can turn it on himself to hear it when it is time to perform the routine. Eventually they will sing or hum the tune and it will become a memory aid.

• **Use videotape and video modeling.** Watching videos of other people performing the task can be a good way for some teens to learn. The tapes can be fun and easy to make with your own camcorder at home—you don't have to be an expert. Watching the tape where someone they know is modeling or where they themselves are modeling the correct way of doing something can be a good way for your child to learn. Popping in a video is cheaper than paying a tutor and less tiring, and may work for your child. There are also a few ready-made videos that you may find helpful. For visual learners on the less able end of the spectrum, the Able Individual Video Learning Series by Child First (www.child1first.com) may be a useful tool. These DVDs and tapes cover hygiene, chores, and dressing.

Resources to help those who are not verbal to communicate about these sensitive issues include:

• The Mayer-Johnson Boardmaker Picture Communication Symbols are very good and have many of the needed pictures for sensitive topics. (www.mayerjohnson.com, tel.: 800-588-4548)

Creating Motor Memory
or
How I Taught My Son Some Basic Motor Skills

Motor initiation and planning has always been a problem for my son Jeremy. When he was a baby in France, I had to get a physical therapist to show me how to teach him to roll over, sit with his back straight, get into the sitting position, crawl; I even had to teach him his reflexes, how to put his arm out when pushed so he wouldn't fall over. I taught him by moving his body parts repeatedly through the sequence of actions needed to accomplish whatever it was he needed to learn. He learned nothing physical on his own except how to twirl toys (I can't take credit for that!). As he got older, through traditional discrete trial methods starting with hand-over-hand prompting, we were able to teach him some physical activities and to make choices independently. However, it would take a long time to teach him, and even with all the behavioral supervision and occupational therapist, there were some physical tasks he never learned.

When doing research for my first book, *Autism Spectrum Disorders,* I had the good fortune to meet Soma and Tito Mukhopadhyay, and I read Tito's book, *The Mind Tree.* In it, Tito described how he is unable to move his limbs, although he wished he could. "Of course from my knowledge of biology, I knew that I had voluntary muscles and involuntary muscles. I also knew that my hands and legs were made of voluntary muscles. But I experimented with myself that when I ordered my hand to pick up a pencil, that I could not do it. I remember long back when I ordered my lips to move I could not do it."

Tito's comments got me thinking about how some stroke patients report "willing" or thinking their affected arm or leg to move, but are unable to do so. Eventually, many regain use of their limbs because the physical therapist moves their limb over and over and they practice, and over time some regain the use of their limb.

I thought that perhaps Jeremy was not learning certain parts of tasks that required physical movement or motor coordination because he was not getting enough motor input from those of us teaching him. I discovered the best way to teach him was to spend a few hours on the same motor skill or task, motoring him very quickly through that physical step of the task over and over, giving him short breaks of a few minutes each doing something he enjoyed that was easy to do (such as favorite puzzles, looking at books) and then getting back to the task. For years he could put his plate of food into the microwave, but could not push the buttons independently. We knew from asking him, using the Rapid Prompting Method, that he understood what to do, but he was not following through. After just two hours of the above motoring-through method, he was able to do it independently, and now he is able to heat up food using the microwave completely unassisted.

• The Slater Software company makes a picture-supported computer literacy program called Picture It and a talking word-processing program that allows students to easily read and write with picture supports. (www.slatersoftware.com, tel.: 877-306-6968)

• The Don Johnston company produces good products for assistive technology, including Write: OutLoud computer software. (www.donjohnston.com, tel.: 800-999-4660)

HEALTH AND HYGIENE TROUBLE SPOTS

Some tweens and teens on the spectrum have a hard time with certain self-care routines because of sensory issues. This may be apparent if your child refuses to participate at all or has a temper tantrum at a certain point each time he is going through a self-care routine. If you have done a task analysis, you can identify where in the task your child is having issues. Some teens who are relatively compliant may tolerate the task when you prompt them through it, but will not independently carry it out. Those on the more able end who are supposed to be doing these routines on their own may just skip them. Here are some examples of a few common sensory issues that come up with self-care, and some ideas to get you thinking about possible solutions.

Washing hair. This could be a problem area for a number of reasons, which you will have to analyze by paying attention to your child's reaction. Remember that it is not necessary to wash hair every day. Washing less often will help keep the discomfort to a minimum.

• He does not like to put his head under the stream of water from the shower and/or refuses to rub the shampoo into his head with his hands, and tolerates you doing it, but doesn't like it. This is most likely because the top of his head is too sensitive. Fix the shower stream to low pressure if possible, let him use a cup to rinse his hair. Apply "deep pressure" to his scalp beforehand by placing your hands on his scalp and firmly applying pressure for a few minutes, and try having him use a big car-washing sponge to soap up his hair. Another idea is to let him know how long he needs to tolerate this, for example, rub five times back and forth, or rinse with three cupfuls. It is always easier to tolerate something that makes us uncomfortable when we are in control of it.

• He seems okay with pressure on his head, but does not tolerate the shampoo. Perhaps he is sensitive to the smell or the texture. Try unscented shampoo, or a bar of soap if it is the gooey texture he does not like. Let him help you shop for shampoos to try.

• He seems to tolerate the shampoo and will rub it into his hair, but does not like water flowing down onto his face, or does not like to have his face wet. He can shampoo sitting in the bathtub, hold his head back, and use a cup to rinse the soap off away from his face. Rolling a washcloth and putting it on the forehead will stop errant trickles of water. Using baby shampoos that will not sting the eyes is one precaution that may be useful as well.

Brushing hair. If your tween is resistant to brushing his hair, it is probably because he has a sensitive head. He may willingly brush the sides and back of his head, but not the top. Again, applying deep pressure (and eventually teaching him how to do this himself) to the top of the head will help. Use a brush with soft bristles. Desensitizing the top of his head by starting off with a stroke, then adding a few at a time, and limiting to a tolerable number, will also help. Keep his hair trimmed and short so that he won't have much difficulty looking neat.

Brushing teeth. Some people on the autism spectrum find this is a real challenge. The teeth and gums are particularly sensitive, and it can be very difficult to convince a person who finds it extremely painful to brush his teeth effectively on a regular basis. Not only is this a hygiene issue, it is a health issue as gum disease and cavities can cause havoc in a person's mouth as time goes on. One way to try desensitizing is to have your tween or teen use his (clean) finger to rub his gums before brushing his teeth. Or, if he will tolerate it, you can wear disposable gloves and try doing this yourself. Using a toothbrush with very soft bristles can help, as can encouraging him to bite down on the bristles. Using a piece of gauze or washcloth dipped in fluoride wash can clean the teeth as well. There are textured teeth wipes for sale that might also be helpful. Adaptive and battery-operated toothbrushes are also available. Visit www.colliscurve.com, www.magicaltoysandproducts.com, and www.bestbabystore.com.

Toileting issues. This is an area that parents of tweens and teens may no longer have to deal with. However, for some teenagers, toileting issues continue to be a problem. Sometimes these issues are physical, other times behavioral and even communicative. Some teens continue to have a hard time controlling their motor functioning or have reactions to extreme light due to sensory processing issues that make it difficult for them to control their bladders (such as walking into a supermarket with strong fluorescent lights from outside where it is gray). Some sleep very soundly at night and do not feel the urge to urinate and wet while they are sleeping. Some teens may not be able to communicate the need to use the restroom in moments of stress and are forbidden to leave their seat in class, and perhaps they can't hold it anymore. Before finding a way to solve or work on this problem, you'll need to understand what the particular issue is. Speaking to a behavior specialist who knows the child can be helpful in implementing strategies.

A useful book that guides you through what to do in an easy-to-understand format is *Toilet Training for Individuals with Autism &*

Related Disorders: A Comprehensive Guide for Parents & Teachers, by Maria Wheeler, M.Ed.

Grooming, Dressing, and Looking Good

WHAT PARENTS NEED TO KNOW

Grooming and Dressing

Looking good is important at any age, but it takes on a whole new meaning during the adolescent years. The teen years are when children start focusing on what they look like, what to wear, what's in and what's not, and being cool. Being "in" is often more important than academics to the neurotypical teen. At the very least, it's important that teens on the autism spectrum look neat and clean; but having an item or two with "cool" labels will help them fit in even more. This is true regardless of whether or not they spend most of the time in a special ed class with a minimum of mainstreaming or they are fully integrated. Parents, your teenager needs your support here.

Luke Jackson and Jerry and Mary Newport, in their respective books, talk about the importance of looking right for the Asperger's teen. The Newports say that right from the first day at school it is important to not look like a misfit, and teenagers on the spectrum need help in this area.

The different aspects that need to be taught to your teen—no matter their functioning level—are as follows:

• The importance of basic hygiene and cleanliness (see previous section).

• What matches and what doesn't. Sticking to solid colors is helpful in this area.

• What's "in" and what's "out." Often the brand name is important. If you have a very small clothing budget, it is better to buy the right thing secondhand from a thrift store than the wrong thing new. However, there are many stores such as Marshalls and Ross where the right labels can be bought for reasonable prices. Have a peer buddy from school, a teenage sibling, or other neighborhood teen go shopping with your teen and be the fashion advisor. Let them show your teen and you what's cool and what's not, what looks good on him or not. You may think you know, but you'd be surprised.

• First impressions are crucial. Jerry Newport talks about the importance of looking right to avoid bullying, in addition to making friends.

• Find out what the current hairstyles are and see if your teenager is amenable to having that look.

Modesty, Privacy, and Personal Safety

Social stories are effective at all levels for teaching about what behaviors are to be done in private and which ones are okay in public, who is allowed to touch the teen and who is not. (See pages 232–233 for more on social stories.) This concept of private versus public is crucial to the child's learning about the body parts that are okay for others to touch, and the parts that are private and should only be touched with his permission. The book *Taking Care of Myself* includes some good social stories you can adapt for all levels of understanding for the concepts mentioned here that every parent and adolescent needs to learn.

Here are some essentials:

• **The concept of privacy needs to be taught and reinforced in all environments.** Teaching the notion of privacy begins with the familiar adults in the teen's life, both at home and at school. At home, it is important to remember to treat them as teenagers and not to continue to treat them as young children when helping them with their daily hygiene routines. At school, it is important that staff unfamiliar to the teen be introduced to them, and that only staff familiar to the teen be involved with any personal, intimate self-care. Staff members should ask permission before touching a student, even if it is an occupational therapist doing sensory integration with the teen. It always amazes me that we expect our children to learn about appropriate behavior in terms of touching or not touching others and about not letting strangers touch them. Yet, sometimes in schools, staff and other professionals unfamiliar to the student (such as substitute instructional aides or occupational or speech therapy interns) are allowed to touch them or invade their personal space, and the student is expected to be okay with it. This is mind-boggling considering not only the safety aspects but also the sensory issues that plague those on the autism spectrum. Neurotypical teens are not expected to allow strangers to handle them in any way, so why should it be different for those with ASDs? Respect and privacy should be practiced and taught to all.

• **Teach your son or daughter to always let you know when someone has seen them naked or causes them to be naked, touched them inappropriately, or physically abuses them.** This determination to tell you should not be a choice. This is how you can keep your child safe and teach him about what is appropriate and what is not. It may be difficult for the less able, but it is nonetheless essential to teach this important skill. Those who cannot verbally communicate can learn to use PECS (Picture Exchange Communications System) icons or point to words. Making sure your child knows that it is not okay for strangers or any adult to touch him on certain areas of his body is vitally important. He needs to learn to be able to tell a responsible person about any inappropriate behavior that someone might be doing to him. It is imperative for your child's safety that he be able to identify appropriate places on his body where people can touch him.

• **Teach the concept of modesty at home, if your tween or teen has not mastered this concept yet.** He needs to learn the appropriate place for private acts (such as dressing, being naked, or masturbation). If he does not understand through an explanation of the concept, then perhaps visual icons will help. Pick an icon or color to represent public and one to represent private (do not confuse him by using smiley and sad faces). Put the private icon on his underwear drawer and his bedroom and bathroom doors, and the public icon on the doors to the rest of the rooms and going outside. If he gets dressed in a place other than the bathroom or his bedroom, or if he runs around the house with no clothes on or in his underwear, now is a good time to teach him what is appropriate to wear in public and in private.

Perhaps you don't really mind at home, but think of when he will be living with others and how inappropriate it will be then, and how your child could possibly put himself in dangerous situations. He needs to learn now, or he won't understand what the fuss is about years down the line. Again, be sure you are teaching him appropriate behaviors that will help keep him safe. If he comes out with no clothes on, you can remind him by showing him to his room or bathroom with the appropriate icon, and pairing it with the icon on his clothes drawer. Similarly, your child needs to learn about using the toilet on his own with the door closed.

• **Masturbation should be contained to private areas in the home.** This is one of those subjects that is difficult for parents to discuss or get information about. Even if your child is not yet masturbating, when you notice his body is starting to change and grow, as explained above, he needs to be told about erections, wet dreams, and ejaculations, as well as why males and females are built the way they are—the birds and the bees talk. Otherwise, he will become alarmed with these body changes and wonder why he is "losing liquid," and may think there is something wrong with him. Masturbation is a common activity for neurotypical adolescents. Your teen needs to be told that it is a normal behavior, okay to practice in specific private places in the house only, but definitely not in public. As a parent, you may be able to control where and when it takes place, but you will not be able to stop it. A parent needs to accept the fact that this is an inevitable and natural activity and make sure it is done in private.

Good communication is necessary with your child's school to ensure that if masturbation is occurring there, the student is redirected to another activity with the knowledge that he can have "private time" when he gets home. Keeping your teen busy with activities he is interested in doing and ensuring lots of opportunities for physical exercise to expend energy will help keep masturbation from occurring at inappropriate moments and places. If masturbation becomes an obsession for someone with obsessive-compulsive disorder, it needs to be addressed as any other obsession. If you are concerned because your son is unable to reach climax and is frustrated and this is affecting his behavior, he may need to be shown what to do. In the section below on sexuality, more information is given, along with some resources in regard to this delicate subject.

• **Teach your teen to say or communicate *no*.** Some children on the autism spectrum are compliant and have learned through years of special education to follow instructions and rules of behavior. However, for safety reasons, now that your child is becoming a young adult, he needs to learn to say no, even to people of authority, when their demands are inappropriate or dangerous. One way to do this is to give him choices (for example, does he want a bar of chocolate or carrots?). When he states his choice, give him the other choice and teach him to say, "No, I want the . . ." This needs to be generalized to all kinds of subjects. Then you can make a list of situations to say no in, some serious and some funny to make it fun (for example, a stranger asks you to get in the car; your dad wants you to eat worms).

• **Teach him to say and communicate "go away."** Invade your child's space when you know he doesn't want you there (for example, when he has closed the door to his room and is watching

TV). Stand very close to where he is sitting, and when he does avoidance behavior (pushing you away, moving to another spot), prompt him to push you and say, "Go away." When you are teaching the concept of "no" and "go away" you must respect his right to choose, but do not confuse him by asking instead of telling in a situation where he really has no choice (for example, "Do you want to get ready to go out now?" instead of "Time to get ready to go out."). You can, however, create choices (for example, "Time to get ready to go out. Do you want to wear your blue jacket or your red sweater?") that he really has.

• **Teach relationship boundaries.** This can be a difficult concept to teach and must be practiced. First your child needs to learn about the various relationships (husband, wife, sibling, aunt, colleague, close friend, neighbor, shopkeeper, etc.). Next comes the concept of appropriate types of conversations and behaviors. One way to teach this is through the idea of Circles, devised by Marklyn P. Champagne and Leslie W. Walker-Hirsch (see resources at end of this chapter). Draw a dot in the middle of a large piece of paper, with ever-increasing circles surrounding it. Each circle defines the acceptable behavior of people in that circle. The different circles represent, starting from the center:

○ Private circle: The circle closest to the center dot represents behaviors of people you are extremely close to, such as immediate family members. When first introducing the concept write in "close hug" in this circle.

○ Hug circle: These are perhaps your extended family and best friends.

○ Faraway hug circle: People you are friends with but not as close as your family or best friends.

○ Handshake circle: People you see at school or people you work with.

○ Wave circle: This could include people you pass every day on the street in your neighborhood, but don't personally know.

○ Stranger circle: People you ignore or do not give a greeting to, because you do not know them.

Hang this up in your child's room and add the people (by name or picture) he knows to the different circles, discussing the concepts at his level. Then, when he meets new people, you can add them to the circle.

Sexuality

WHAT PARENTS NEED TO KNOW

Sexuality is a topic that many parents would rather avoid, even with their neurotypical children. It's a sensitive subject because of all the different religious, philosophical, and ethical beliefs that affect what our thoughts are on sex education and what is taught in school and how it is taught. As parents, you are responsible for your child's ethical and religious upbringing. Before teaching or explaining to your tween or teen about sexuality, parents will need to reexamine their own ideas and attitudes about sex, sexuality, and what they believe teenagers should know.

It is possible to teach some essential information about sex without giving him permission to enact those behaviors in the present. In other words, your teens should learn from you about your ethical and religious beliefs concerning sex as well as about the birds and the bees. However, as a parent you must keep in mind that one day your child will be an adult and will have the right to make his own decisions in this area. And who better to learn from than Mom and Dad?

Sexual feelings are natural, and everyone has them, regardless of whether we are on or off the autism spectrum. According to a Danish study published in 1992 (*Sexuality and Autism, Danish Report,* Demetrious Haracopos and Lennart Pedersen), 74 percent of all autistic residents of different ability levels living in a group home for autistic adults demonstrated definite signs of sexual behavior.

Adolescents become young adults, and some young adults on the autism spectrum want intimacy and want to get married; some do not. Many want friends and to date; some may not. For those who are unable to communicate on these matters, it is hard to know. But when they become adults, it will be up to them to choose, and it is up to us as parents to teach them about this touchy and personal topic. If we don't, who will?

Even if your teen is very able and has been through some aspects of sex education at school, it will be necessary to see what he has learned and understood. The good news is that even if your teen is on the more able end of the spectrum, he will be physically developing at the same rate as his peers; however, emotionally he will be younger and may not be interested in dating or sex until his early twenties.

Even if your young adult is not interested in relationships or intimacy or sex, these topics need to be addressed. First off, everyone at school will be talking about sex, and sadly, people who have intellectual disabilities are at a high risk of sexual abuse and of catching sexually transmitted diseases. The very nature of ASDs makes it difficult for someone with the condition to read the social cues and understand appropriate versus inappropriate behavior. These cues need to be taught. There are various ways to teach them, depending on the person's level of ability.

TEACHING ABOUT SEXUALITY

Dr. Isabelle Hénault, a researcher in this area, wrote a chapter in *Asperger Syndrome in Adolescence,* edited by Liane Holliday Willey. In this chapter, Hénault suggests that parents start with topics they feel comfortable about and keep it simple, that is, general knowledge about hygiene and anatomy, gender issues (what it means to be a boy or a girl), sexual characteristics (physical, emotional, etc.). Speak in a positive manner about sexuality and give explanations that are concrete, simple, and effective. Avoid being overprotective, which may lead to ambivalence and misinformation about sexuality. Also, by explaining to teens the consequences of sexuality, parents can guide their teenagers. Information presented in a positive format will help the teenager form his own impressions and judgments. Remember that open communication is a process that needs to be worked on over time.

Dr. Isabelle Hénault's book, *Asperger's Syndrome and Sexuality: From Adolescence through Adulthood* (2005) is a wonderful resource for parents to address sexuality including masturbation, intimacy, and comprehending appropriate and inappropriate sexual behavior. Although written with Aspies in mind, parents of teens more impacted by autism will find this book helpful for understanding more about sexuality for those on the spectrum and as a springboard for thinking about what to explain to your teen.

WHAT PARENTS NEED TO KEEP IN MIND

• Sex education given at school for the mainstream population covers many areas including bodily changes, contraception, sexual orientation and identity, birth control, emotions related to sexuality, values and steps to decision-making (Sexuality Information and Education Council of the US, 1991). These same areas should be explained to those on the autism spectrum in a way they can understand.

• Hyposensitivity or hypersensitivity due to sensory processing challenges may affect how a person on the spectrum handles intimacy.

• Gender identity can be an area of concern for some as they are trying to work out who they are and how they relate to or feel about others.

• Sometimes teens on the spectrum get in trouble with law enforcement agencies because they do not understand what constitutes inappropriate behavior in public toward others or even touching their own private parts in public.

• Some individuals on the spectrum may be homosexual or bisexual, just as some neurotypicals are.

SPECIFIC AREAS TO CONSIDER TEACHING YOUR TEEN

- As discussed earlier in this chapter, puberty and changes to the body must be discussed.

- Contraception and protection against sexually transmitted diseases.

- Recognizing what is appropriate "dating" or friendly behavior toward your teen.

- Knowing what is appropriate behavior toward an admired person.

- Appropriate masturbation and ejaculation.

TEACHING MASTURBATION/EJACULATION

The issue of masturbation is a sensitive one for most people, but I would be lax not to address it here, as it is a subject that parents often ask about. One of the questions often asked is about the male teens who masturbate and are not able to ejaculate, whether or not this could be a contributing factor to more frustration and anxiety, and what can be done about it.

Dr. Isabelle Hénault says that when teenagers are not able to ejaculate, there is a possibility of an increase in anxiety and frustration. Some teenagers lack experience, combined with low muscle tone and/or sensory issues. Some medications may be influencing the ejaculation potential as well, and this should be discussed with the treating doctor. They may be hypersensitive or hyposensitive, and this has a direct effect on their potential to ejaculate. In her book, Dr. Hénault discusses ways to address this issue and teach your teen the necessary skills. For more practical and visual resources that are educational and respectful, consider the books and videos *Hand Made Love* (men) and *Finger Tips* (women) at www.diverse-city.com.

Here are some resources to help you in teaching your teenager in the area of sexuality:

• *Autism-Asperger's and Sexuality: Puberty and Beyond,* by Jerry and Mary Newport. This book is a wonderful resource for the more able teenager and young adult, although parental guidance is recommended. The publishers suggest photocopying individual sections of the book to give to your child to read. In this way you can give him only the information he is ready to handle.

• *Asperger's Syndrome and Sexuality: From Adolescence through Adulthood,* by Dr. Isabelle Hénault (with a foreword by Tony Attwood). This book covers puberty through adulthood. The information is helpful for parents, professionals, and individuals with Asperger's, with many practical resources as well as a sex education program, divided into twelve workshops.

• *Sexuality: Your Sons and Daughters with Intellectual Disabilities,* by Karin Melberg Schwier and Dave Hingsburger. This is a good resource for the parents of less able children, although some ideas could be incorporated for the more able as well. Even though this book is not written specifically with individuals with autism in mind, many concepts and strategies can be adapted.

• *Circles* is a commonly used program (on video) for teaching appropriate social and sexual behaviors to people with developmental disabilities. It is an expensive, three-part video system and would be a good program for a parent group or resource center to buy. The Circles videos are published by James Stanfield Publishing and are devised by Marklyn P. Champagne and Leslie W. Walker-Hirsch. (www.stanfield.com/sexed)

• *Hand Made Love* (men) and *Finger Tips* (women) books and videos. These resources are educational, and provide practical and visual information on masturbation and reaching climax. Available at www.diverse-city.com.

FOOD FOR THOUGHT

Why Talking About Sexuality to Teenagers Is Important

That is how many of our people will experience puberty in school: left behind and alone and feeling steadily worse about it. People who had time to before, now don't. That time is now shared with people who go around in groups of social pairs. There are rumors of social and even sexual activity that usually only serve to make our kids feel more left out. True, the people telling the stories are usually not nearly as active as they claim to be. Listening to a group of schoolboys in locker rooms is like listening to a blind man teach defensive driving. But to the people totally left out, especially autistic boys who have little personal experience to compare with what they are hearing, it sounds true enough.

—Jerry and Mary Newport, *Autism-Asperger's and Sexuality: Puberty and Beyond*

4

The Middle and High School Years

My teenage memories are stuffed with good times and good people.
Even when I start to remember something raw and ugly that might
have tried to ravish me then, I am able to toss it off as a bad memory
that had little effect on me. The experiences I've had in high school
prepared me for a bright future. They gave me strength and insight
and confidence to look at myself as an individual and not a parallel
image. The only thing my close community of friends and teachers
and counselors and mentors did not give me, the only thing they could
not give me, was protection from the chill that would nearly undo me
when I left them all behind.

—LIANE HOLLIDAY WILLEY, *Pretending to be Normal:*
Living with Asperger's Syndrome

I had high hopes for my son Jeremy's first year at the local middle
school. The special education teacher was a former tutor of Jeremy's.
He really liked her, and I thought she was one of the best he'd ever
had. However, within the first two months, Jeremy was hurt in two
different instances in circumstances beyond the teacher's control,
once due to being left in the restroom unsupervised and unprotected
with another student who had problems keeping his hands to himself,
and another time by a young professional trying out a technique she
was not properly trained in.

When Jeremy started at the local high school, I was very appre-
hensive. He was starting in a new environment with unknown staff

and administrators we had no reason to trust, following the middle school experiences, which had not been handled well at all. By now my expectations about school were more about Jeremy coming home unharmed and uninjured than about learning anything. I started teaching him at home after school using the Rapid Prompting Method. The teacher visited our house and observed one day, and pretty soon they were incorporating it in the classroom. The following school year, there was a different teacher, a male this time, who really bonded with Jeremy. Thanks to him and to the rest of the educational team—his instructional aide, the speech therapist, occupational therapist, his general education teachers, and his peer tutors and buddies—Jeremy has grown into a confident student. As his experience illustrates, students blossom when they know they are respected and supported.

The Individualized Education Program (IEP)

The middle school and high school years are interesting in that they are both transitions to another world. Middle school is, in effect, preparation for high school, and high school is preparation for the real world. While the student is focusing on the academic lessons and life skills to be learned, the educators and parents are focusing on what the student needs to be successful in an environment that holds more challenges, as well as prepare the student for transitioning to high school. In high school, again the focus is on doing well there, but also in preparing for life as a responsible adult.

In order to ensure that the tween and teen on the autism spectrum is learning what he needs to know—for now and the future—specific instruction in areas discussed in chapters 3 and 6, must be included and addressed in the Individualized Education Program (IEP) with measurable goals. Future needs and options discussed in chapter 5 should be considered in preparation for transition planning.

For the teenager to be successful in high school and the future, both parents and professionals need to work together to ensure that the teenager is well prepared. Hopes for the future can become a reality, but the road map is the IEP and the Individualized Transition Plan (ITP). After analyzing the teenager's strengths and weaknesses, goals need to be written into the IEP to ensure that the needed skills are taught.

In school, neurotypical tweens and teens learn academics from their teachers; social skills and how to look good from naturally interacting with their peers; self-care, life skills, organizational skills, self-esteem and responsibility from their parents. Self-esteem, organizational skills, and responsibility are naturally generalized and reinforced at school through the learning process.

However, for adolescents with ASDs, nothing is learned naturally from interacting with their peers, and nothing is naturally generalized from one environment to another. For Asperger teens and the more able with autism, there are strategies that can be put into place to help in these areas and allow the child to continue to develop to his potential. For the less able, these tactics can be modified and used when appropriate for the teen. Examples will be given throughout this chapter.

Another important consideration is that as our tweens grow into teens and toward adulthood, we must remember that they should have more and more input into their IEP and preparation for adulthood. This is not only legally mandated but makes sense as a preparation for adulthood. Much as our neurotypical teens have more and more say as the years go by, we must remember to do the same for our children with ASDs. This may seem obvious for the more able on the spectrum, but extra care must be taken to ensure that for the less able and less communicative we allow them choices and give them opportunities to think about their future and what they envision in order to prepare them for their adult lives.

ADVOCATING FOR THE MOST APPROPRIATE
PROGRAMS FOR YOUR CHILD

Parents need to be aware that when students reach the tween years around middle school time, school districts tend to put special education students on different tracks depending on their academic successes or lack thereof. When the student reaches high school, these tracks are even more clearly divided. If your child is on the less able end of the autism spectrum, you must be clear on what your philosophy is in regard to the need for integration or mainstreaming, and you will need to be able to convince school administrators of the benefits of having your child participate in certain areas regardless of your student's rights. Obviously, all mainstreaming and integration should be based on goals and objectives that the student is working on. Check your school district's philosophy about occupational and speech services. Although we all know these services are supposedly based on the student's needs, it is surprising the number of students arriving from middle school into high school who, quite suddenly, don't need occupational therapy (OT) anymore, according to certain school districts.

Make sure that the IEP team's decision about whether or not OT and speech services will continue for the student is based on the student's need and not continued simply because he has always had it—or discontinued because it's "not offered in high school—the students don't need it."

Along with the need for facing and embracing their teen's situation, parents must also continue to advocate for the education, services, and supports their teen needs. This is based on two simple facts: the budget and the perceived closing of the "window of opportunity." School districts are stretched with more and more cases of young children diagnosed with autism. Because early intervention has been proven to be important for children with autism, that is where most of the funding goes. But remember, your child *can* continue to learn. Our brains don't stop growing and taking in information. Stroke victims who have lost the use of their limbs can learn to

FOOD FOR THOUGHT

Why I Drive an Old Car

It's a typical gorgeous Southern California summer morning and by all rights I should be heading toward the beach with my kids and a couple of boogie boards. But instead, I'm sitting in a school district boardroom attempting mediation in regards to my severely autistic, practically nonverbal teenager's school program. My son's special education attorney is sitting next to me in a very pretty pink sweat suit drinking Dr Pepper out of a coffee tumbler (this is California, after all). She is discussing the tax benefits of her new BMW with the mediator, while I am calculating how much I will have to increase my yearly income if I'm going to stay in this school district.

The school district administrator arrives, and each side gives a ten-minute explanation on why we are sitting in mediation. After both sides speak, the mediator recaps to make sure he has understood correctly: I am requesting an occupational therapist for my son that won't give him rug burns (like the last one did), and that staff working with my son be trained on autism and the effective teaching methods that work for him. The mediator looks at the school district administrator and asks her if that isn't what is normally provided in a program of this kind.

After spending two half days in a stuffy boardroom and thousands of dollars in legal fees split between the school district and me to obtain what my son—by all rights—should be normally receiving, I leave feeling saddened and drained. I think of how much quality staff training (which would have benefited every student in the class) could have been bought with the money the school district and I have just spent on legal fees. As my son's attorney drove away in her well-earned BMW (she did, after all, get my son an occupational therapist who isn't going to hurt him), I climb into my nine-year-old station wagon, wondering if I have enough money left for badly needed new tires.

use them again. It's called neuroplasticity, and we all have it, so don't believe you can't teach someone at any age, because you can. It may be easier when they are younger, but they can learn when they are older, too.

Preparing for the Transition to Middle School and High School

Regardless of where on the autism spectrum a student may fall, every student has needs for being successful at school, whether it be modifying the curriculum or teaching a student how to organize his time or recognize when he is getting close to sensory overload.

In middle school, students are usually confronted with a larger number of students and have different teachers and classrooms for every class, and this requires adjustment on the part of the student. Whether your tween or teen is mainstreamed for just one class or totally included, some adjustments are necessary due to the change in school campus. What follows are some ideas for facilitating a smooth transition to middle school.

For all students, at the transition IEP from elementary school to middle school, bring up your concerns about transitions, and what supports, modifications, or adaptations your child may need as well as what information the teachers will need to have in regard to your child. Make sure these are specifically noted in a clear and specific manner in the IEP. Remember, your child is changing schools and perhaps even administrative school districts, and you must be sure to give them the information they need. Here are some practical tips to help plan for a smooth transition:

• Make sure that all necessary assessments have been made for the students in terms of academic strengths and weaknesses; functional assessments of behavior, sensory, language, and social skills; and life skills.

• Early in the year before the transition should take place, evaluate and select the appropriate new school placement and environment, based on your tween or teen's need. The local neighborhood school will provide more opportunities for continuing social relationships developed in the elementary school. Magnet schools may have a specialty program that coincides with an interest that an Asperger's student may have. A private school may be the best provider for the student's educational needs. School placement should be decided before the transition meeting.

• Make sure that a transition planning meeting is taking place with personnel from both the school transitioning from and transitioning to. At this meeting, any supports needed should be discussed. Staff and teacher training as well as accommodations or modifications for the student should also be discussed. The next section will describe this transition meeting in more detail.

• During the summer, when the school is empty or almost empty, take your child to the new school and show him where his classrooms are and how to get from one place to another. It is helpful

---

FOOD FOR THOUGHT
Accommodations Can Help

All through secondary school I would wait until the very end of lunch break, when there would only be a few people left in the queue, to get my lunch and on some days I would be unable to face it at all. Allowing a child to "queue jump," to have a seat on an aisle in exams, or to always sit in the same seat in the classroom could make a remarkable difference in their ability to cope. Simply making sure a child has access to "sensory retreats" during the day (being able to spend time in a quiet library, for example) can make a dramatic difference.

—Clare Sainsbury, *Martian in the Playground*

to do this a few times, if you live nearby, explaining to him about the coming year. This is an informal way to start getting him ready for learning how to get around the school and giving him a chance to get to know the physical environment without the crowds and noise. Introducing one new element at a time is helpful for our tweens and teens.

MAKING THE MOST OF THE TRANSITION MEETING

No matter where your tween or teen is on the spectrum, there are areas that need to be addressed and planned for, and this should take place at the transition meeting with personnel from both schools.

• Put together the student's schedule. For students who are based in a special education classroom, discussion of which mainstream classes would be appropriate for the student to be participating in should be discussed. If they are receiving adapted physical education (APE) services when does that take place? If your child will be fully included and moving from classroom to classroom, ask if it is possible to schedule his classrooms near one another at least during the morning and afternoon periods, so that your child does not need to cross over long distances through crowded areas too many times during his first semester. In schools with large populations and many classes repeated throughout, this should be easy to work out. Also, can your child be scheduled in classes where he has known friends or buddies from elementary school? This can be helpful as well.

• Discuss and review any supports, modifications, or accommodations your student will need. Be clear as to what these are, and who is responsible for implementing them. Think of everything that helped your student in elementary school, and use that as a starting point. Later in this chapter, you'll find some suggestions for ensuring student success.

• For students who are fully included, identify who the case manager or primary contact will be, and identify who the "safe persons" are for your child to approach if needed, as well as a safe quiet place the child can go when he needs to.

• Make sure it is clear what your student's areas of strengths are and what his learning style is. Ensure that everyone is clear about what has worked with the student in the past, what modality of communication (such as, verbal, pecs, Dynavox, alphabet board) the student uses, and what type of schedule and method of organization has worked best for him. Remember that many students with autism have challenges with generalization and with changes. Now that the student is changing environments, it is probably not the best time to experiment with new methods or systems. Once he is comfortable in his environment, changes can be made. For now, don't mess with what has been working.

• Make sure training for school personnel is discussed in terms of your student's needs. Who will be trained and when they will be trained should be specified. It is best if training takes place before start of the new school year.

• Student orientation needs to be discussed as well, regardless of whether or not your child will be fully included or in a special education class.

Preparing the student ahead of time, to lessen the stress, is a good idea. It's helpful to have photographs and names of the various teachers and other personnel to review with the student before the start of the school year.

Preparing Your Child for the New School Environment

Many students with ASDs have trouble finding their way around. Learning to navigate around the school campus is important, regardless of ability level. For those on the more able end, practicing getting around the school will alleviate some of the stress of being in a new environment. For the less able, this will help students with autism learn how to figure their way around places without always following someone else or being prompted by an instructional aide. Here are some tips:

• A walk-through of the student's daily schedule (or schedules if they change every day) should be done a few times. Videotaping of the different paths to take for the student to watch at home is also helpful. Even if the student will be mostly based in a special education class or will have an aide, he needs to start learning some independence in recognizing where he is and planning how to get from one place to another.

• Have the teen walk through the school a few times before the start of the school year. It helps if someone who is already familiar with the campus goes with the student. If possible, walk the route the teen will have to take.

• Take pictures or draw the different landmarks that are on the path from one place to another. List on a piece of paper or dictate into a mini-recorder the order of the landmarks and where the teen needs to turn or stop or take another direction.

• Make a small guidebook with the pictures and notes, including the times the student has to leave one place and go to the next.

• Draw a map, if you think it will be helpful to him, of all the corridors or alleyways or streets and landmarks.

• Practice navigating through the school site that has been mapped out.

Parents of Asperger's students may wish to consult the book *Asperger Syndrome and Adolescence: Practical Solutions for School Success,* by Brenda Smith Myles and Diane Adreon. The book has a transition checklist that is useful for the student with AS.

Planning for Future Success

KEEPING THE BIG PICTURE IN MIND

In terms of any child's education, the two most important factors that your child's future depends upon are early intervention and transition planning to adulthood while still in high school. The reasons for this are simple. First of all, for neurotyical children, school is where they learn about living in society with others and is a preparation for future life. Although parents might be concerned about the student's grades, in reality whether or not their child earns an A+ in algebra is really not going to determine the child's success or happiness later in life. What's more important is learning how to be responsible, how to relate to other people, how to use common sense as well as developing interests and strengths into a marketable career skill.

In essence, our schools should be preparing students for the future, to be independent, employable, and responsible citizens. With most neurotypical students, this happens naturally because they model the people they are surrounded with. They have mentors and peers and adults to help guide their way. For students with autism, however, this does not come naturally. Everything must be taught or explained at their level.

Federal special education law requires that school districts help students with disabilities make the transition from school to work. The Individuals with Disabilities Education Improvement Act (IDEIA)

FOOD FOR THOUGHT

The Not-So-Smooth Transition to Middle School

It was the end of the school year and my son Jeremy was finishing up sixth grade and would be starting at the middle school the following September. This entailed an administrative transfer from the elementary school district to the high school district as well as a change of school. A transition planning meeting was set up, with about fifteen people present. My husband and I arrived and met the new administrators from the school our son was transitioning to. Unfortunately no one showed up from the school district my son was transitioning from. It seemed the program specialist had gotten her days mixed up, and the director of special education did not know this meeting was taking place.

To our dismay, this meeting turned out to be unproductive, because at the time, Jeremy's program was being supervised by an outside agency, and it appeared the new district administrator had no idea about this, nor that Jeremy required a one-on-one behaviorally trained instructional aide. In the end, the only purpose served was us having an opportunity to meet the new district educators and for them to learn about Jeremy from our perspective. However, another transition planning meeting had to be called. Unfortunately, because it was the end of the school year, this new meeting had to be scheduled during the summer when not many school personnel were available for input and planning.

The moral of the story is, make sure your ducks are all lined up. Don't leave it to other people to plan. Have the meeting far enough in advance so that if there are mess ups (such as ours), you will still have time to work things out before the start of the new school year.

2004 signed into law by the president in December 2004 stipulates that the first IEP after the student turns 16 must include appropriate postsecondary goals that are measurable.

Another reason why transition planning for after high school is an important factor is that once your child reaches the age of eighteen, there is no federal requirement under IDEIA to continue special educations services. Some states may continue provisions until the age of twenty-two for some students. It is important for parents to realize that once your child leaves the school system, he may be eligible for other services, but there is no federal mandate for your child to actually receive them. So the school years are the only years that your child is actually guaranteed by law to receive the support and help needed. Thus parents and teenagers must make the most of this opportunity.

In the next chapter, IDEIA and the Individual Transition Plan will be explained. Parents of teenagers sixteen and above may wish to read that section when planning for their teen's ITP and IEP. An overview of what is currently available in terms of work structures, supports for college students, and living arrangements as an adult is also provided, as are helpful tips on how to find out more or create some possibilities more in line with your teen's desires and needs.

FIVE THEMES FOR SUCCESS

Even for the younger teens, it's never too early to start thinking about the future and how to prepare them for success. For this reason, I'm including this section to help you think in terms of what could be incorporated into your teen's IEP and taught to him at school.

Many skills contribute to success, but according to Paul Wehman in his book *Life Beyond the Classroom*, there are several themes that characterize adults who do well compared to those who do not. In this instance, "doing well" means feeling good about oneself and having a positive impact on others. Wehman identifies the following themes for future success:

- **Personal responsibility.** This can include self-control around a person he or she is attracted to, ability to save money and have good financial habits, arriving at work on time and being able to take criticism from a supervisor. The list of responsible behavior is long, yet it seems to define well those students who succeed after leaving school.

• **Self-determination and initiative.** Self-determination is being able to make choices and to act on them. The components necessary for self-determination include knowing yourself, valuing yourself, planning, acting and experiencing outcomes, and learning. Most people develop self-determination during childhood and the teenage years as they receive more responsibilities and more freedom from their parents and teachers. People who are self-directed have the initiative to be successful, have some ambition, practice a reasonable amount of work ethic, and do better in life than those who do not. Self-determination and self-advocacy are important skills and must be taught, regardless of the ability level of the individual.

• **Social competence.** Getting along with people, interpersonal skills, and social competence in a variety of environments may be the most important features of success in life. Knowing the socially appropriate way to behave in a variety of social situations can make the difference in successful outcomes in the community, at home, and in the workplace.

• **Vocational competence.** Work is the key to a successful and fulfilling life as well as a paycheck. People with Asperger's or autism such as Temple Grandin write and talk about how their work provides meaning in their lives, which is true for many neurotypicals as well. We live in a country that expects people to be productive in work, and individuals in the United States are largely defined by the type of work they do, their earning power, the regularity with which they are employed, and long-term work potential.

• **Postsecondary education.** Ongoing education and lifelong learning are important for continued success. Earning an associate's degree or bachelor's degree from a four-year college is an outstanding asset to add to a résumé. However, there are many other options for individuals who do not wish to work toward a degree but still want to learn and add to their knowledge and skill base.

Here are some suggestions for addressing these five themes within the school environment with students on the autism spectrum:

Personal responsibility: It's important that the curriculum at school include developing good habits and patterns of personal responsibility, across environments and in collaboration with all members of the educational team. Classroom instruction should include new experiences and information about current events that can influence student behavior. Parents can teach personal responsibility at home by giving the teenager more and more responsibility for his own self and his room as well as chores that contribute to the household. Teaching personal control over behaviors, such as teaching a teen to know when he is approaching sensory overload or close to losing his temper and what he can do about it, is an important part of learning personal responsibility. Being able to make his way around school based on recognizing landmarks and making decisions as to which way to go and being able to follow a schedule, yet deal with some changes are necessary skills for personal independence that all need to learn.

The kind of strategies that help the teen organize their schoolwork can also help with his daily living skills as well as in their future work. Learning to schedule and color code school projects and paperwork can help the teen prepare for the necessary scheduling of daily, weekly, and monthly activities and chores for independent living.

Self-determination and initiative: These attributes are important, regardless of the ability level of the individual. It is up to the school and parents to ensure that the student is learning to value himself, learning the skills of planning, having the opportunity to act and experience outcomes, and learning from those experiences. Self-advocacy goes hand in hand with self-determination and needs to be developed during the tween and teen years.

In addition, IDEIA 2004 mandates that students be invited to participate in transition planning, which includes self-advocacy and self-determination. In order to participate, the student will need to be familiar with these concepts and what they mean for his future. This means that both the students and the parents or guardian should be involved in determining desires and wishes for the future and taking the necessary steps to accomplish those goals.

An excellent resource is the book *Ask and Tell: Self-Advocacy and Disclosure for People on the Autism Spectrum,* edited by Stephen M. Shore, which gives specific steps for how a teen on the spectrum can become his own self-advocate, including representing himself during the IEP process.

Every student with ASD, regardless of ability level, will need to learn about self-advocacy. Eventually, even the less able child will be living away from home and not under parental protection and will need to stick up for himself. It is important that all students be introduced to these notions as teenagers if it has not already been done.

Some parents who have a child on the able end of the spectrum do not want to have their child's autism or Asperger's Syndrome disclosed to the school staff or other students as they want their child to fit in and be considered as just any other student. They do not wish their child to be singled out as different. This type of nondisclosure works only if the student can have his needs met without the people around him knowing about his uniqueness.

In order for a person to be able to advocate for his needs, he must develop a sense of self-awareness of his strengths and weaknesses as well as how he is different from others. For those who are visual learners, drawing a map of where the teenager is now, what his goals are, and what is needed to reach those goals can be useful. For some, creating lists of words of what works and what doesn't work can be helpful. It is also important to list or make notes of a person's strengths.

Stephen Shore has written about how his parents noted his skill for taking watches apart and putting them back together again. Shore never became a watchmaker or repairer, but that technical skill was transferred to bicycles, which provided him with employment in middle and high school and through college.

Of the resources listed below, only *Ask and Tell,* edited by Stephen Shore, is specifically written for people on the autism spectrum. However, the other resources offer ideas that can be adapted in the school environment for ASD students of different ability levels:

• *Ask and Tell: Self-Advocacy and Disclosure for People on the Autism Spectrum,* edited by Stephen M. Shore.

• *Life Beyond the Classroom,* by Paul Wehman, describes a self-advocacy program titled *Whose Future Is It Anyway?* by Wehmeyer and Kelchner.

• *The Transition Handbook: Strategies High School Teachers Use that Work,* by Carolyn Hughes and Erik Carter.

• Self-Determination Lesson Plan Starters, which you can download and adapt or read to get some ideas, is at www.uncc.edu/sdsp/home.asp, the website for the Self-Determination Synthesis Project at the University of North Carolina at Charlotte.

• www.self-determination.com: This self-determination website has informational resources, including some listed by state.

Websites run either by people with autism or their families that also touch upon advocacy and self-determination, as well as provide other information, include:

• www.grasp.org—The Global and Regional Syndrome Partnership—an educational and advocacy organization started by and serving individuals on the autism spectrum.

• www.ani.autistics.org: An autistic-run self-help and advocacy organization for autistic people.

• www.autistics.org: Resources by and for persons on the autistic spectrum.

• www.aascend.net: The Autism and Asperger's Syndrome Coalition for Education, Networking, and Development.

Social competence: We all know how difficult an area this is for people on the spectrum, from the less able to the very able. Some of the less able may be taught just the bare minimum of social courtesies to function in a job or social situation. Others, on the more able end, need to learn more complex social competencies in order to have jobs or careers that match their intelligence, or to be able to attend and be successful in college. Well-known individuals with autism or Asperger's such as Temple Grandin, Liane Holliday Willey, and Stephen Shore have described work situations that were difficult because they didn't know the social rules. The social skills that are necessary to network, ask questions, and understand the true meaning (as opposed to the literal meaning) of what is being said, as well as interpreting nonverbal communication, are areas in which those on the spectrum are often lacking. However, there is much that can be done to help in these areas, and these are discussed below.

School is a good place to foster relationships with other peers. Even for those who are more impacted by their autism, many schools have a "Best Buddies" program that matches students with a disability to a nondisabled peer to foster friendships and to accompany them to school activities. Peer tutors can help with socialization. Many towns have community centers and YMCA-type organizations that offer classes and activities that your teen might enjoy taking part in. These are all helpful in cultivating that needed social competence as well as teaching your teen how to enjoy recreational and leisure activities with others.

Vocational competence: This is an area much discussed in chapter 5. Even those on the less able end of the autism spectrum can have meaningful jobs or work. The preparation in high school is important, and if there is a job coach involved, they should be familiar with the strategies to help someone on the spectrum be successful in their job placements while still at school. Adult mentors in the community who are experienced in careers or jobs that a teenager with autism might be interested in can be very useful for working toward vocational competence. Although the following resources are written for the more able, it is possible to find an appropriate job or develop a microenterprise around a person's likes or obsessions even if they need support, and this is discussed in chapter 5.

For further information, see the following resources:

• *Developing Talents: Careers for Individuals with Asperger Syndrome and High-Functioning Autism,* by Temple Grandin and Kate Duffy.

• "Choosing the Right Job for People with Autism or Asperger's Syndrome" and "Making the Transition from the World of School into the World of Work," both by Temple Grandin at www.autism.org, the website for the Center for the Study of Autism (Stephen M. Edelson, Ph.D.).

• Planning and Self-Marketing for People on the Autistic Spectrum, by Lars Perner, Ph.D. (www.aspergerssyndrome.org/self-marketing.htm).

• "Survival in the Workplace" and "A Day in the Life," by Stephen Shore (www.udel.edu/bkirby/asperger/survival_shore.html).

Postsecondary education: Some people with Asperger's or autism do well attending two-year or four-year colleges. For others, opportunities exist elsewhere to attend classes and take courses to add new skills to a person's knowledge base. Taking classes can also help to identify new interests and hobbies as well as connect with people who share the same interests. This is covered more in depth in chapter 5.

For further information, see the following resources:

• "Preparing to Be Nerdy Where Nerdy Can Be Cool: College Planning for the High Functioning Student with Autism," by Lars Perner, Ph.D. (www.professorsadvice.com)

• "Understanding College Students with Autism," from *Chronicle of Higher Education,* by Dawn Prince-Hughes. (www.ohiou.edu/oupress/aquarticle2.htm)

• The website for University Students with Autism and Asperger's Syndrome (www.users.dircon.co.uk/~cns) is a great resource including first-person accounts and links to other websites.

Curriculum Ideas and Strategies to Help with the Challenges of ASDs

Now that the big picture is a bit clearer, keep it in mind as you plan your teen's curriculum for the school year. You want your teen to be successful at school and prepared for the future. Many of the challenges explained in chapter 1 are discussed below.

ASSESSMENTS AND WRITTEN GOALS

Curriculum-based assessments are important in determining the skills the student has as well as those he needs to learn. Some of the less able students on the spectrum are unable to respond to or take these assessments. For the more able students on the spectrum, the usual norm-referenced standardized tests used by many school districts may not always be an accurate measure of a student's strengths and weaknesses. For example, a particular reading test may measure the number of words read correctly as well as the number of factual questions answered correctly, but does not paint an accurate picture of the student with Asperger's skill level. The student with AS may have trouble making inferences or drawing conclusions, and these types of difficulties would not show up on the test.

The kind of assessments your teen needs depends on which areas are of concern: cognitive, behavioral, vocational, and so on. A professional familiar with autism spectrum disorders should be able to help you with assessments if you are concerned about challenges your teen is facing at school. Check with parents and professionals in your area, as well as the local chapter of the Autism Society of America, for the names of capable professionals that can assess your student.

The assessments will show what your teen's strengths and weaknesses are and will help identify useful strategies. Make sure that areas your teen needs to work on are addressed in his IEP with well-written goals, as these goals form the basis of your teen's placement and services. There are many good books available that offer advice on writing goals and the IEP process. A recent one is *How to Compromise with Your School District without Compromising Your Child: A Field Guide for Getting Effective Services for Children with Special Needs,* by Gary Mayerson.

There are a few books geared specifically toward the more able individual on the spectrum and the challenges faced at school. Some of the information and ideas can also be adapted for use with the less able.

- *Asperger Syndrome and Adolescence: Practical Solutions for School Success,* by Brenda Smith Myles and Diane Adreon

- *Asperger Syndrome and Adolescence: Helping Preteens and Teens Get Ready for the Real World,* by Teresa Bolick, Ph.D.

- *Incorporating Social Goals in the Classroom: A Guide for Teachers and Parents of Children with High-Functioning Autism and Asperger Syndome,* by Rebecca A. Moyes

A good resource for the less able student is:

- *Social Skills Training for Adolescents with General Moderate Learning Difficulties,* by Ursula Cornish and Fiona Ross

USE OF PEER TUTORS

When looking at strategies for the student, consider the use of peer tutors and "best buddies" for some of the learning. It's good for both

FOOD FOR THOUGHT

Advice for Peer Tutors

by Susan J. Moreno, M.A., and Cathy Pratt, Ph.D.

When you do not know how to help, ask a teacher, a program assistant, the parents or a sibling of the student with autism, or another peer tutor who has known the person longer. Know to whom you may turn for help or advice for your classmate with autism before you start working with him/her.

Treat classmates with autism like people first. People with autism are just that: people who happen to have the disability of autism. Please avoid references to "the autistic" or "the disabled." Rather say, "the person with autism" or better yet, use their name. These individuals have the same feelings and personalities as you. They just cannot always show it as clearly.

Be consistent in how you refer to your classmate with autism. Use whatever name he/she prefers. Avoid calling him/her by their given name one time and by a nickname like "pal" or "buddy" the next.

Be specific when discussing plans or directions. For example, do not say, "I'll meet you near the room after class." Instead say, "I'll meet you at locker number 220 at 12:05 P.M."

Do not be late! Many people with autism have a hard time understanding the concepts of time and waiting. Therefore, when you are late, they are not able to figure out on their own that an emergency or some other event may have delayed you. The result is that they may feel confused, upset, and insulted. If necessary, plan to be early and wait for him/her.

Remember that taking a little extra time or trouble to include your classmate with autism in your social plans could be very important to him or her. They need and want friends and social opportunities, and do not always know how to show that need to others.

Do not tease or be sarcastic with the person with autism. In order to understand the humor in teasing or sarcasm, people must be able to detect double meanings. The person with autism may not have that knowledge. Teasing has probably already been a very unpleasant part of that person's life.

If you see others teasing, laughing at, or making fun of a person with autism, try explaining a little about the person to them. They may only be laughing because they do not understand the person or the disability.

Do not make promises that you cannot keep. Avoid phrases like, "Maybe we'll go to the show together someday." This may be interpreted as a promise. They seldom process all of the qualifiers, such as "maybe" or "someday."

Do not borrow things from the person with autism. Having others borrow items can be frustrating for any person—mainly because people seldom return what they have borrowed on time and/or in the same condition that it was before it was borrowed. The person with autism already handles too many frustrations in daily life. This is one frustration that easily can be avoided.

Remember that you can play an important role and make a wonderful difference in the life of a person with autism.

Dr. Cathy Pratt is the director of the Indiana Resource Center for Autism at the Indiana Institute on Disability and Community located at Indiana University. Susan Moreno is the founder and president of MAAP Services for Autism and Asperger Syndrome.

the student on the spectrum and the neurotypical peer, as long as the tutor or best buddy has been given some information and explained how to best assist the person on the spectrum. Peer tutors can be mentors and become friends. The most important consideration is to make sure that the peer understands about autism spectrum disorders in general, and specifically how it affects the particular student they are tutoring.

SPECIAL INTERESTS AND OBSESSIONS

The special interests that students on the spectrum tend to have can be useful in teaching academic subjects. If a student is into trains, math skills can be taught by figuring out the number of hours or minutes it takes to get somewhere, and history or geography can be taught by using the kinds of trains from different historical eras as a starting point, or which cities and rural terrains the different train lines go through, for example.

When the student reaches the teen years, it's time to start thinking about how to channel special interests or talents into a career or job skill. There are many jobs and possibilities that require specific skills; parents need to do much research into different lines of work. This will be discussed more fully in the following chapter.

USING MENTORS

Channeling a special interest into a career or at least looking at the possibilities that exist is best done with the use of a mentor. A mentor can be anyone in the school or community that is knowledgeable about the teen's area of interest. If your teen is into trains or air conditioners, find a person who works in that field who would be willing to help your child realize the different applications of his interest. Retired people in the community make wonderful mentors. There may be a science teacher, engineer, or musician (retired or not) willing to mentor your child and help with contacts, as well. Developing a relationship with a mentor can also improve social skills.

BULLYING AND SAFETY

Research shows that bullying is a pervasive problem in our schools, and we know that bullying is a major problem for students on the autism spectrum. Bullying, which can range from verbal taunts to actual physical encounters, is very upsetting to the victims and should not be treated as a fact of life. Jerry and Mary Newport, Kenneth

Hall, Luke Jackson, Clare Sainsbury, and Liane Willey, all authors on the spectrum, discuss bullying in their respective books, at some length.

Students on the spectrum are at high risk for bullying because they are poor at picking up social cues and predicting behaviors. Sometimes they are the planned targets of bullies, and at other times they put themselves in unsafe situations because they do not recognize the situations as being unsafe. It can happen simply because the teenager with an ASD appears different to the neurotypical teens because of his dress and grooming. Often it is because as the other teenagers start to question authority, the ASD teen is still in the mentality of following the rules and thus seems to be "nerdy." Sometimes bullying is due to the misinterpreted behavior of the teen on the spectrum. Some teens with ASDs have monotone voices, and sound rude, or mimic the person they are speaking to, which makes it appear as if they are making fun of someone. A teenager on the spectrum may appear sneaky or manipulative because of some of his body language when stressed (avoiding eye contact, shifting from foot to foot, speaking in a flat voice). The teen, usually a stickler for rules, may correct another student, thus irritating the teacher, who does not realize that he has no sense of hierarchy, only a sense of what is right. If a teen on the spectrum has good language skills, others tend to forget that his comprehension of the language is different—that he only has a literal understanding of language, which can lead to trouble.

It is sometimes hard for teachers and other students to comprehend that someone who is verbally astute and gets good grades for his work is unable to pick up all the nonverbal cues. Neurotypical peers need to be told about ASDs and how they manifest themselves. It needs to be made clear that bullying will not be tolerated. Adults need to take more responsibility in creating a safe environment. Parents can help by teaching their students with Asperger's more about social cues, predicting behaviors, and teaching the meanings of metaphors used on a regular basis by peers (this is addressed later on in this section).

Rebekah Heinrichs, author of *Perfect Targets: Asperger Syn-*

drome and Bullying, says that successful bullying programs need to incorporate a strong emphasis on awareness and understanding as well as consequences that help the bully learn to think differently and change their behavior. According to Heinrichs, components of a successful bullying-prevention program include increased awareness and understanding; surveying students, staff, and teachers; creating a coordination group, providing staff training, and holding class meetings with students; increased supervision of high-risk areas; and promoting social competence skills for targets, bullies, and bystanders.

There should always be a safe place and a safe person that the student has access to. Because students with autism can be gullible, it is important that parents establish a code word, so that if there is a change in plan, and a parent sends someone else to pick up the student, the student knows not to get into the car unless the person tells him the code word.

For more information, see Rebekah Heinrichs, *Perfect Targets: Asperger Syndrome and Bullying.* This book is a good resource for schools as well.

Health and Puberty

As mentioned in chapter 3, hygiene and puberty as a curriculum may be covered if your tween or teen is in a life-skills type of special education class setting. In that case, as the parent you and the teacher will need to decide what will be worked on at school and what you will be doing at home. As mentioned in chapter 3, *Taking Care of Myself: A Hygiene, Puberty and Personal Curriculum for Young People with Autism,* by Mary Wrobel, is a great book to use in this area. In order to facilitate the establishment of routines at home as well as to promote independence and a sense of responsibility in the teenager, Mary recommends creating a hygiene book for each individual student. This book can show the products the teen uses, step by step instructions as well as schedules or photos of the student carrying out hygiene routines. Students can create their own books with pictures of the products they would like to include in their routine.

Students who are fully included may have seen some films or attended some classes about hygiene, sexuality, puberty, and so on. This does not mean that they have understood all the information, and parents may wish to check on their student's understanding.

Sensory Issues at School

Most students with autism have sensory integration or sensory processing issues, as discussed in chapter 1. For optimum learning, it is important that the students not feel sensory overload. In middle school and high school, students need to start learning how to recognize their sensory issues especially as they relate to arousal or awareness. Then they can learn to change their level of alertness in response to academic or social demands. A good resource for this is *How Does Your Engine Run? A Leader's Guide to the Alert Program for Self-Regulation* by Mary Williams and Shelly Schellenberger.

As they are learning to recognize and take control of their sensory

---

FOOD FOR THOUGHT
Sensory Overload

The lunch queue is a key example of a daily feature in school of which sensory problems can turn into a nightmare, but which is rarely even considered in discussions of education. The importance of school as a sensory/motor environment is rarely considered and so the idea that something as ordinary as a lunch queue could be a source of major stress for a child with Asperger's syndrome rarely even occurs to neurotypical people.

—Clare Sainsbury, *Martian in the Playground*

---

issues, students need a way to communicate about their sensory over-stimulation and need for either leaving the environment or learning to regulate their response. Even if it is a simple card that they can hand to the teacher or instructional aide, being able to communicate about their sensory overload is a first step toward learning how to deal with it.

Occupational therapists trained in sensory integration and experienced with adolescent issues and the middle and high school environments can help at school with teaching the student sensory activities that might be helpful in keeping them from being overloaded. While they are learning to regulate themselves, a sensory diet on a regular basis overseen by the OT can be helpful and a necessary part of the curriculum for some.

Other therapies and treatments listed in chapter 6 may be helpful. Some of them may be available through the school, while others may be provided by the parent.

Both Temple Grandin (*Thinking in Pictures*) and Liane Willey (*Pretending to be Normal*) have much information to share about sensory difficulties. Some ideas they have may be appropriate for the high school environment, some may not. There is always a balance to be made between desensitizing the person and adapting the environment. Here are some of their suggestions:

• Auditory sensitivity can be minimized for some through auditory integration training. Meanwhile, wearing earplugs may be helpful in curtailing sensitivity to sound. However, the student must still be able to hear people talking to him and emergency vehicles and signals such as fire bells. If it doesn't distract the teen from work or studies, wearing headphones and listening at low volume to music can be helpful during study periods. Grandin cautions against using these strategies all the time, as some exposure to noise can help desensitize a person, and there is a need to get used to some everyday noise.

• For visual sensitivity, try Irlen colored lenses. If they are too expensive, try on different pale colored sunglasses until the best color is found. Pale pinks, purple or tans often work best. Wearing a hat or visor helps block flicker from fluorescent lights.

• If the student suffers from tactile sensitivity, those who are around him every day should be made aware that the student does not like to be touched. Carrying a heavy backpack or shoulder bag or sewing pockets of little weights into the student's coat or sweater may help with the need for deep pressure. If the student feels the need to put things in his mouth, he should carry gum with him.

• For those with olfactory sensitivity, try putting some of his favorite scent on a small piece of material, the inside of your elbow, or a cotton makeup-remover pad, so that he can smell this scent when other smells overwhelm him.

• If food sensitivity is an issue, see if the foods the student can tolerate are available at school. If not, be prepared to have available foods that the student can pack to take to school.

Behavior Problems

As discussed earlier, behaviors are a form of communication and there may be different reasons for the same behaviors exhibited by different individuals. For behavior challenges at school, a functional behavior assessment can be extremely useful. A functional behavior assessment is a precise description of a behavior, its context, and its consequences. It looks at the antecedents prior to the behavior, the actual behavior, and the consequence of the behavior. The intent of the assessment is a better understanding of the behavior and the factors influencing it. A functional behavior analysis should include the added step of systematically changing the antecedents to and the consequences of the behavior to determine precisely which are the driving forces behind that behavior.

You may ask your district to provide a functional behavior analysis. Again, make sure that the person doing the assessment is experienced with adolescents on the spectrum at the same functioning level as your child.

Behavior plans can be effective if there is good communication between the different classroom teachers and home and if it is followed through by all. A Travel Card can increase productive behavior in teens and facilitate communication and collaboration between all staff members and the family at home. A Travel Card lists four or five targeted desired behaviors across the top, with a listing of the classes the student attends on the left-hand side. At the end of each class period, the teacher notes whether or not the student performed the desired behavior, and at the end of the day the points are tallied and graphed. Points are accumulated toward a choice of reinforcers already discussed and agreed upon between the student and the responsible adult (this could be a staff person at school or parent at home).

Cognitive Challenges

By the time your child has reached middle or high school, you will have a pretty good idea of what kind of learner he is—auditory, visual, or kinesthetic. If your child is seriously impacted by autism, shows severe academic difficulties, and is not responding or apparently learning through traditional methods, it is important to reevaluate how he learns. Often, methods such as TEACCH are used in teaching autistic students because it is assumed that all children with autism are visual learners. This is not true. Many are, yet some are auditory learners, and for them, TEACCH is not helpful unless it is paired with verbal language. For those students who are not successful with the more traditional methods of teaching students with autism, serious consideration should be given to trying the Rapid Prompting Method as described in chapter 6. It is important to keep trying to find a way of communicating and reaching the students who appear to be severely cognitively challenged in order to prepare them for their future as functioning adults.

GENERALIZING/PROBLEM SOLVING

For the less academically able, it is important to start giving functional meaning to the academics they are learning and generalizing them to the community, since generalization can be difficult. Math, reading, and following directions are all skill sets that can be practiced in the community to help prepare for independence in later years. Shopping, taking the bus, and figuring out if they have enough money to buy a wanted item are a few examples of important skills.

Whether a student is more or less impacted by autism, he needs to be taught about generalizing and problem solving. Those on the more able end can be given a list of situations for generalizing, but it will still need to be seen if they can follow through functionally. It may have to be practiced. Problem solving also needs to be practiced; writing social stories together at the student's ability level can be helpful. (For more about social stories, see pages 232–233.)

MEMORY AND SEQUENCING

For help with sequencing and memory (that is, remembering steps in a sequence or rules of behavior in a certain situation), mnemonics can be useful. As discussed in chapter 2, sometimes using music and favorite songs can help with this, as can social stories. More ideas to help with memory are discussed under executive functions below.

EXECUTIVE FUNCTIONS

As discussed in chapter 1, planning, organizing, shifting attention, and multitasking are common areas of difficulty for the student on the spectrum, yet they are important for daily living as well as academic areas and future jobs of all kinds. For students learning life skills, planning the next steps in a sequence or a recipe, or learning how to organize the needed materials for a certain task or to organize their schedule for the day are important for when they are no longer living at home. AS students need to learn how to plan timelines for ongoing school projects and how to organize their backpacks and notebooks to find needed assignments, and how to shift their attention from individual work to listening to the teacher. Many of these ideas were developed for the more able on the spectrum, but many of the strategies can be adapted for the less able.

There are some practical solutions for this area, depending on the student's ability level. Provide organizational supports depending on the need of the student. This can mean:

• Have different-colored folders with sections for papers going home and papers to take back to school. A sticker of the same color can be put on the spine of the corresponding textbook.

• Consider having different backpacks for days with different schedules. Backpacks should have different compartments for different school supplies, folders, money, and so forth.

• To-do lists and timelines for tasks or recipes or long-term assignments are good for organizing now, and can be a lifelong tool. Students can learn to cross off or date when each step is completed. This can be as simple or as complex as needed.

• Social stories created by the student (and teacher or aide at first) with "What comes next?" or "What do you need for this task/ assignment?" can help students learn to think ahead and plan.

Providing visual supports can help with attention shifting and multitasking for many students (auditory learners will need auditory input of the following) and can be helpful in all class situations. Think about what visual strategies help you in your job or at home and how that can help your student.

• In mainstream classes, homework assignments should be given in writing to the student and a content outline and notes be provided at the start of class.

• A map of the school outlining where the needed classrooms are and the student's class schedule can be taped inside the first pages of student's planner or primary notebook.

• A written list of names of classes, room numbers as well as needed supplies and books, and a list of the teacher's expectations and routines for each class can be helpful.

• Sample models of assignments and a list of test assignments will lessen the student's anxiety level.

• A cue card for the teacher or aide to place on the desk when she recognizes that the student is entering a meltdown or tantrum cycle. This will prompt the student to leave class and return to home base to lower his stress level.

Social Communication Challenges

Communication can be complex and entail body language, double meanings, and idioms. The area of social communication can be particularly difficult for those on the spectrum and starts to become more of an issue during the teen years. As discussed in chapter 1, there are areas of social competency that are particularly difficult for individuals on the spectrum. These are discussed particularly in terms of the more able teen with autism and the teen with Asperger's Syndrome. For more information see chapter 6 under "To Teach Social Skills and Social Communication."

THE TEENAGER IN THE SOCIAL WORLD

For teens with ASDs, the social realm—school, community, place of worship, after-school activities—is particularly difficult. Individuals with an ASD do not naturally pick up nonverbal language or emotional cues such as facial expressions, nor are they capable of "reading between the lines" or understanding more than the literal meanings of the spoken or written words. Remember how difficult it was in the teenage years learning to fit in although you knew what the rules were? It isn't possible for the ASD teenager to know the rules by osmosis; he needs to learn them, and his peers needs to learn about tolerance and that being different is not a negative thing. This not only makes life difficult but can be dangerous as they are often victims of bullies or inappropriate sexual behavior.

The family unit is the first social circle that people have experience with. Next comes school, which is usually the first formal social unit outside the home. School is the place where children and adolescents learn about navigating the social world, and this is why it is so important that the school address the issue, teaching your child what it takes to take part in society. Some of the strategies useful for teaching these skills to those on the more able end of the spectrum are useful for those on the less able as well, while others are not.

PERSPECTIVE TAKING AND SOCIAL COGNITIVE DEFICITS

According to Michelle Garcia Winner, a speech and language pathologist who runs a clinic for students with social cognitive deficits, general problem solving is usually not a problem for those on the more able end of the spectrum. However, personal problem solving is another can of worms because it requires perspective taking as well as thinking in terms of the whole picture, and not in terms of details as most of these individuals do. Besides perspective taking, a person needs to choose an action path based on anticipated consequences, which requires abstract thinking as well as perspective taking. Then, if we are solving a problem that involves another person, we need to use personal communication skills to negotiate, which requires that we formulate, interpret, and respond to language appropriately. This is actually quite complex. The following resources offer some suggestions parents and teachers might find useful.

For more information, see *Inside Out: What Makes a Person with*

FOOD FOR THOUGHT
Perspective Taking

All this gets very tricky! The very heart of AS is that we are not able to decipher other people's thoughts and feelings and motivations—we can't put ourselves "in their shoes" (if you saw some of my teachers, believe me, you definitely wouldn't want to—phew!). Because of this problem, it really does make it very difficult to know who is likely to be helpful and supportive and who is likely to make things worse, either by accident or on purpose. I can't work that out at all. So usually I just keep my mouth shut and hope that Mom sorts stuff like that out. After all, I am only thirteen so I may get better at working out this stuff as I get older.

—Luke Jackson, *Freaks, Geeks & Asperger Syndrome:*
A User Guide to Adolescence

Social Cognitive Deficits Tick? and *Thinking About You, Thinking About Me: Philosophy and Strategies for Facilitating the Development of Perspective Taking for Students with Social Cognitive Deficits*, both by Michelle Garcia Winner.

RECOGNIZING EMOTIONS AND CONTROLLING EMOTIONAL RESPONSES

In order to recognize emotions in others, we need to be able to recognize the nonverbal cues that show what emotional state a person is in. Even the less able need to know about recognizing facial expressions of different emotions, so they can know how to "read" the emotion of someone they are dealing with. Some auditory learners may pick up more easily on the difference in the tone of voice for each emotion (such as happy versus angry), and visual learners may notice the facial changes. By using their stronger learning modality for teaching the emotions and cues, they can learn to pick up the other cues when paired with it.

I've listed some resources below, including games that use flash cards with photos of different emotions that can easily be used with all ability levels, and a computer program or two as well. New products are coming on the market all the time in this area. It's important to remember that regardless of what type of teaching tool is used, the knowledge must be generalized to real people.

For more information, see the following resources:

The Incredible 5-Point Scale: Assisting Students with Autism Spectrum Disorders in Understanding Social Interactions and Controlling Their Emotional Responses, by Kari Dunn Buron and Mitzi Curtis. This book is intended for younger students on the more able end of the spectrum. However, the ideas in here can be used and adapted for a wider range, including the less able. The idea of assigning feelings a number between one and five can be very useful for those who are less communicative.

Exploring Feelings: Cognitive Behaviour Therapy to Manage Anger and *Exploring Feelings: Cognitive Behaviour Therapy to Manage Anxiety,* by Tony Attwood. Cognitive Behavior Therapy encourages the cognitive control of emotions. Tony Attwood developed the Exploring Feelings Cognitive Behavior Therapy Programs to be highly structured, interesting, and successful in encouraging tweens and teens to learn how to control their emotions. Dr. Attwood developed this program as a treatment of anger management and/or anxiety disorder in children with Asperger's.

Feelings and Faces Games, by Lakeshore. These games use photos of different emotions that can easily be used with all ability levels.

UNDERSTANDING THE UNSPOKEN RULES OF THE "HIDDEN CURRICULUM"

People on the spectrum have difficulties with unstated rules in social situations, also known as the Hidden Curriculum. Having lived in

FOOD FOR THOUGHT

The Hidden Curriculum

As long as things followed a set of rules I could play along. Rules were—and are—great friends of mine. I like rules. They set the record straight and keep it that way. You know where you stand with rules and you know how to act with rules. Trouble is, rules change, and if they do not, people break them. I get terribly annoyed when either happens. Certain things in life are givens. "Thank you" is followed by "You are welcome." You hold doors open for other people. The elderly are treated with respect. You do not cut in front of other people, you stay in line and wait your turn. You do not talk loud in libraries. Eye contact is made when you talk to someone. The list goes on, but the intent never changes: rules are maps that lead us to know how to behave and what to expect. When they are broken, the whole world turns upside down.

—Liane Holliday Willey, *Pretending to be Normal:*
Living with Asperger's Syndrome

three different countries, I can testify to the fact that when changing cultures, one often is confronted with unstated rules that must be learned in order to understand what one is supposed to do or say in social situations as well as the true meaning of people's actions and conversations. For individuals on the more able end of the spectrum, the school environment is like a foreign country, as they don't naturally pick up on the unstated rules. During the teen years, this can be quite a challenge as much of the teen world and teen social conventions are based on not what is said but what is meant, and by body language, and sometimes even by what is *not* said. That is why it is so important to teach our teens with ASDs about the subtext of social situations.

A great resource is *The Hidden Curriculum: Practical Solutions for Understanding Unstated Rules in Social Situations,* by Brenda Smith Myles, Melissa L. Trautman, and Ronda L. Schelvan.

IDIOMS AND METAPHORS

Even teenagers on the spectrum with good language skills have a tendency to interpret words or phrases concretely. Understanding implied meaning is something that must be taught. Students with ASDs do not learn metaphors just by hearing them and figuring them out. It is similar to students of a foreign language who, when they finally travel to the foreign country, find that they do not understand some of the expressions and try to translate them word for word. Having access to a dictionary and learning the meanings of commonly used expressions can be very helpful.

An Asperger Dictionary of Everyday Expressions, by Ian Stuart-Hamilton, provides explanations of more than 5,000 idiomatic expressions plus a guide to their politeness level. Each expression is accompanied by a clear explanation of its meaning and when and how it might be used. The expressions are taken from British and American English, with some Australian expressions included as well.

FOOD FOR THOUGHT

Transition Planning for Aspies

by Valerie Paradiz, Ph.D

Adolescence is an important time of growth in any young person's life. It's a vulnerable time, during which self-esteem can be exceedingly fragile. For teens with AS, HFA, or PDD, the quality of support and education they receive during this formative period can make or break future success as an adult, be it on the job, in relationships, or in independent living. While more and more young Aspies (a term coined by Asperger self-advocates) have access to crucial social skills curricula and practice of social skills in schools, opportunities for building self-advocacy skills are scarce.

Self-advocacy is a lifelong endeavor, and the teen years offer a particularly fruitful moment for cultivating self-awareness, self-monitoring, and deeper exploration of what it means to be autistic, by way of peer discussion groups. Self-advocacy differs from advocacy in that the individual with the disability self-assesses a situation or problem, then speaks for his or her own needs. Learning how to do this takes practice and direct instruction. Too often, we raise our kids, treat our patients, and educate our students without ever speaking to them directly about autism. Perhaps we've made assumptions or even harbor fears that they aren't capable of self-reflection. Yet if we deny kids this very important aspect of identity, we limit their ability to become the successful adults we want them to be. As with any academic subject, teaching self-advocacy takes training as well as knowledge of and respect for the disability movement. Parents can model self-advocacy at home, teachers can offer curricula in school, and most important, peers on the autism spectrum can offer strategies for good living and share mutual experiences.

I'd like to talk a moment about these fellow travelers on the spectrum. Increasingly, adults with AS and HFA are coming together with the recognition that autism is not only a medical, neurological, or psychiatric condition, but that it is a way of life possessing a particular culture and history. Many peer support organizations run *by* autistic people *for* autistic people began springing up in small pockets around the country in the mid 1990s, around the same time that AS was first included in the *DSM IV* (*Diagnostic and Statistical Manual of Mental Disorders*).

The first known peer support group, AGUA, was founded by Jerry Newport in Los Angeles, where he also met his future wife, Mary Newport. Soon thereafter the couple became important voices in the self-advocacy movement, authoring two books that offer important insights and advice on learning many adult life skills. In San Francisco, Adam Pollack developed the AUTASTICS. Here in New York state there is Autism Network International, based in Syracuse, which hosts a retreat each summer in the Adirondacks, offering conference workshops presented by and for folks on the spectrum. Finally, there is GRASP, a new nonprofit in New York City, directed by Michael John Carley, that is about to launch a major campaign of setting up peer support groups across the nation, conducting a large-scale outreach campaign to educate the general public about Asperger's Syndrome, and offering a list of speakers who can visit communities, institutions, and schools as a means of modeling successful adult living. GRASP is also putting together a database and referral list of professionals, schools, and services that pass standards developed by folks on the spectrum.

At ASPIE (a school for academically able teenagers on the autism spectrum), we have culled information from many of the sources I've mentioned here to create a self-advocacy curriculum for our students. Some of our kids weren't aware of their diagnosis until very recently. Others have known for years, though they really haven't had the opportunity to learn what autism or Asperger's syndrome is. At ASPIE, they are now beginning to get a good working knowledge of autism's medical and psychiatric history, and they're learning about important role models, both living and dead, from Albert Einstein to Andy Warhol to Temple Grandin. They also have the opportunity to speak about their strengths and about the challenges they face, and to share difficult, often traumatic experiences from the past, which they had no previous opportunity to discuss with peers. This process can carry a fragile teen from a place of shame and fear about his or her difference into a more powerful position of self-knowledge, self-expression, and the confidence everyone needs for a successful adult life.

To give a few examples: students at ASPIE have been learning and discussing key terms like "perseveration," "eye contact," and "sensory sensitivities." With time and practice, they have begun to have words for experiences they often didn't understand in the past. Important self-advocacy concepts, such as neurotypicality and self-disclosure, are also explored in a safe, confidential group setting. Our students are beginning to see that, along with their parents and professionals in the autism field, *they, too,* have a perspective on their own lives, and one day they will be "experts" on themselves! In essence, they are practicing crucial skills that are the foundation for future success in employment and living situations.

In addition to the examples I've mentioned, our self-advocacy curriculum at ASPIE features the following:

- Adults on the autism spectrum regularly visit ASPIE to meet with kids and share life stories and to meet with parents and staff for training and development.
- Our therapeutic staff conduct sensory profile questionnaires to help kids learn self-monitoring skills.
- Students are preparing to attend their own special education planning meetings.
- Students attend autism society meetings and conferences.

• Future topics will include self-advocating for services, introduction to self-run organizations, the ADA (Americans with Disabilities Act), the history of the disability movement, etc.

Valerie Paradiz, Ph.D., is the executive director of the ASPIE School and Institute located in Boiceville, New York. For more information visit www.aspie-school.org.

5

Transition Planning: Preparing for Life After High School

Work is more than just a livelihood or paycheck; it is the key to a satisfying and productive life. For many on the autism spectrum, it is the glue that keeps our lives together in an otherwise frustrating and sometimes confusing world. Certainly, my life would not be worth living if I did not have intellectually satisfying work.
—TEMPLE GRANDIN (AND KATE DUFFY), *Developing Talents: Careers for Individuals with Asperger Syndrome and High-Functioning Autism*

WHEN he was little, my son Jeremy loved following the patterns in our old Persian rug or the mosaic tiles in the old buildings in Paris, and we used to joke that when he grew up he could be a quality-control person in a carpet factory. Jeremy is not that big on task completion, and he can twirl and flicker just about anything he can get his hands on. He hates sitting and doing the same thing over and over, so Jeremy is not "workshop" material. He would be bored to tears. I don't expect his neurotypical sister, Rebecca, to have a job she is not cut out to do; why should I expect Jeremy to?

Jeremy is learning about different jobs and careers from his teacher at school, and he has a few options we are all thinking about, including perhaps owning his own small business. Now, thanks to his teacher, his instructional aide, the rest of the professionals at school, and his individualized transition plan, he is enjoying success at his first small entrepreneurial venture, which is varied enough to keep his interest for now. Jeremy is making a little money, but he is also learning about the cost of doing business: that expenses can eat up a portion of your earnings. Lessons such as this one are necessary no matter what he chooses to do later in life, and is a crucial part of envisioning—and ensuring—a productive and happy future.

The Individualized Transition Plan

It really does take a village—or, more precisely, a team—to prepare teenagers on the spectrum for a fulfilling and successful life. Parents need to get involved to ensure that an individual transition plan will be created that fits their teen's aspirations and dreams. The student in question has to share his dreams and hopes, his interests and obsessions, his likes and dislikes. Brainstorming and thinking outside the box will be necessary on the part of all of those who know the student in question. The Individualized Education Program (IEP) and the Individualized Transition Plan (ITP) and goals set forward must reflect these dreams and hopes to ensure a solid transition.

In reality, the ITP is the "business plan" for the teenager's life. The mission statement should reflect the student's dreams and aspirations. The goals should tell you how to get there and what is needed to make the dream a reality.

The challenge faced in the teenage years is that the student must learn what he needs to know to survive adolescence and high school, but he must also learn the skills necessary for his future, his transition to the adult world. Whether the teenager will attend college, hold a job, be in a sheltered work environment, live independently or in a group home, he must prepare during his high school years for every aspect of everyday life. While the teenager is in the quasi-sheltered environment of school, his future hopes and dreams need to be looked at and prepared for now. However, the reality of the situation is that in the United States today, our transition programs and plans are wholly inadequate for preparing our students for real life after high school.

CHALLENGES, EXPECTATIONS, AND DEMANDS

Today, there are work, college, and living options and concepts available that never existed before, as well as a growing awareness of the value of individuals with ASDs and how to support them in order to help them be successful as adults. Even for those on the less able end of the spectrum, creative options exist. The students who are now teenagers are the children whose parents once fought for early intervention and ABA. These parents are not going to give up on their children. The expectations of many families and students is that they will have a better quality of life than their predecessors. These are exciting times, when "self-determination" and "person-centered planning" are routinely discussed and gives hope for the future of our children. "Self-esteem" and "self-advocacy" are two other buzz words we are hearing more and more in connection with our ASD students.

Unfortunately, we still have a long way to go. Most schools are unable to keep up with the philosophy of self-determination and aren't fully preparing the majority of our ASD students for life after high school, regardless of the path the student has chosen. Students and parents are given few options for transitioning toward the future and are told what is available (not very much). Again, we are dealing with the "one size fits all" mentality that many of us are already familiar with. All this is why parents must arm themselves with information and a game plan.

ADULT SERVICES TODAY

As discussed in my previous book, *Autism Spectrum Disorders,* although the future looks brighter than ever in terms of possibilities of creating what our children need, the reality of what is available in terms of adult services today is a different story. There are not enough residential and work programs that are tailored for the needs of individuals on the spectrum. Dr. Ruth Sullivan authored a position paper published by the Autism Society of America in July of 2001 that gives information about the critical state of adult services and recommendations as to what should be done to improve them. Recently, The National Association of Residential Providers for Adults with Autism (NARPAA), founded by Dr. Sullivan, has developed a "Train the Trainer Project" in response to the severe shortage of trained staff for adults with Autism. For more information, visit their website at http://www.narpaa.org/.

It is important as you and your teenager are planning transition services to keep in mind the reality of what is out there, to take a look at the new funding models, and to think of the possibilities that you may need to create with other like-minded people.

FACTS AND CONCERNS

In October 2001, President Bush ordered the creation of the President's Commission on Excellence in Special Education. This commission held thirteen hearings and meetings throughout the nation and listened to the concerns and comments from parents, teachers, principals, education officials, and the public. The commission published its report in July 2002. One of its main findings was: "The focus on compliance and bureaucratic imperatives in the current system, instead of academic achievement and social outcomes, fails too many children with disabilities. Too few successfully graduate from high school or transition to full employment and postsecondary opportunities, despite provisions in IDEA providing for transition services. Parents want an education system that is results-oriented and focused on the child's needs—in school and beyond."

In terms of postsecondary results for students with disabilities and effective transition services, the commission found that:

• **Young people with disabilities drop out of high school at twice the rate of their peers.** Students with disabilities are unemployed and underemployed upon leaving school compared to their peers who have no disabilities.

• **Too many students with disabilities leave school without successfully earning any type of diploma** and attend postsecondary programs at rates lower than their nondisabled peers.

• **Adults with disabilities are much less likely to be employed than adults without disabilities.** Unemployment rates for working-age adults with disabilities have hovered at the 70 percent level for at least the past twelve years, which the commission found to be wholly unacceptable.

• **Employed adults with disabilities earn markedly less income than their nondisabled peers.** These statistics reflect failures of the present system structures.

In terms of IDEA 1997 transition regulations, the commission found that:

• **IDEA 1997 transition regulation requirements are too convoluted** to implement in practical ways and should be revised.

• **The fundamental failure of federal policies and programs to facilitate smooth movement for students from secondary school to competitive employment and higher education** was the overriding barrier preventing a smooth transition from high school to adult living for individuals with disabilities.

• **Several federal programs fail to direct the necessary resources to increase a successful transition of students with disabilities.** For instance:

1. IDEA 1997 and the Rehabilitation Act vocational rehabilitation program have no links based on student results. While

each mandate some level of cooperation, the lack of postschool data tracking under IDEA as well as the lack of a Rehabilitation Act obligation for active involvement of vocational rehabilitation counselors in each student's transition planning contribute to poor student outcomes.

2. In addition to IDEA 1997 and the Rehabilitation Act, programs authorized under the Higher Education Act do not sufficiently provide transition services to meet the needs of students with disabilities.

• **Poor implementation.** If existing federal policies and laws were more effectively implemented, the low rates of individuals with disabilities currently obtaining competitive employment or accessing higher education would dramatically improve.

• **Poor targeting of resources.** Funding for more focused transition services now exists; however, these funds are spread across multiple agencies and programs. They do not target transition services or foster coordination with other federal programs. The commission found that these programs did not provide states the flexibility needed to develop comprehensive programs to use general funds already available. Federal programs must be required to

---

FOOD FOR THOUGHT

Underemployment Starts Here

Requested by a mother to attend her son's IEP and ITP meeting, I sit listening to the team discuss Roger's intellectual capabilities and the strategies put in place that make him a successful high school junior. It is the end of the year, and the team is planning for next year, his last year in high school. Roger, who has Asperger's Syndrome, will be graduating with a high school diploma, making him ineligible for further special education services under California law. The discussion moves on to Roger's current "workability job" where he is wiping tables in a "volunteer" capacity. This may be good for a first job to teach responsibility, but uses none of his capabilities. His mother brings up the fact that Roger loves to bake; he is constantly baking at home. He has shown interest in pursuing this as a career. Roger says that perhaps he can get a job at the local bakery to learn how to make bread and pastries for a wider market than friends and family, learn about the business, and eventually own his own bakery. One of the school staff members, a wonderful, caring person who has been there for many years, says that perhaps he can get a job for Roger at a local bakery—wiping tables.

To parents of ASD teenagers who are now juniors and seniors in high school, this will come as no surprise. We are used to having to broaden the narrow perspectives inherent to the systems that are in place. We are now advocating to get job coaches who understand about autism, who know strategies to put into place to make the work experiences successful; advocating to have job experiences for our teenagers than can actually help them in their career choices, jobs that can turn their interests, talents, and obsessions into gainful employment or micro-ownership when they leave school for the real world. Even if they are severely impacted by their autism, we expect them to contribute to society and have a happy life. We are, after all, expecting them to live the American Dream, just like any other American, disabled or not.

The big question is, why are we spending millions of taxpayer dollars on special education and workability programs to turn all these hopeful teenagers and young adults into janitors, bookshelf stockers, or fast-food workers? I am not saying there is anything wrong with doing that kind of work—if that is what you like doing, and if you are getting well paid to do it. Why does our society still expect individuals who are a bit different—yet able—to be happy doing jobs they would never think of doing themselves or of having their own children do for more than a summer break?

There needs to be real commitment from all of us—parents, school administrators, and business owners—to think outside the box. Parents can help by using their contacts and connections, their knowledge about their teenagers' strengths, talents, and dreams, and find options for work experiences in the community.

better coordinate their services to focus on reaching people with disabilities early.

• **Transition services are not being implemented to the fullest extent possible.** IDEA's 1997 federal requirements were too complex for educators, students, parents, and others (such as vocational rehabilitation program counselors) to understand what the law required.

The reauthorized Individuals with Disabilities Education Act (IDEA) 2004 was signed into law on Dec 3, 2004, by President George W. Bush, and is referred to as the Individuals with Disabilities Education Improvement Act (IDEIA) 2004. Hopefully, the federal regulations to implement IDEIA 2004 (not yet released at time of writing) will be clearer than the IDEA's 1997 federal requirements with regard to transition services.

The recommendations of the commission were:

• **Simplify the federal transition requirements in IDEA.** These provisions should provide clear steps for integrating school and non-school transition services and should closely link the transition services to the goals in each student's IEP.

• **Mandate federal interagency coordination of resources.** Multiple federal policies and programs must be required to work together to improve competitive employment outcomes and increase access to higher education for students with disabilities. An executive order mandating agency coordination and pooling of existing funds would improve transition services. Further, the bridge between federal special education policy and rehabilitation policy must be strengthened.

• **Create a Rehabilitation Act reauthorization advisory committee.** The secretary of education should create an advisory committee to examine the reauthorization of the Rehabilitation Act.

• Support higher education faculty, administrators, and auxiliary service providers to more effectively provide and help students with disabilities to complete a high-quality postsecondary education. Support and hold accountable all postsecondary institutions receiving federal funding for using evidence-based programs and practices. Fund programs to educate postsecondary education personnel to modifications and accommodations for students with disabilities that have been proven to increase graduation rates and entry into the workforce.

Hopefully, the implementation of IDEIA 2004 is creating positive change and reflecting the recommendations made above by the commission.

Specifically in terms of individuals on the autism spectrum, there is not that much specific employment data available. However, this is what we do know:

• The autism population remains the most unemployed population despite the fact that, according to the U.S. Department of Education, Office of Special Education Programs, the dropout rates for students fourteen years and older with autism were lower than students with any other disability. In the Indiana Parent/Family 2003 Needs Assessment Survey, 69 percent of the individuals with autism represented in the survey over the age of eighteen were unemployed, 8 percent worked in sheltered workshops, and 23 percent worked in community jobs. Those who were employed worked an average of nineteen hours per week and had a median annual income of $3,500.

• Estimates of unemployed or underemployed individuals with ASDS in other parts of the world are high as well. In the UK, these estimates are as high as 85 percent. Even for those who have formal qualifications, employment levels and occupational status are low (Goode, Rutter & Howlin, 1997).

• In a study of eighteen individuals who had Asperger's, HFA, or PDD, all participants reported lengthy periods of unemployment and underemployment, although they all described themselves as hard workers and good workers. The majority had held multiple jobs. Almost all described their work experience in negative terms. Mastering the job application process, acclimating to new job routines, and navigating social interactions with supervisors and coworkers were considered to be the main obstacles to successful employment for them (Muller, Schuler, Burton, and Yates, 2003).

• A national study of effective transition practices in local districts (Hasazi et al., 1998) validated the importance of self-determination, effective and substantive interagency collaboration, extensive cross-agency professional development, a climate that supports transition, coordination across educational as well as other agency programs, and sustained leadership. Among the challenges to effective transition planning were the lack of available community programs and the often fragmented and unsystematic nature of the planning.

CONCLUSION

• Parents of adolescents with an ASD need to know the facts of unemployment and underemployment for adults on the spectrum in order to understand the failings thus far of the system.

• In order to better prepare their teenager for a successful future after high school, parents will need to be an active member of the transition planning process and understand the shortcomings of the system

• Creative thinking outside the box and teamwork with all members of the ITP will be necessary in order to ensure a successful future outcome.

• More connections with businesses and people and entrepreneurs in the community are necessary to ensure more access to job opportunities.

How to Get the Transition Services Your Teenager Needs

Federal special education law, specifically the Individuals with Disabilities Education Act (IDEA), requires that school districts help students with disabilities make the transition from school to work. As a parent, it is necessary for you to take an active role in the planning process to ensure your child has a good preparation for his future as an adult. However, remember that the school district remains ultimately responsible for ensuring that transitional services are provided. The following section is not intended to be legal advice, but is provided for informational purposes only. Parents are encouraged to check with their state's protection and advocacy office for the regulations in place in their state.

FOOD FOR THOUGHT
They Are Counting on Us

It is uncomfortable for me to think back to my late teens and early twenties. Hindsight has taught me a few things about those years but it has not taken away the bad memories or the deep embarrassments.

The future is often blinding for eighteen-year-olds, blinding with unending brightness and possibility or blinding with a potential to scorch and burn. Which experience is met depends not just on the abilities or potential of the young person, but so very much on the support friends, family members, guidance counselors, mentors, employers, and continuing education specialists legitimately offer. This is especially true for those with any special need, even those whose needs are often invisible to the unknowing observer.

—Liane Holliday Willey, *Pretending to be Normal: Living with Asperger's Syndrome*

DEFINITION OF ITP AND
TRANSITION SERVICES PER IDEA 1997

The Individual Transition Plan (ITP) is a term used to describe the written plan designed to help prepare students for passage from school to postschool life. The 1997 Reauthorization of IDEA defines transition services as a coordinated set of activities for a student with a disability that:

• Is designed within an outcome-oriented process, which promotes movement from school to postschool activities, including postsecondary education, vocational training, integrated employment (including supported employment), continuing and adult education, adult services, independent living or community participation.

• Is based upon the individual student's needs, taking into account the student's preferences and interests.

• Includes instruction, related services, community experiences, the development of employment and other postschool adult living objectives, and, when appropriate, acquisition of daily living skills and functional vocational evaluation.

Keep in mind that:

• Special education is not mandatory between the ages of 18 and 21, but some states continue to provide special education services to those that have not received their high school diploma or passed exit tests.

• Vocational education is a term that refers to organized educational programs that are directly related to the preparation of individuals for paid or unpaid employment, or for additional preparation for a career requiring other than a college or advanced degree. Vocational training is included within the definition of transition services. Vocational service should be considered as a long-range process starting with developing the awareness in the student of possible career choices and work attitudes even as young as elementary school if appropriate.

YOUR STUDENT'S RIGHTS AND RESPONSIBILITIES

At time of writing, federal regulations for IDEIA 2004 in regards to transition planning and services were not yet released. Once the federal regulations are released, each state will publish its own guidelines. It is important to be knowledgeable about your teenager's rights to ensure a useful transition program. Readers are advised to find out about the regulations in effect in their state. Sources of information include:

- Your state's protection and advocacy office. Find it on the Autism Society of America website: www.autism-society.org.

- http://www.ideapractices.org/law/index.php

- www.wrightslaw.com

Points that are being made in IDEIA 2004 include:

- The first IEP after the child turns 16 must include appropriate postsecondary goals that are measurable.

- These goals must be based upon age-appropriate transition assessments related to independent living skills, if appropriate, as well as assessments related to education, training, employment.

- The IEP must also include the transition services needed in order for the teenager to reach these goals, and the IEP must be updated annually.

GETTING THE TRANSITION SERVICES YOUR ADOLESCENT NEEDS

It is important for parents and the student to realize that although IDEA mandates services and programs for all children with special educational needs, there are no mandated programs or services for individuals after they leave the school system. Eligibility does not provide entitlement—unlike the mandatory services funded under IDEA. This means that your teen needs to make the most of this transition period to learn all he needs in terms of life skills and what he would like to do careerwise.

It's important that your teen have a few work experiences while in high school, doing different types of jobs in different environments. This will help him become aware of what he likes and doesn't like and what he is good at.

In preparation for his ITP, your teen needs to learn some self-advocacy skills as discussed in chapter 4. When planning for the ITP, find out from the case manager who will be at the ITP meeting. The meeting could include someone from the department of vocational rehabilitation or the U.S. Social Security Administration. Each case is different, depending on the age and need of the individual students. Do not be afraid to ask for the presence of an agency or person you think would be helpful in helping to plan your teen's future.

Remember during the transition planning process that the agencies and staff involved (for example job coaches) may be knowledgeable about developmental disabilities, but not necessarily about autism spectrum disorders. Just as you did for school staff, you will need to make sure that the people helping your teen are knowledgeable about ASDs and the particular strategies that have been helpful to your teen and the educators that work with him.

Parents must empower themselves with knowledge about what a good transition plan looks like, the possibilities in your community, resources in your state, what agencies can help you, your child's legal rights, and your legal rights. Here are some resources that will help you find out what you need to know:

• "Life after High School." A four-page document, this is a good, short summary of transition planning from junior high to after high school. (Autism Society of America, www.autism-society.org)

• "Transition: Adulthood." This is an excellent free detailed document on transition planning on the National Dissemination Center for Children with Disabilities website, www.nichcy.org. This is a more detailed overview of what should be included in transition planning, who the "players" are that should be invited to the ITP table, and examples of different types of services that could be helpful to your teenager.

• Protection and advocacy. Every state has a protection and advocacy agency (though it might have a different name in certain states) that gives free information and advice in regard to your rights as well as your teenage student's. It is important to check with your state because although IDEA is a federal act, each state applies it differently within the parameters. Also, the state regulations do change. Make sure you are getting current information, wherever you get it from; check the dates on any papers. The National Dissemination Center for Children with Disabilities, www.nichcy.org, lists information by state of all the offices and administrations that are there to help, including the contact information for protection and advocacy offices.

• Quality Mall (www.qualitymall.org). This organization provides free information about person-centered supports for people with developmental disabilities. Each of the "mall stores" has departments you can look through to learn about positive practices that help people with developmental disabilities live, work, and participate in our communities and improve the quality of their supports, or you can type in a search word such as "employment."

• The Consortium for Citizens with Disabilities (www.c-c-d.org) is a coalition of national consumer, advocacy, provider, and professional organizations headquartered in Washington, D.C. Since 1973, the CCD has advocated on behalf of people of all ages with physical and mental disabilities and their families. CCD has worked to achieve federal legislation and regulations that assure that the fifty-four million children and adults with disabilities are fully integrated into the mainstream of society.

In the following sections, we'll explore the issues involved in determining your teen's transition needs, as well as descriptions of some employment, college, and living options. Coping strategies and practical tips based on the experiences of those with an ASD and other experts are also included.

DETERMINING YOUR TEENAGER'S TRANSITION NEEDS

As mentioned earlier, planning your teenager's transition into the real world of adult life is one of the most important aspects of his educational life. In order to prepare him as best you can for transition into adulthood, you must determine what his transition needs are. Here is a short summary of what you need to take into consideration, with a more detailed explanation in the following section:

- **Your teenager's hopes and dreams.** Where he thinks and hopes to be in five years and in ten years. Does he know what kinds of jobs or type of work he is interested in? What kind of living arrangement does he see himself having? As his parent, you know your son well. What do you see him being successful at? Discussing this question with other family members and people that know and love him will be helpful. For those who are less able or have difficulty communicating, Person-centered planning can help to figure out what the person's likes and dreams are.

- **Your teen's talents, obsessions and interests.** These should be the starting point for any planning. As for any individual, why spend a lifetime doing a job you are unhappy with and maybe not as successful, when you have a talent or interest to capitalize on? Even for the less able, there are options for creating self-employment opportunities based on what they like to do.

• **Other successful people on the spectrum and their experiences.** This is crucial knowledge when thinking about the possibilities for your teen. Neurotypical teens look at successful individuals in the fields that interest them; they have their role models. So do teens on the spectrum! Reading the experiences of successful adults with an ASD can give ideas on what might work with your teen as well as what he needs to learn to prepare for a successful life. Practical tips offered in these life experiences can be helpful for the less able as well and provide ideas for needed supports.

• **Your teen's academic interests.** College is a good option for many on the more able end of the spectrum. Some have even become professors in their field of interest.

• **Employment options currently available in the community.** A look at what currently exists in the community will give you and your teenager some ideas. If you see work opportunities that fit his dreams and his interests, find out what kinds of skills he should learn and what kind of supports he will need in order to be successful in those environments. If you see that nothing appears appropriate for your son, you will know that you will need to create something that works for him, and ideally the transition team at his school will help in this effort.

• **Living arrangements currently available in the community.** Just as for employment opportunities, a look at what is out there and your teen's skill level as well as his ideas for what kind of living situation he envisions can give you an idea of the kind of planning you need to do and what your teen needs to prepare for his chosen living arrangement. Again, perhaps you can create options with other like-minded community members.

YOUR TEENAGER'S HOPES AND DREAMS

At age sixteen transition services must begin and your teen must, by law, give his input. As discussed in the previous chapter, self-determination is a necessary component for having a successful life, and your teen should be learning to express his wishes in regard to the future as well as learning some of the responsibilities of being a good citizen and neighbor.

Some students may find it easier than others to give input and speak for themselves. For those with good communication skills, the parents and educators are probably aware of the student's wishes and dreams for the future or can draw them out by asking the right questions. For the many who have only basic communication skills, it will be harder and require more effort, patience, and active observation.

For those with very limited communication skills, there are some tools used to help figure out through observation of the person and input from the people who know him well. It is important to make sure that input is given from all who know him well (friends, relatives, tutors, teachers, neighbors, peers at school, etc.) and care for him, not just the parents. Some useful tools are Making Action Plans (MAPS), Planning Alternative Tomorrows with Hope (PATH), and Circle of Supports. Simple courses and explanations of these tools can be found at the Person-Centered Planning Education Site at www.ilr.cornell.edu/ped/tsal/pcp.

Another good site is www.allenshea.com, which has examples of Essential Lifestyle Planning, which is also a person-centered approach.

Some good books to help you, your teen, his teacher, and the ITP team:

• *Becoming Remarkably Able: Walking the Path to Independence and Beyond,* by Jackie Marquette, www.independencebound.com. This book has practical information for parents and professionals, and some ideas and worksheets to help the teen and those who love him think about future possibilities based on the teen's ideas about his future.

• *The Transition Handbook: Strategies High School Teachers Use That Work!* by Carolyn Hughes and Erik W. Carter. This book offers practical models that can be used in everyday life. It offers specific strategies for how to implement training techniques and support strategies in the context of community and social living. It is not specific to ASDs, but can easily be adapted as a model.

• *Life Beyond the Classroom: Transition Strategies for Young People with Disabilities,* by Paul Wehman. This textbook is geared toward educators and is not specific to the autism spectrum. However, parents who are interested may wish to peruse this for factual and practical information.

The World of Work

YOUR TEEN'S TALENTS, OBSESSIONS, AND INTERESTS

Many people with autism or Asperger's have written about the importance of having a meaningful career or job that uses their interests in talents as a necessary ingredient for a fulfilling adult life. This is true for all adults, neurotypicals included. However, without guidance in developing their talents or the proper supports to be successful on the job, most individuals with autism or Asperger's are unemployed and underemployed.

It cannot be overemphasized that future employment success is dependent on starting to develop the tween's and teen's interests in middle and high school, if it has not already been done. Even if it is not known what employment structure the student will eventually find a good fit, developing talents and teaching skills that are necessary in all jobs (such as organization, scheduling, etc.) must be taught and emphasized during the transition period.

Even if your teen is on the less able end of the spectrum, you can find a way, with supports, for your teen to have a job or micro-enterprise based on what he likes. But don't expect someone else to come up with the ideas. You, as the parent, will have to get those creative juices flowing and think outside the box.

PEOPLE WITH ASDS AND THEIR WORK EXPERIENCE

In order to prepare for future employment, it is important to not only look at the existing structures in place but to reflect upon what those on the spectrum have to say about their work experience, how they came to be in the job they are in, and what was helpful in preparing for it.

A great book for a teen, his parents, and his teachers is *Developing Talents: Careers for Individuals with Asperger Syndrome and High-Functioning Autism,* by Temple Grandin and Kate Duffy. This book is full of practical information such as rules for success on the job, how to find a vocation the teenager can love, and a discussion of how the characteristics of ASDs relate to the workplace. For the more able on the spectrum, it gives plenty of ideas about the types of careers that are out there depending on the kind of talents and interests the teenager has and what kind of thinker he is.

Another good resource is Jerry Newport's book *Your Life Is Not a Label*. In it, Newport writes that no matter what job you have, you should do it well, and shares many useful tips for teens. He suggests that even low-entry-level jobs are important as they can teach you things that are necessary for all jobs, namely how to follow instructions, how to be on time, how to dress appropriately, and how to work independently.

Stephen Shore's article "Survival in the Workplace" describes the various careers he attempted before finding the one that fit him and what it was about the jobs that he found difficult. This kind of analysis is helpful in determining a good fit. www.udel.edu/bkirby/asperger/survival_shore.html

Liane Holliday Willey's book *Pretending to be Normal: Living with Asperger's Syndrome* has a great section in the back titled Employment Options and Responsibilities to stimulate creative thoughts and viable options.

Other places to look for information about people on the spectrum's work experiences include:

- "Survival in the Workplace" and "A Day in the Life," by Stephen Shore (www.udel.edu/bkirby/asperger/survival_shore.html).

- "Marketing a Person on the Autistic Spectrum: Some Business School Lessons," by Lars Perner, Ph.D. (www.larsperner.com).

- *Thinking in Pictures,* by Temple Grandin.

- The video *Asperger Syndrome: Transition to College and Work,* at www.coultervideo.com.

ADVICE FROM A PROFESSIONAL

In the Coulter video *Asperger Syndrome: Transition to College and Work,* Drew Coulter, who has AS, Dr. Peter Gerhard, who has published and spoken widely on the needs of adults with autism spectrum disorder and the school-to-work-transition process and Mary Beth Berry, a teacher and advisor at North Hunterdon High School, discuss getting ready for the world of work. Some points they make include:

- **Job matching:** Lots of neurotypicals don't like their jobs, but they are motivated by money. To someone on the spectrum, money may not be as big a motivator. They need to like the work they do; consequently, a good match between the individual and the job is particularly important.

- **Personal inventory:** Making a list of likes and dislikes, strengths and weaknesses as well as what is important in the physical environment can be helpful when thinking about potential jobs.

Questions to ask include: Can I check my own work? How independent am I? If I need help, can I get help? How long can I work without taking a break?

• **Personal disclosure:** Disclosure about having AS is a personal choice. However, it is important to keep in mind that in order to be eligible for accommodations under the Americans with Disabilities Act (ADA), you must tell the potential employer during the interview or shortly after being hired. Otherwise, your "window of opportunity" for reasonable accommodations on the job closes. Disclosure is discussed in chapter 4 under "Planning for Future Success."

• **Reasonable accommodations under ADA:** These can include such things as longer training periods and leaving for breaks and coming back a few minutes earlier to avoid the crowds and noise.

• **Understand business speak:** If you are helping people on the spectrum to find work, you must learn to understand the mentality of the business world. You must learn to understand "what's in it for them" so you can understand how to sell the idea of hiring a person in their company.

• **Safety:** Workplace safety issues include everything from understanding fire drills to learning about how not to let people take advantage of you.

• **Social skills:** Even if these are not important for the actual job, these are important for keeping the job. As Drew Coulter says, "Work isn't just about work, it's about dealing with people." Certain social skills may be different at different workplaces, but there are some basic skills every employee should know. For example, a person may need to learn who and how to ask for assistance (that is, don't bother someone every five minutes or when they are on the phone).

• **Training of coworkers:** Sometimes the coworkers of the person with AS need to be given some information about the person with

AS they will be working with, much as the coworkers of a blind person will be trained on how to accommodate or work with the colleague. Information such as, "He needs thirty seconds to respond because of processing challenges; he is thinking about the answer," can be very helpful for facilitating the job placement.

• **Transition strategy:** Gerhardt attributes an important transition strategy for work to Paul Wehman, author of *Life Beyond the Classroom: Transition Strategies for Young People with Disabilities*: If you can teach the skill, teach it. If you can't teach the skill, adapt it. If you can't adapt it, figure out a way around it. To this strategy, Gerhardt likes to add: If you can't figure out a way around it, teach the neurotypicals to deal with it.

Obviously, not everyone has the capabilities of Temple Grandin or Stephen Shore; however, the concerns of finding a good fit and a job or career that is interesting to the individual are the same whether the person is more or less able. Many of the ideas and supports mentioned can be adapted for the less able as well.

EMPLOYMENT STRUCTURES CURRENTLY AVAILABLE IN THE COMMUNITY

This is not meant to be an exhaustive list, but rather a glimpse at what structures are commonly available so that you can have a starting place from which to expand your knowledge base. Different states may propose different opportunities or use different labels to describe what structures are available, so check to see what is offered in your area. You may get some information from your state's department of vocational rehabilitation. Again, the individual's personal choice and interests should be the guiding force.

Competitive employment. These types of employment opportunities are usually good for people who can work at a job with some adjustments but who will not need support on a continual basis. People who have an employable skill will find it easier to find work. Net-

Transition into Work
Tips from Temple Grandin

Temple Grandin says that work based on her talents and interests is what makes her life worth living. Grandin says that she knows and understands the social manners inherent to neurotypical society, but will never have the social-emotional relatedness that comes naturally to most people. Therefore, Grandin believes, "I am what I do, not what I feel," and credits her success as an adult to having work based on her talents and interests. To find the right job match, sometimes it is necessary to use, as Grandin calls it, "the backdoor approach": getting your first job or work experience by asking around the people you and your family know. This is what most neurotypicals do, and for people on the spectrum it works as well. Grandin got her first job in her field after meeting the wife of the insurance carrier of a cattle-handling facility.

To get ideas about what possible jobs they could do, teenagers need access to trade magazines. All industries have them. Some are available at the local libraries. Parents can send in to school the copies of whatever subscriptions they have, for example, computer or construction industry magazines. This can give ideas to both the students and the educators.

In the book *Developing Talents: Careers for Individuals with Asperger Syndrome and High-Functioning Autism,* which Grandin cowrote with Kate Duffy, Grandin states that teaching children at a young age to be responsible for their belongings and carrying out tasks will help them in being more successful and therefore fulfilled in their lives. To make a successful transition to work, Grandin had these tips to offer:

- **Make gradual transitions** by starting to work for short periods while in high school. Finding volunteer or paid work a few hours a week based on an interest, such as working in a pet store if the teen wants to be a veterinarian, is a good start.
- **Seek out supportive employers** by finding employers who appreciate special talents and who need these talents to keep their

businesses open. Parents can help with this by networking and using their contacts.

- **Find mentors** that can help your teen learn important social and job skills. Mentors can be teachers, neighbors, college students, anyone who takes an interest in you and can motivate you in your area of interest.
- **Educate employers and employees** about autism spectrum disorders so they can offer support when necessary.
- **Consider freelance work** so that the environment can be organized and structured to the individual's needs.
- **Make a portfolio** in order to show the talents and skills the candidate can bring to the job.
- **Make your own web page** to showcase the capabilities on offer.
- **Develop skills that other people will value and need** and it will be easier to find work.
- **Keep your chosen career in your talent area** to ensure that you are successful in what you do.
- **Get help with financial records and other official record keeping** if this is something you find difficult.
- **Manage your temper, anxieties, and social skills** as this is critical to success in the workplace.

In her book *Thinking in Pictures*, Grandin gives some useful information about how she was able to transition from college to work. Grandin suggests developing a special interest or obsession into an employable skill. Even though social skills may be lacking, prospective employers or clients can be impressed with your talents, strengths, and abilities and then hire you. People respect talent, and the focus can be on selling skills instead of personality. Employers will have to understand the person's needs in order for a job or career to be successful, but having a special ability will convince someone that the person is worth employing. Employers should be reminded of the positive attributes that most people on the spectrum have such as honesty and diligence, as well as the challenges they face.

In *Developing Talents*, Grandin says that autism/Asperger brains tend to be specialized, and that there are three different specialized brains: visual thinkers, music/math brains, and verbal/nonvisual thinkers. She goes on to list the types of jobs and careers that use the talent of each type; some of them are mentioned here:

- Visual thinkers: architectural and engineering drafter; photographer; graphic artist; animal trainer, jewelry maker and other crafts; web designer; auto mechanic; computer troubleshooter; landscape designer.
- Music/math brains: computer programmer; engineer; musician/composer; scientific researcher; music teacher; chemist.
- Nonvisual thinkers with more verbal brains: journalist; translator; librarian; accountant; stock and bonds analyst; speech therapist; bookkeeper and record keeper; inventory control specialist.

working through family members, friends, and people from church can perhaps lead to employment. Jobs may be found through contacts made at school, mentors, and other people who admire the student's abilities and may know others who can use his talents. Local unemployment centers, the classifieds, and job posting websites are also places to look for openings.

Supported employment. This provides assistance in areas where people with ASDs need help: job finding, job coaching, skills training, employment advice and guidance. The goal is to place the person in a job in the community that fits in with their interests and abilities. These kinds of programs, regardless of the ability level of the person, provide each person with the training and support to maintain employment in the chosen career field.

Micro-enterprise or self-employment. Working as a freelancer or owning a micro-enterprise is possible, even for the less able. Generating income based on a person's skills, talents, or particular area of interest is a possibility. Some may need only mentors to refer work to them, others may need to contract out the part of their work that they cannot fulfill. Even if the person is on the less able end of the spectrum and needs much assistance, the assistant can be an employee of the micro-enterprise, thus creating a shift in the power structure and hopefully eventually lessen the dependence on the government or service providers. This is a great concept as it provides a way for the individual to do something he is interested in doing and not be constrained by what "the system" has or doesn't have available for him and gives him more control over his environment. For more information about self-employment see the following resources:

- Income Links: Doreen Rosimos and Darcy Wilson put on conferences on micro-enterprise to help people come up with ideas get started on their business (www.incomelinks.biz).

- "Self-Employment for People with Developmental Disabilities," by Patricia Okahashi in *Rehabilitative Review,* April 2001 (www.vrri.org/rhb0401.htm).

- "Influencing Self-Employment Success for People with Developmental Disabilities," by Patricia Okahashi in *Rehabilitative Review,* May 2001 (www.vrri.org/rhb0501.htm).

- "Marketing a Person on the Autistic Spectrum: Some Business School Lessons," by Lars Perner (www.larsperner.com).

- *Making Self-Employment Work for People with Disabilities,* by Gary Griffin and David Hammis

The World of College

Many of the more able people with ASDs are successful at college. Some of the interests or obsessions they have can be pursued in a course of study. The challenge may well be translating that knowledge or degree into stable employment, but that is a challenge all students face. Some feel so comfortable at college that they develop their interests into a career on campus. Both Stephen Shore and Lars Perner in articles on the web describe college as being "heaven" either for themselves or for others they know on the spectrum.

There are different types of colleges: vocational or technical colleges, community colleges, and universities or four-year colleges. Vocational or technical colleges usually teach a skill in preparation for a specific job or employment goal. Community colleges are only for two years, with students transferring to four-year colleges or universities to complete their education. There is also the possibility of online college courses over the Internet.

Some students prefer community or local colleges as they can continue to stay at home. Dormitory living can be difficult unless the student has a private room. Living with unknown roommates in a rental unit also can be tricky. Community colleges, however, can be a challenge if the student wishes to continue at a four-year college. The student will have to make sure to plan carefully what classes to take to make sure they apply. Also, if adjusting to different environments is a challenge or stressful, the student will be going through that step twice.

Here are some resources to help with transitioning to college:

• "Preparing to Be Nerdy Where Nerdy Can Be Cool: College Planning for the High Functioning Student with Autism," by Lars Perner (www.larsperner.com).

• The website for University Students with Autism and Asperger's Syndrome (www.users.dircon.co.uk/~cns) is a great resource including first-person accounts and links to other websites.

• *Aquamarine Blue 5: Personal Stories of College Students with Autism*, edited by Dawn Prince-Hughes.

• Liane Holliday Willey's book *Pretending to be Normal: Living with Asperger's Syndrome* has a helpful section in the back titled Survival Skills for AS College Students.

• *Beyond the Wall: Personal Experiences with Autism and Asperger Syndrome,* by Stephen Shore.

• *Succeeding in College with Asperger Syndrome*, by John Harpur, Maria Lawlor, and Michael Fitzgerald

• *Asperger Syndrome: Transition to College and Work,* (www.coultervideo.com).

• *Realizing the College Dream with Autism or Asperger Syndrome: A Parent's Guide to Student Success,* Ann Palmer

In the Coulter video *Asperger Syndrome: Transition to College and Work,* Drew Coulter, who has Asperger's Syndrome, describes the difference between attending high school and attending college as the difference between taking a commercial flight and flying your own plane. During high school, a student has the help of parents and the community he lives in, and the parents are piloting the plane. When the student is in college, he has to fly his own plane. Some of those differences are:

• **Under IDEIA 2004, everyone has a right to a high school education, but not a college education.** Although a college may not discriminate against any individual, there is no such thing as a "right" to attend college. The college may not ask the student if he or she has a disability; however, if a student needs and wants to have special accommodations, the special need must be disclosed.

• **In high school, the whole community recognizes the student.** The teachers are familiar with the student, perhaps even with the family if there was an older brother or sister who attended a few years earlier. They know the students from being in the neighborhood. However, at college, the professors and staff do not know the student's family and there are many more people. The college campus is usually a lot bigger than the high school's.

• **At college, the student's schedule is much different from high school.** Peter Gerhardt says that the changeover can be difficult, especially if the student is going away to school and living on campus. The student will have roommates and needs to have independent skills to be able to take care of himself. The student will need to be able to stick to a schedule. Gerhardt says in the past, a student might have scheduled only one hour for home-work, whereas in college he may have to schedule four to five hours for each class that he takes.

Drew Coulter also gives these tips for picking a college:

• **Identify what kind of program you're interested in attending.** Search out the colleges that have that type of program.

• **Decide whether it would be easier for you to attend a four-year program or a two-year program and then transfer.** Some students might find it helpful to attend community college, and then transfer to a four-year college. They then can still live at home and deal with only one change at a time. However, it may be difficult for some students to change to another campus two years later. They might find it easier to go directly to a four-year college.

• **Some students may benefit from shorter certificate programs to obtain a hands-on job at the end.** There are many certificate programs out there that teach technical skills and medical skills. Such programs are also a good way to meet people with similar interests.

• **Find out if the college has or can provide the type of accommodation that the student will need.** It is important that the student be able to articulate his needs once he's at college because at age eighteen, colleges are not allowed to disclose information to parents, only to the students, unless the parents have conservatorship or guardianship.

• **Find out which professors are most flexible.** It is important to remember that the student needs to learn to communicate with the professors. The professors may not be familiar with Asperger's Syndrome.

• **Take a reduced load the first quarter or semester.** Ann Binder, director of Special Needs Services at Delaware County Community College in Media, Pennsylvania, advises students with Asperger's

Syndrome to take a reduced load, because the schedule is so much different, as noted by Peter Gerhardt above. Students attended high school for six hours a day five days a week, while in college, much of the work is done outside the classroom. Students must be able to schedule their study time and organize their schedule and make sure they fit enough time in for their studies.

GETTING SUPPORT

Colleges offer services and supports for students with special requirements. However, not all colleges are familiar with ASDs and the student's particular needs. Here are some suggestions for making college a rewarding experience:

• Give information about the ASD and how it affects the student, the challenges he faces, and what strategies can be used to help him to those you think he may need to know. This is where the student's self-advocacy skills get put to good use. Disclosure is necessary for getting needed assistance.

• Find a sympathetic guidance counselor or mentor. This person can help in many ways, for example by helping the student find a group on campus that shares a special hobby or interest.

• Ask a guidance counselor or mentor which teachers would be more accepting of the student's difficulties and willing to make him comfortable with learning in their class.

• The same kinds of strategies that helped in high school will be of benefit at college. For the visual learner, written schedules, lists, and visual aids for studying such as graphs, charts, and videos are helpful. For the auditory learner, tape-recording lectures or having a note taker works well. Textbooks on tape can be another useful tool.

• Tests or exams can be modified to take into consideration any difficulties a student may have with test taking.

Living Arrangements Currently Available in the Community

For all of us, where we live and sleep—our home—is our sanctuary, where we need to feel comfortable; a place where we can rest, but also be inspired; a place where we can feel contentment. Living arrangements should be based on the individual's desires and comfort level. Many types of options are theoretically available, as are ways to fund them. Again, the guiding principle should be what the individual wants, what kind of living arrangements he would like to have. Even the most disabled person can live independently with supports, if that is what he desires.

Researching this now, while your teen is still in school, will help you realize the kinds of possibilities that exist out there, as well as what skills your teen may need to be learning in order to live the life he dreams of living. There is the very real fact that your teen may need to get on some waiting lists, and you will need to find out about financial help that may be available. Whatever option he is leaning toward, preparation and planning is necessary. The world is full of opportunities, but many times you have to create your own.

Here is an overview of some of the different types of living structures that exist in most communities, or that can be created. Keep in mind that this is just a starting point to get you thinking:

• **A room:** Some able individuals prefer to rent a room in a home owned by someone else, with kitchen privileges.

• **Room and board:** Some live in a room-and-board situation in another person's home, and no services other than a service coordinator who sees the person from time to time.

• **Independent living:** This is usually in an apartment rented or owned by the individual. Outside training and support is provided to help learn and become independent with money management, getting around town, learning to recognize health issues and how to make the necessary medical appointments, grocery shopping, and all the basics needed for independent living.

• **Supported living (SL):** SL is about living with extra support in the person's own place or in the family home. SL can mean living with another person who has a disability or a neurotypical roommate. The necessary level of care is provided by an outside person, and can range from not very much care to 24/7 if needed. SL is similar to assisted living for elders. Needed services and supports come to the household instead of the person going out for them. This is the most popular option, although it is still relatively new in some parts of the United States.

• **Supervised apartment living:** People who need some assistance and supervision may prefer living in a larger apartment complex open to other renters without disabilities. Typically, there is an agency staff person or service provider that lives in one of the apartments who responds to emergencies and assists the residents in small ways.

• **Supervised group home living:** These are typically homes for three to six persons and are run by agencies, although some may be family enterprises. These homes are staffed by trained personnel who assist the residents based on each individual's need. The residents usually have some type of daily activity outside the home during the day.

• **Adult foster care:** One or two individuals may live with a family that has been recruited to serve them. An agency oversees the recruitment, certifies the home, and provides supports to the family.

Websites that provide additional information:

TAC (www.tacinc.org) is a national nonprofit organization that works to achieve positive outcomes on behalf of people with disabilities, people who are homeless, and people with other special needs. Affordable housing is an area they address.

The Allen, Shea & Associates website (www.allenshea.com) has information and ideas on Essential Lifestyle Planning, which includes housing.

FOOD FOR THOUGHT

Acceptance

The biggest thing I have had to admit to myself is I am not, nor will I ever be, like other people. No matter how hard I try, I will always have Asperger's syndrome. But the miracle is I'm finally okay with that. Today I have friends. Today I share my life with others and they share their lives with me. All I have to do is be honest.

—Benjamin Levinson, in *Finding Ben:*
A Mother's Journey Through the Maze of Asperger's, by Barbara LaSalle

---

There are many ways we can help our adolescent live up to their potential. Finding the right strategies as well as nontraditional or traditional medical approaches to help them and keep them healthy is not always easy, but it is important. In the next chapter, treatments, therapies and strategies are discussed and analyzed based on what is known in regards to their usefulness with teenagers.

6

Therapies, Treatments, and Strategies to Help Adolescents on the Autism Spectrum

If eating different foods, taking enzymes, taking vitamins, or anything else helps this kind of stuff, then it is surely worth a try. It has made a massive difference to my life, in the lives of many others, and if it doesn't help, then no harm has been done.

—LUKE JACKSON, Freaks, Geeks & Asperger Syndrome: A User Guide to Adolescence

WHAT wouldn't a parent do to help his or her child? Basically, I had my son Jeremy try anything that had clinical research or strong anecdotal evidence to support it, was a match for his autistic symptoms, and was not dangerous. He has been a very patient and willing participant to much of the alphabet soup: ABA, DTT, TEACCH, FC, GFCF, OT, SI, RPM, MB12, traditional medications including depakote, and more. Most everything has helped, some more than others. We have added only one treatment on at a time, and I've taken data on the results or lack thereof.

Now that Jeremy is a teenager, it's necessary to get his buy in for anything we're doing. We've recently tried methyl-B$_{12}$ shots as well as vitamin and mineral supplements, and everyone is reporting positive changes in his attending behaviors, initiation, follow-through, and communication. Now, at the movies, instead of averting his eyes from the screen and just listening, he has been looking directly at the screen for most of the movie. As well, he has spelled out, "Something is doing good to my eyes, I don't know what it is . . . I can hear and see at the same time." I'll keep taking data and videotaping to make sure it's really making a difference. Jeremy must feel it's helping. Why else would he, at his age, gladly accept to swallow all these supplements twice daily and submit to a shot every few days?

Finding Treatments That Can Help Your Adolescent

Whether your child is just beginning to hit puberty or is firmly entrenched in the teenage years, your goal for him as a parent is different than when he was a toddler. Back then, perhaps, you were intent on attempting to cure or recover your child. Or perhaps it is now as a preteen that your child has recently been diagnosed with Asperger's. Whatever road you have been on, your goal as a parent now is to support your child, alleviate any sensory stresses or physical aliments he may be having, and help him learn the skills he needs to be as independent, functional, and social as possible. This includes figuring out what your teen's behaviors are telling you about what his needs are.

This chapter will not go over every single treatment, therapy, and intervention available or purporting to be beneficial to individuals with autism. For a more complete overview of what is available for all ages on the spectrum, see chapter 5 in my previous book, *Autism Spectrum Disorders: The Complete Guide to Understanding Autism, Asperger's Syndrome, Pervasive Developmental Disorder, and Other ASDs.*

Unfortunately, because there is no treatment or strategy that works for every person on the spectrum, it is still up to parents, in consultation with credentialed experts, to decide what to try. In the past, there was not much out there to choose from; now there are so many options that it can be confusing and even overwhelming. Many of these options may already be familiar to the well-educated parent. However, now as your child is changing and growing, perhaps his needs are different and you may want to review what is helpful to the older child and teen. If your tween or teen was diagnosed as a child, then by now you have a pretty good idea of how to analyze treatments and therapies and decide what may work with your teen. You also know about your teen's learning style and what types of interventions or strategies will help him. However, many children with Asperger's may not get diagnosed until they are tweens or teens for various reasons as discussed in chapter 1. For those who are new to this kind of information gathering and decision making, or what to remember and what to focus on when deciding what to try, I am including the following overview.

WHERE TO START

The first thing to do is to look at the tween or teen on the spectrum. Here are some things to consider:

The teen's behaviors and symptoms: It is important to look at his behaviors and any symptoms he may have and try to understand what they indicate. Is the teen covering his ears frequently when there is a lot of activity in the room or complaining that it's too loud? Does he often have diarrhea or an upset stomach? Does he have meltdowns when there is a change in his routine? Does he appear clumsy and uncoordinated and find it difficult to play sports? Does he speak obsessively on just one topic? Does he have trouble understanding body language and cues? Is he showing aggression?

The teen's functioning level or ability: The autism spectrum covers a wide range of functioning in terms of behavioral characteristics, communication and social awareness, and sensory integration issues. If a formal diagnosis has been made, any assessments made at that time may give you more information about the child. There are many different assessments that are used depending on the age and ability of the person: speech and language, occupational therapy, functional be-havior analysis, neuropsychiatric tests, developmental, intelligence, and academic tests. A parent of a tween or teen with an ASD has a good knowledge base of what their child is able or unable to do just from living with him and observing his capabilities and deficits.

Whether he is a visual or an auditory learner: Often parents and educa-tors assume that all people on the spectrum are visual learners and therefore that visual strategies will work with everyone. This is not the case. Some people are auditory learners. It is helpful to establish which sensory-processing modality works best for your teen.

What his strengths and weaknesses are: Every person has strengths, and if you can identify them, you can build on them to fortify the weak-nesses. When he is a teenager, you need to reinforce his strengths, be-cause that is what is going to get him through transition and into the real world, and he will be able to base his future work experience and career on this success.

What treatments he has already had: Looking at what has been helpful and what has not in earlier years can be useful at times in analyzing whether or not a particular treatment is worth pursuing now that your child is a teenager.

What is your goal; what challenge are you attempting to address with a treatment you are thinking of trying: If you are concerned about certain health issues, you will perhaps be considering particular biomedical treatments. If you are concerned about certain organization chal-lenges or behavioral issues, you may be looking at behavioral and cognitive therapies, but also certain biomedical interventions or sen-sory integration or even traditional medications.

What hopes and dreams your teen has, and what your goals are for him: As a teenager, your child needs to start thinking about his hopes for the future and how they can be realized. As a parent, you need to help him translate that into reality. If you have not broached these topics with your child before, you need to start doing so now in preparation for transition. Even the less able have opinions about what they want out of life. Just because someone cannot talk does not mean he isn't thinking; however, you need to start the ball rolling. Is your teen college material? Does he want to start his own micro-enterprise? Will he live in a group home or independently? Once you have an idea of where your teen is headed, you will have an idea of what he needs to learn to reach his dreams.

WHAT TO CONSIDER WHEN LOOKING AT TREATMENT OPTIONS

As Donna Williams explains in her book *Autism: An Inside-Out Approach,* all these therapies, treatments, and interventions truly need to be looked at with a department-store mentality, rather than a main-street approach. Autism spectrum disorders are all invasive, and rarely does one therapy or strategy alone provide all the help a person needs. Therapies or treatments are not exclusive of others, and a visit to different "departments" or types of therapies is often needed.

After looking at the needs of the person on the spectrum, there are other factors to consider before deciding on what treatments and therapies to pursue at this particular time. Some of these are:

- **The potential risk to the teen.** Does the therapy have side effects? Is it risky to mental or physical health? Do the possible risks outweigh the possible gains? If a therapy has potentially serious side effects, you want to ensure that you are seeing strong positive results, or else it is not worth the risk.

- **The family.** ASDs are a family matter, as they affect everyone in the household either directly or indirectly. But so does the treatment. The parents have to think about how the treatment or therapy fits into the family. What kind of involvement is expected from others? How will this treatment affect any siblings? Is the family going to be able to follow through with whatever the professional deems necessary (such as giving supplements on a regular basis, adhering to a diet, generalizing skills learned, having a daily schedule posted)? Can the family commit to the prescribed treatment or therapy for whatever time it takes or is recommended? Are all responsible adults in the household in agreement about the particular treatment and supportive of seeing it through? If the treatment fails, how will it affect the family?

• **The financial cost of the therapy.** Money does not grow on trees, and as our children get older, so do we. Your earning potential needs to be taken into account. Do you have to sell your home to provide this therapy or intervention? Is insurance going to cover it? Are you asking the school district to fund the treatment or therapy, or to train staff in a particular strategy? If yes, do you have the tenacity to advocate effectively to obtain the appropriate type of service?

• **Can the strategy or treatment be integrated into whatever educational program the teen already has, and if so, how?** For example, in the case of a special diet, can it be carried over to all of the teen's environments and will the teen learn to take responsibility for this? Will including this treatment or strategy be at the expense of other equally important aspects of the teen's program?

• **What evidence exists to validate this method of treatment, and in particular for the tween or teen age group?** Is the therapy being touted as a miracle cure for everyone and for every age? Is there scientific validation of this treatment? What does the anecdotal evidence have to say?

• **Is this treatment or therapy autism specific, and if not, has it proved effective with teens on the spectrum?** Some treatments may not be specifically created with ASDs in mind, but can nonetheless be very beneficial. However, it is important to verify how others on the autism spectrum have done with this treatment, and in particular how adolescents have fared.

FOOD FOR THOUGHT

Puberty and Anxiety

This is what we have in common with animals. Our fear system is "turned on" in a way a normal person's is not. It's fear gone wild. In my own case, overwhelming anxiety hit at puberty. From age eleven to age thirty-three, when I discovered antidepressant medication, I felt exactly the way you feel when you're about to defend your dissertation, only I felt that way all day long, every single day. I was in a constant, daily state of emergency. It was horrible. If I hadn't gone on medication I couldn't have had a life at all. I certainly wouldn't have been able to have a career.

—Temple Grandin and Catherine Johnson, *Animals in Translation:*
Using the Mysteries of Autism to Decode Animal Behavior

• **How is the effectiveness of the therapy or teaching strategy going to be measured?** With any treatment, therapy, or strategy, there should be record keeping in order to track effectiveness. Parents need to ask who is responsible for taking data, how data is taken, how often it is recorded, and how often is it reviewed.

• **What is the track record of the treatment provider of the therapy or treatment?** How long have the practitioners been doing this therapy and with what age group? What level of ability has this person worked with?

• **Does the professional prescribing the treatment or supervising the course of treatment have all pertinent information about the teen being treated?** Make sure the person knows as much about your teen as possible. It's a good idea to write down anything you think the provider should know, especially if he is dealing with someone who is unable to communicate independently and dependably about himself. Information that is helpful includes other treatments that may have been tried, the person's likes or dislikes, and particular behaviors the practitioner should know about. Any allergies to food or medication, phobias, chances of seizures, special diets, etc., are all valuable information.

• **Do you have your teenager's buy in?** The older your child or teenager, the more you need his consent. For some treatments and strategies perhaps he has nothing to say about it because there is no choice and it is absolutely necessary. However, as they get older, they ethically do have more to say about certain treatments. They are bigger, too, and not wanting to participate can mean it won't happen. As a parent, you will have to "convince" your teenager about trying treatments or strategies. Hopefully, he will see the positive results and be a willing participant.

Treatments, Therapies, and Strategies

Discussed below are most of the therapies, interventions, and treatments that may be used to help an adolescent on the spectrum with difficulties and challenges they face as described in chapter 1. Strategies specific to the school or home environments are discussed more in depth in those chapters, although some may be touched upon here. Strategies to help with puberty and hygiene are discussed in chapter 3.

Again, as autism is a spectrum with different causes, the treatments useful for each individual will be different. There is not much research out there about the effectiveness of any treatments for adolescents; practically all clinical research is based on the younger population. Some anecdotal information exists about the older population.

Inclusion in this chapter does not mean the intervention is endorsed by the author; neither does noninclusion signify a treatment may not be effective in your child's particular case. Consider this information as a starting point to begin your own search for knowledge. The only fact that is certain when it comes to autism spectrum disorders is that some of these treatments work for some people, and not all of the treatments work for everyone. Parents are urged to research their options carefully.

WHERE TO GET MORE INFORMATION

New discoveries are being made all the time, and it is important to keep current. Below are some resources that can help you find out more about treatment options, the latest research, and the experience or opinion of other parents and professionals. These resources are not specific to tweens or teens; however, as new treatments or helpful strategies are discovered, they will show up on these websites. It is important, also, to be able to go directly to the source when it comes to any research studies and to not rely solely on the media. Any media will reflect the opinion of the person interpreting the research. Once you hear about a study through the media, you can go to the original source and read the report yourself, along with the actual conclusions as written by the researcher.

• The National Library of Medicine PubMed: To locate any research articles concerning autism, visit the National Library of Medicine PubMed at www.ncbi.nih.gov/entrez/query.fcgi. Use the search engine to find abstracts of articles you are interested in reading. There are tutorials on the site with instructions for more advanced search techniques. Some abstracts will link you to the full article on the website of the journal where it is published. Some journals will provide full text for free while others require a subscription or fee.

• The Lenny Schafer Report is the largest daily (almost) newspaper on ASDs; it is edited by Lenny Schafer and available free through the Internet. To subscribe, go to www.SARnet.org; for archives, groups.yahoo.com/group/AuTeach/messages.

• Autism Research Institute International Newsletter: Dr. Bernard Rimland publishes a quarterly newsletter with summaries of current research. These are archived at and can be read at www.autism

website.com/ari/arri/arriindex.htm. The ARI website has information on some research studies and new biomedical treatments (www .autismresearchinstitute.com).

• The Autism Society of America (ASA) website www.autism-society.org often has information about the most important ASD issues being discussed by the media.

• Autism One Radio at www.autismone.org/radio/ is a radio station over the Internet that you can hear anywhere in the world over your computer. There are many different hosts and shows and a wide range of topics all having to do with autism, many dealing with treatment as well as practical issues. Shows are archived so if you miss them live, you can tune in at your convenience.

• Talk About Curing Autism (TACA, www.tacanow.org) is a great website to find out about treatments and therapies and other information valuable to families. There is helpful information about medical and health insurance, which you may wish to consult in trying to get services reimbursed. TACA also has a Yahoo! discussion group where you can discuss biomedical and other therapies with other parents.

FOOD FOR THOUGHT

Medications and Autism

by Temple Grandin, Ph.D.

One of the keys to my success was finding the right medication. When puberty hit I felt like I was in a constant state of stage fright and panic attacks. I was one of the types where anxiety and panic worsened as I became older. Socializing with other people and other activities were difficult when my heart was pounding and I had a lump so big in my throat that swallowing food was sometimes difficult. The autism/Asperger spectrum is very variable. Some people will really need conventional medications and others remain calm and c̲

In my early 30s I took the old-fashioned antidepressant̲

My panic attacks were due to faulty biology and they subsid̲e

most went away within a week. I have been on this medicatio̲

twenty-five years. Since I am stable I do not dare stop taking it.

Low-Dose Principle

Today Prozac (fluoxetine) or Zoloft (Sertraline) are probably better choices. Top autism specialists, Dr. Eric Hollander of Mt. Sinai Hospital in New York and Dr. Ed Cook in Chicago, both use Prozac in teenagers and adults who have either high-functioning autism or Aspergers. I know several people on the spectrum for whom Prozac reduced their anxiety attacks, and really helped them.

Individuals on the spectrum often need much lower doses of anti-depressants than normal people. Some need only ½ to ⅓ of the normal starter dose. Parents often report that their child did well on a low dose and became agitated on a higher dose. Insomnia and feeling like one has drunk fifty cups of coffee is the first sign of too high a dose of an antidepressant. If this occurs the dose must be *lowered*.

There is controversy about the safety of antidepressants in children. Most hazards are caused by too high a dose and they will occur within the first few weeks. Paxil (paroxetine) has been associated with a higher risk of suicide. Prozac and Zoloft are the only SSRI antidepressants that have FDA approval in children. If an individual is doing well on Paxil or some other drug, which would usually not be the best first choice, they should continue to take it. Switching medications may cause problems.

Another class of medications that are often used are the atypical anti-psychotics. The five drugs in their group are Risperdal (Risperidone), Zyprexa (olanzapine), Geodon (ziprasidone), Seroquel (quetiapine), and Abilify (aripiprazole). These medications may have severe, long-term side effects such as high weight gain and tardive dyskinesia (shaking palsey). However they are the most effective medications for severe rage attacks. They should also be given at *very low* doses. Other extremely useful medications are beta-blockers such as Propranolol and Valproic Acid. Propranolol is an old blood pressure medication that works well for anxiety and panic attacks. Valproic Acid is an anticonvulsant (epilepsy) drug. It works well for rages that occur totally at random. These rages are caused by tiny, difficult-to-detect seizures. The seizures may not show up on the EEG if the individual is sedated for the test. Dr. Joe Huggins, an autism specialist in Canada, works with the most difficult, non-verbal teenagers and adults who have been kicked out of their school or group home due to rage. In this population he uses the three drugs, Risperdal, Valproic Acid, or Propranol. For each person he usually uses one or two of these medications. He avoids the SSRI drugs such as Prozac in low-functioning individuals. Prozac usually works best in cases of high-functioning autism and Aspergers.

Treatment of Different Rage Types

1. **Random Rage:** Depakote (divaloproes sodium) or Depakene (Valproic Acid). Random rage is not related to a particular person, place, or situation. Must do blood tests to monitor for liver damage. Random rage is caused by small seizures.
2. **Directed Rage:** This type of rage is directed at a particular person, place, or situation. Low doses of atypical medications such as Risperdal.
3. **Undirected Hot and Sweaty Rages:** The individual may breathe heavily and be hot and sweaty. When he is in this state he may lash out at any nearby person or object. Use Propranol.

If rage or anger attacks occur in a non-verbal individual who has previously been cooperative, he/she *must* be examined for a hidden painful medical problem that he/she cannot tell you about. One boy died because he had an undiagnosed burst appendix. Some of the most common undetected medical conditions are dental problems, constipation, heartburn (acid reflux), and ear infections.

Alternative versus Conventional Medication

I am sick and tired of the debate between alternative bio medical treatments and conventional medications. Sometimes a combination of the two is most effective. Donna Williams, a well-known person with autism, takes a tiny, ¼ milligram of Risperdal per day and eats the casein (dairy)-free and gluten (wheat)-free diet. The two together work better than either treatment alone. This combined treatment has allowed her to tolerate large convention centers. The diet alone helped but not enough to enable her to go to large, noisy meetings.

In very young children it is probably better to try some of the alternative approaches first. The casein- and gluten-free diets should be tried in all children as soon as autism symptoms are detected. Do not use soy products, and sugar should be reduced. The diet really works well in a subgroup of children. If the diet is going to work, *obvious* improvement should be seen in 4 weeks. Other supplements that work in some individuals are B$_6$ and magnesium and Omega 3. Chelation is a common alternative treatment. This is one alternative treatment that can be hazardous. Chelation removes toxins such as lead and mercury, but it also removes minerals that are essential for life. A child died after undergoing an extreme chelation procedure in 2005. Most doctors do not recommend chelation as a routine treatment because it requires extremely careful monitoring to make it safe.

Principles in Using Medications and Biomedical Alternative Treatments

1. Try one thing at a time so that you can see if it works. Different agents usually only need a few weeks separation to determine effectiveness. Do not start a medication, diet, or supplement at the same time a new school or ABA program started.
2. A medication should have an *obvious* beneficial effect to make it worth the risk. It should be "*wow*—this works." A diet should have an obvious benefit, or else it is not worth the hassle.
3. Be careful when switching brands of medications or supplements.
4. New is not always better. If an individual is doing well on a reasonable dose of something old it is usually best to stay with it.
5. If a person has been on a drug for many years it must never be removed suddenly. Taper the dosage over several months.
6. Parents must work with a good doctor to tailor treatments that will work for their child.

References

Donavon, S.J., Steward J.W., and Nunes EW. 2000. Divalproex treatment of growth with explosive temper and mood liability. A double-blind placebo controlled crossover design. *American Journal of Psychiatry.*
157: 818–820

Lindsay R.L. and Aman MG. 2003. Pharmacological therapies and treatment of autism. *Pediatric Annals.*
32: 671–676

McCracken J.T., McGough J., Shah B. Cronin P., and Hong D. 2002. Risperdone in children with autism and serious behavior problems, *New England Journal of Medicine*.
347: 314–321

Ratey J.J. et al. 1987. Autism, The treatment of aggressive behaviors. *Journal of Clinical Psychopharmacology*.
7: 35–41
Describes the use of propranolol.

Richardson A.J. and Montgomery P. 2005. The Oxford-Durham study- A randomized controlled trial of dietary supplementation with fatty acids in children with developmental coordination disorders. *Pediatrics*.
115: 1360–1366

Sheehan D.V., Beh M.B., Ballenger J., and Jacobsen G. 1980. Treatment of endogenous anxiety with phobic, hysterical and hypochondriacol symptoms. *Archives of General Psychiatry*.
37: 51–59
(Note from Temple: This paper saved my life. This is where I discovered the use of antidepressant drugs.)

Trivedi H.K., Wang B., and Gonzales-Heydrich J. 2005. Anti-epileptic drugs (AEDs) in the treatment of aggression in children and adolescents. *Child and Adolescent Pharmacology News* Vol 10 No 1 p. 8–10.

Wild J. 2005. Adult Suicides linked to popular antidepressant, *Nature* 436: 1073 (Note from Temple: Paxil linked to increased suicides. Prozac was not linked to this hazard).

Temple Grandin, Ph.D., is the author of *Thinking in Pictures, Developing Talents,* and *Animals in Translation.* Temple is also an associate professor of animal science at Colorado State University, as well as the founder and president of Grandin Livestock Handling Systems, Inc.

For Health Concerns

Effective teaching methods are extremely important, but so is the individual's physical and neurological health. As there is a definite connection between the body and the brain, a healthy body is a priority. If the teen is healthy and calm, he will be more ready for learning whether his educational needs are academic or life skill in nature.

In the last decade, dietary and biomedical interventions have been developed and have shown promise with people on the spectrum. Some young children have even been recovered from autism using biomedical interventions in conjunction with an intensive applied behavioral analysis (ABA) program as well as other therapies. Some of these treatments have no side effects, while others do. Some are expensive, while others are cheap. Some have empirical research to back them up, while others have only anecdotal reports. Some of these interventions are noninvasive and worth trying; others should be done only under the care of a knowledgeable health professional.

More and more health practitioners are learning about these interventions and how to treat patients with ASDs from a dietary and biomedical perspective. In the last few years an increasing amount of credence has been given to the positive effects of these interventions on many individuals with ASDs. Bear in mind that most research and anecdotal evidence available on these interventions and diets is based on younger children. However, some authors on the spectrum, including Luke Jackson and Donna Williams, have written about the positive effects these interventions have on their ability to cope with daily living.

These types of interventions are effective in helping people whose metabolic systems may not be functioning properly. It may be that their systems are not processing essential nutrients properly, possibly because of a food allergy or intolerance, or a "leaky gut" (where the wall of the intestine does not do its job of keeping its contents separate from the bloodstream), or high levels of mercury or other toxic metals. It is possible to check for food allergies by adding or removing the suspected culprit from the person's diet and taking data, before and after, on their behavior. Essential nutrients can be tested in the same way. However, there are specific tests and analyses that can be done that are more indicative of what is going on in the metabolic system. A medical professional can administer these tests.

Before starting any of these interventions, data should be taken over at least a two-week period on all of the person's negative (tantrums, hyperactivity, self-stimulatory behaviors, obsessive-compulsive) and positive (communication, staying on task, eye contact) behaviors. This will give a baseline of the behaviors before treatment. During and after treatment, the same types of notes should be taken. This will enable you to judge whether or not the treatment is having an effect.

Some good resources on biomedical interventions in general are:

• "Parents Ratings of Behavioral Effects of Drugs and Nutrients" at www.autismresearchinstitute.com. Since 1967 the Autism Research Institute has been collecting information on the usefulness of the interventions parents have tried on their children.

• For those wishing to read studies regarding dietary and biological interventions for ASDs, Karyn Seroussi of the Autism Network for Dietary Intervention (ANDI) has compiled most of them on the website www.autismndi.com/studies.htm. Research results are also available from the Autism Research Institute (ARI).

• There is a Yahoo! discussion group at health.groups.yahoo.com/group/autisminterventionsocal/ about biomedical interventions based in Southern California. This is a great place to exchange information with other parents and to ask advice of another parent.

• *Autism: Effective Biomedical Treatments—Have We Done Everything to Help This Child? Individuality in an Epidemic,* by Jon Pangborn, Ph.D., and Sidney MacDonald Baker, M.D. This April 2005 version of the DAN! Clinical Options Manual replaces the previous editions on the biomedical approach to the diagnosis and treatment of autism, PDD, and related disorders.

• *Children with Starving Brains: A Medical Treatment Guide for Autism Spectrum Disorder,* by Jaquelyn McCandless, M.D., a psychiatrist and neurologist who became interested in treating autism with biomedical interventions after her grandchild was diagnosed.

• *Treating Autism: Parent Stories of Hope and Success*, edited by Stephen M. Edelson, Ph.D., and Bernard Rimland, Ph.D. consists of thirty-four chapters by parents, eight of whom are physicians, describing their success in treating their own children.

FOOD FOR THOUGHT

Puberty, Aggression, and Seizures

by Bernard Rimland, Ph.D.

Puberty in autistic children is often accompanied by the onset of seizures or an increase in seizures and/or aggressive behavior. These problems have been addressed in many previous issues of the *Autism Research Review International*. The back issues of the *ARRI*, volumes 1 through 18, 1987 through 2004, may now be accessed, along with an extensive index, free of charge at www.ARInewsletter.com or may be purchased from ARI (see subscription form). Readers are urged to refer to our previously published articles on puberty, seizures, and aggression, as well as on self-injurious behavior (SIB) for much more comprehensive discussions than can be provided here.

Our immediate purpose in this article is to provide an overview of the issues, as well as to discuss several previously undiscussed, or underdiscussed, ideas that merit your attention.

A great many cases of aggression or self-injurious behavior have been found to be the child's response to physical pain. In one case a child's decades-long severe SIB was found to be caused by a chronic painful mastoid infection. In recent years, late-onset autism, which comprises the autism epidemic, has often been characterized by severe abdominal pain, frequently accompanied by constipation, diarrhea, or both. Gastroenterologists Andrew Wakefield, Tim Buie, Arthur Krigsman, and other speakers at our Defeat Autism Now! (DAN!) Conferences have addressed these issues in considerable detail.

A pediatric gastroenterologist may perform a colonoscopy to determine if a patient needs treatment. A highly effective treatment protocol has been developed by Tim Buie and colleagues at the Massachusetts General Hospital and Harvard Medical School. A consortium of other medical schools in various parts of the United States, known as the Autism Treatment Network, has been formed to implement this treatment approach for the GI issues of autism.

Migraine headaches and the pain of hypersensitive hearing have also been found to cause aggression or self-injurious behavior in many individuals. Food allergies are a frequent cause of migraines and seizures. Keeping a food diary may be helpful in identifying foods that cause migraines and seizures. Avoiding common allergenic foods has been found to be helpful.

Joseph Egger et al., in a 1989 study, found that forty of forty-five patients with migraines and epilepsy reported improvement on what Egger referred to as an "oligoantigenic" (few foods) diet. The foods found to be most troublesome (most important to eliminate from the patient's diet) were cow's milk and cheese, citrus fruits, wheat, artificial food colorings and flavorings, eggs, tomatoes, pork, and chocolate.

Hypersensitive hearing can be painful and often is exacerbated in puberty. Covering the ears when certain sounds are heard is an obvious clue. Since hypersensitive hearing is a common sign of magnesium deficiency, simply supplementing the diet with magnesium should be the first priority. Irritability may also be a sign of magnesium deficiency. I suggest giving 4 mg of magnesium per pound of body weight (for example, 400 mg of magnesium for a 100-pound person) per day. Magnesium citrate and magnesium glycinate are the two best absorbed forms of magnesium. In purchasing magnesium supplements, be sure you read the label correctly. Look for the number of milligrams of *elemental* magnesium in the tablet or capsule. The magnesium should be given with a B vitamin supplement to help the body absorb the magnesium properly.

If magnesium supplements do not correct the hypersensitive hearing in a few days, ear plugs, purchased at drugstores or hardware stores, may be helpful. Berard-type auditory integration training (AIT) is often helpful for hypersensitive hearing and many other problems common in autistic children and adolescents. (I do not recommend the Tomatis type of auditory training. The Tomatis approach does not have the extensive research validation that provides support for the Berard method. For a review on the research on Berard auditory integration training go to www.SAIT.org.)

The increase in seizures that accompanies puberty is well known, but not at all understood. Puberty has been found to increase the need for vitamin B_6 in both boys and girls. In my opinion the top priority in responding to aggression, self-injurious behavior, and seizures in adolescence should be to increase the dosage of B$_6$ and magnesium in those already on B$_6$ and magnesium, and to initiate B$_6$ and magnesium treatment in those not already on it. The same is true for dimethylglycine (DMG), another very safe and effective nutritional supplement. In a number of cases, patients with multiple severe seizures while on four or five anticonvulsant drugs have experienced complete relief from seizures upon being given B$_6$ and magnesium and/or DMG.

In his book *Nerves in Collision,* Walter Alvarez, M.D., "the Sherlock Holmes of medicine," reports that "nonconvulsive epilepsy" (seen only on an EEG) may cause fits of sudden explosive aggression. He observed that remorse was common in such cases, while rare in violently aggressive persons with normal EEGs. Small maintenance doses of the anticonvulsant drug Dilantin were found to be helpful in such cases.

Although there are many newer anticonvulsant drugs (see Parent Ratings of the Effectiveness of Biomedical Interventions in Autism, at www.AutismResearchInstitute.com), Dilantin may nevertheless be especially useful in autism. In our first study on B$_6$ in autism, the six children who responded best to vitamin B$_6$ had, as it turned out, also been taking Dilantin.

High-dose vitamin B$_6$ and magnesium, which has been reported as helpful in autism in twenty-one of twenty-two studies to date, is even more likely to be helpful in adolescents and adults than in children. B$_6$ and magnesium are immeasurably safer than any of the drugs used to treat autism, including the anticonvulsant drugs. See "Vitamin B$_6$ in Autism: The Safety Issue" (*ARRI* 10/3/3). See also "What Is the Right 'Dosage' for B$_6$, DMG, and Other Nutrients Useful in Autism?" (*ARRI* 11/4/3). To summarize our findings on the dosage of B$_6$ and of DMG: every individual is unique, and the "right dose" varies enormously from person to person. Since these nutrients are very safe, trial and error is a valid approach. On average, 8 mg of vitamin B$_6$ per pound of body weight per day seems to work well for many, but some individuals need much more, and some need much less. Read the article! DMG is classified by the FDA as a food. No toxicity has ever been reported. Read the article!

A 2004 study at Emory University reported that patients with uncontrolled epilepsy had low blood levels of DHA, an essential fatty acid. Studies of autistic children also frequently find essential fatty acid (EFA) deficiencies. The moral is clear: if the kids won't eat salmon, give them EFA supplements!

If other approaches fail, consider medical marijuana, which has proven to be a lifesaver, literally, for many desperate families. See *ARRI* 12/2/7, 16/2/7, 16/3/7, and 17/1/2–4 for discussions. As well, see the book *Jeffrey's Journey*, by Debbie and LaRayne Jeffries.

In this brief overview I could only touch on various topics that have been covered in depth in previous issues of the *ARRI*, which are now readily available.

Bernard Rimland, Ph.D., is the founder of the Autism Research Institute and editor of the Autism Research Review International. *This article appeared in the vol. 19, no. 1, 2005 edition of the* Review.

GLUTEN-FREE/CASEIN-FREE (GFCF) DIET

This has been developed for individuals who have allergies or a toxic response to gluten (found in wheat, oats, rye, and barley among others) and casein (found in dairy products). Some indications of allergy or a toxic response to gluten and casein are diarrhea, constipation, hyperactivity, red face or ears, breaking wind frequently, pale skin. (However, it is important to note that these symptoms can be an indication of other problems.) Basically, peptides that are derived from an incomplete breakdown of certain types of food are affecting neurotransmission within the central nervous system. Research studies as well as hundreds of anecdotal reports have shown dietary intervention as a useful treatment for alleviating some of the symptoms of autism in children. It is less clear what the effect is on teenagers, although there have been some written reports by both teenagers and adults that they benefit from being on the diet.

This type of treatment, though constraining in terms of diet, is not harmful and it may be worth removing your child from gluten and casein to see if it has an effect on his behavior. However, there are urine and blood tests that can give information as to the level of peptides your child has, which would be a helpful indicator of before and after trials to see if the diet is helping.

GFCF diet website: www.gfcfdiet.com

Coeliac disease and gluten-free diet online resource center: www.celiac.com

Autism Network for Dietary Intervention (ANDI): www.autismndi.com

There are many interesting books on gluten- and casein-free diets, as well as recipe books. The above websites give details of many of them. In addition, the following are worth looking at:

A User Guide to the GF/CF Diet for Autism, Asperger Syndrome and AD/HD, by Luke Jackson. A book by a teenager with an ASD who is on this diet.

Unraveling the Mystery of Autism and Pervasive Developmental Disorder, by Karen Seroussi. *Special Diets for Special Kids,* by Lisa Lewis.

THE SPECIFIC CARBOHYDRATE DIET

Some autistic children who have not responded to the GFCF diet have benefited from this diet, which forbids grains of any kind but allows some dairy products. Strict adherence to the diet is necessary to see improvements. If the diet is beneficial, some improvements should be seen within the first one-month trial period.

For more information, visit www.breakingtheviciouscycle.com. Also see *Breaking the Vicious Cycle: Intestinal Health Through Diet,* by Elaine Gottschall, B.A., M.Sc. The sourcebook for the Specific Carbohydrate Diet (SCD).

ANTI-YEAST (FUNGAL) DIET

This is helpful for those individuals who have an overgrowth of yeast (*Candida albicans*) in their system. Children who have autism and have had frequent ear infections treated by antibiotics may be likely to have an overabundance of yeast in their gut. While the antibiotics may reduce the bacterial flora naturally present in the gut, the candida increases, as it is not affected by the antibiotics. Physical symptoms of yeast overgrowth may include gastrointestinal distress, headaches, skin rashes; behavioral symptoms may include irritability, confusion, and hyperactivity. As these may be characteristics of other difficulties, testing for yeast overgrowth is advisable.

Anecdotal reports show that this diet has been effective in more than 50 percent of cases. There are some antifungals such as luconazole that may be useful for more persistent yeast overgrowth.

For more information, see *Biological Treatments for Autism and PDD,* by William Shaw.

Feast Without Yeast, by Bruce Semon and Lori Ornblum.

THE FEINGOLD DIET

This diet was developed by Dr. Ben Feingold to treat hyperactivity in children. In his book *Why Your Child Is Hyperactive* he recommends removing artificial colorings and flavorings, salicylates, and some preservatives from children's diets. (Salicylates are a group of chemicals related to aspirin and found in certain fruits and vegetables.) His hypothesis is that more and more children are being seen and treated for hyperactivity due to the increase in artificial ingredients being added to our food and the increase in the consumption of processed foods.

For more information, see the Feingold Association of the United States at www.feingold.org, and *Why Can't My Child Behave? Why Can't She Cope? Why Can't He Learn?* by Jane Hersey.

MERCURY DETOXIFICATION TREATMENT (CHELATION)

There has been growing concern over the last few years about a possible connection between mercury and ASDs. Mercury is present in dental amalgam, certain types of seafood, and in thimerosal, a preservative found in some vaccines. It is highly toxic and some individuals are extremely sensitive to it. If the mercury exposure has been fairly recent, urine, hair, and blood analysis may show some trace. However, provoked excretion of mercury and heavy metals is necessary to estimate the amount in the body. Defeat Autism Now! and the Autism Research Institute brought together the expertise of twenty-four experienced physicians and researchers to come up with a mercury detoxification protocol, published in June 2001. It is suggested that before starting the mercury detoxification treatment, patients must correct as much as possible any nutritional disturbances, or "leaky gut" problems. This is because many of the drugs and supplements used for mercury detoxification can increase the growth of bacteria and fungi.

For more information, see "Mercury Detoxification Consensus Group Position Paper" on the ARI website at www.autismresearchinstitute.com.

VITAMIN B$_6$ AND MAGNESIUM

This is one of the treatments you can try without worrying about possible negative effects. Since 1965, twenty studies on these supplements have been published. These studies have shown benefits to taking vitamin B$_6$ (often combined with magnesium) and none have shown harm. Some of the benefits reported have been improved eye contact, improved language, reduced self-stimulatory behavior, reduced aggression, and reduced self-injurious behavior.

See the Autism Research Institute at www.autismresearchinstitute.com for more information.

METHYL-B$_{12}$ SHOTS

Methyl-B$_{12}$ is the most powerful member of the B$_{12}$ family. According to Dr. James Neubrander (the first person to describe the effects of methyl-B$_{12}$ for children with autism), there is no risk of toxicity. Side

FOOD FOR THOUGHT

Methyl-B$_{12}$

by James A. Neubrander, M.D.

Methyl-B$_{12}$ is the most powerful member of the B$_{12}$ family because of the numerous ways it affects the brain and the body. Its power lies in its ability to donate one-carbon units known as *methyl* groups to key components that are necessary for synchronous and normal brain activity. Examples include *methylation* of neurotransmitters, RNA and DNA, creatine, myelin, phospholipids, and proteins. Additionally *methyl*-B$_{12}$ has been found to form active glutathione, a requirement to detoxify the body and properly handle oxidative stress due to runaway electrons that "rust" the body. It is only the *methyl*-B$_{12}$ form that interacts with the enzyme methionine synthase that can be used by the brain to accomplish these processes.

Since May of 2002 I have treated more than 500 children and have prescribed more than 75,000 subcutaneous *methyl*-B$_{12}$ shots. I have used *methyl*-B$_{12}$ to effectively help neurotypical children, children with neurodevelopmental delays, cerebral palsy, those on the autistic spectrum, and children with ADD and ADHD. Though benefits may be observed from other routes of administration, significantly more symptoms are improved when the subcutaneous route of administration is used once every three days. This is due to the establishment of a *slow and continuous leaching effect of methyl-B$_{12}$* from the fat into the body.

Four areas of the brain are affected, resulting in the positive changes. The most common observation is an increase in executive function due to activation of the cerebral cortex, things like increased cognition, awareness, the ability to think abstractly rather than just concretely, and so on. Speech and language centers are affected. Hippocampal and limbic system stimulation results in more normal socialization and emotion. Cerebellar activation results in better fine and gross motor skills and spatial orientation. *Methyl*-B$_{12}$ affects the immune system very strongly. In addition, *methyl*-B$_{12}$ helps normalize low glutathione levels and render them once again "active" or reduced.

At this time there is no laboratory test that can predict which child will and which child will not respond to a *methyl*-B$_{12}$ clin[...] to its safety, ease of administration that is essentially pair[...] cause of its effectiveness in such a large percentage of [...] my strong opinion that every child and adolescent be g[...] portunity to see if they might benefit from *methyl*-B$_{12}$ sho[...].

James A. Neubrander, M.D. was the first person to describe the effects of methyl-B$_{12}$ for children with autism and other neurodevelopmental disorders. For video documentation and more information, refer to www.drneubrander .com.

effects do occur in about 25 to 30 percent of the subjects, the most common being hyperactivity, increased stimming, changes in sleep patterns, and mouthing of objects that usually diminish or disappear after about four to six months. More research is needed, but preliminary results on adolescents show that it may be effective if given as subcutaneous injections and that better results are seen over time, when this route of administration is the one used. See Food for Thought on page 212.

See www.drneubrander.com for more information.

DIMETHYLGLYCINE (DMG)

This is a naturally occurring substance in the body and is involved in a number of important biochemical reactions. Much anecdotal evidence exists that DMG has been helpful for some people with autism, although there have been no scientifically valid trials to show efficacy. Reported benefits are positive changes in behavior, improved language, and even in some cases reduction of seizures. Some parents have reported increased hyperactivity, and in those cases it is suggested that small amounts of folic acid be added to alleviate the problem. As DMG is not harmful, it is one of those therapies that is often worth trying. For information, go to www.autismresearchinstitute. com and www.arinewsletter.com.

FATTY ACIDS

It has been recognized that fats have a very important role to play in the metabolism and development of the body. However, due to the way our foods are now processed and the widening use of antibiotics that alter the intestinal flora, plus the fact that we do not swallow a daily spoonful of cod liver oil the way our grandparents did, it has become apparent that most of us are not getting the fatty acids our bodies need. Omega fats, cod liver oil, and evening primrose oil may be of benefit to all individuals, not just those with autism. Cod liver oil has the added benefit of containing vitamin A.

SULPHATE IONS

Dr. Rosemary Waring at the University of Birmingham has been studying the levels of sulphates in children with autism and was the first researcher to produce scientific evidence of abnormal sulphate levels in such children. (It was the UK parent group Allergy induced Autism that first brought concerns of a possible link between sulphation and autism to the attention of Dr. Waring.) Some children with ASDs show a deficiency of sulphates in their plasma. Sulphate is a substance the body produces that helps break down and get rid of compounds it no longer needs, such as the residues that are left once medication has done its job. This deficiency may contribute to "leaky gut." Sulphates appear to be important for hormone effectiveness as well as good intestinal function. As sulphate ions are not easily obtained from food but may be absorbed through the skin, magnesium sulphate (Epsom salts) is added to bathwater as a way of facilitating absorption.

ENZYMES

The stomach enzymes of some people with autism may not be working properly. It could be that in some there are insufficient levels of peptidase enzymes, or insufficient acid in the stomach for the enzymes to break down proteins. Some parents of children with hyperactivity have for many years been using enzymes taken orally to help with some of the problems associated with hyperactivity. Enzyme therapy is usually administered in conjunction with other dietary interventions.

Traditional Medications

PSYCHOPHARMACOLOGIC TREATMENTS

Medications can be used to treat some of the behaviors associated with autism. Certain drugs are used to control seizures. For some people, drugs can be helpful for reducing anxiety, obsessive-compulsive behaviors, hyperactivity, self-injurious behaviors, attention deficits, and depression. Medications used include anticonvulsant drugs, stimulant medications, tranquilizers, antidepressants, and opiate antagonists. No medication should be tried without the advice of a knowledgeable physician familiar with ASDs and the person being treated. Most of these medications should be tried in very tiny doses, less than the manufacturers' recommendation. Care should be given especially when treating young children, as many of these medications have been researched for use in adults only.

For more information, see *Straight Talk About Psychiatric Medications for Kids,* by Timothy E. Wilens, M.D. Parent Ratings of Biomedical Interventions (including 50 drugs commonly used in autism) at www.autismresearchinstitute.com.

FOOD FOR THOUGHT

Why Medicate?

by Joshua D. Feder, M.D.

Some would say "why not?" There is a reasonable body of research demonstrating that some medicines, specifically the neuroleptics haloperidol (Haldol) and risperidone (Risperdal) help persons with autism learn better and socialize better. The occasionally spectacular results seen with these medicines make some physicians feel that is it their duty to offer these medicines to persons with autism spectrum disorders (ASDs). That said, medication treatment in persons with ASDs can be complex, tedious, and frustrating. People with ASDs may be sensitive to side effects, yet may require very low or relatively high doses of medications to have benefits.

Use of medication should be preceded by a full evaluation and a full understanding of the major problem areas (target symptoms) to address. Examples of target symptoms include everything from sleep, attention sensory sensitivity, and processing to obsessive and perseverative thinking and behavior, mood problems, anxiety, and mood instability, and even learning and social function.

While no medicine is FDA approved for marketing for use in autism, many medicines from many different classes are used to treat specific symptoms, and combined pharmcotherapy (use of more than one medicine) is very common. It is important to understand what each medicine is for, and to think about how the different medicines and all other treatments combine (herbals, vitamins, and nonmedical therapies). For example, a person may be using guanfacine to soften their "fight/flight" response, and this may help anxiety, concentration, and sensory sensitivities, but might be sedating and interfere with speech therapy.

Many people see medication as a last resort, and indeed medication does not make up for an inappropriate placement or a teacher or therapist who does not understand how to help. Many times when we pay attention to regulation, joint attention, and social reciprocity, in that order, and in every interaction, then we do a much better job at engaging people with ASDs. Then, such things as anxiety, self-stimulation, and many other common symptoms are ameliorated.

That is, when we engage people better, we make more progress with less reliance on medication.

Now add puberty and adolescence. The surge of sex hormones can destabilize any plan, and the possibility of a spike in seizure activity may also play a role, especially in persons with more involved symptoms of ASDs. Social expectations change, and for many the gulf between their own function and that of peers becomes painfully apparent. Natural tendencies in adolescents to separate from parents and rely on peers are thwarted by the social and dissocial aspects of the condition itself (that is, uninterested, or interested but awkward) as well as by necessary-but-not-developmentally-normal dependence on family and others that comes from having those challenges. Vulnerability to mistreatment (teasing, bullying, or physical or sexual abuse) may increase as an adolescent is given more freedom, whether because we are encouraging it or because services are taken away. So, in addition to treating the usual target symptoms, in adolescence medication may have a role in everything from treating emerging depression when peers reject a person; seizures that are peaking at this age; or perhaps cooling off a hot libido that is getting the person in trouble.

The ethical issues that arise in the treatment of persons with autism are multiplied by those inherent in the treatment of adolescents (where people start participating in their choices and are more likely to want privacy in their care). In the end, it is most important to:

- have a good overall picture of a person and the context,
- have a good working relationship with your doctors and other helping professionals,
- brainstorm the set of possible interventions, including medications, nonmedical therapies, environmental circumstances and supports,
- sort all the above out and create a workable plan for each individual.

Joshua D. Feder, M.D., is a child and family psychiatrist in San Diego, California, specializing in the treatment of neurodevelopmental disorders with medications and interactive therapies (DIR, ICDL). His comments are often seen on Valerie's List, an email forum based in San Diego. To be added to the list email Valerie at ValeriesList@aol.com

For Help with Sensory Processing Challenges and Sensory Motor Issues

As mentioned in chapter 1, the auditory, visual, tactile, taste, and smell senses are what give us information about the world around us. Individuals with sensory disorders have senses that are inaccurate and send false messages. Children and adults with hypersensitivity overreact to stimuli, while others have hyposensitivity, which prevents them from picking up information through their senses. Sensory malfunction can also be an inability to understand and organize sensory information when it is received. Sensory processing disorder symptoms are many and varied depending on which sense or senses are perturbed.

Sensory issues are not autism specific, and therefore the methods below were not specifically developed for people with autism. Many children and adults who have sensory disorders do not have an ASD. It is important that you choose therapy providers who have experience with adolescents and the type of teen on the spectrum you have. If the

---

FOOD FOR THOUGHT

Why Sensory Integration Is So Important

But one of the biggest reasons autistic children (and more than a few autistic adults) seem so "untamable" is that they're terrified of so many things. It can take years for an autistic child to lose his fear of the most ordinary events, like getting a haircut or going to the dentist, if he ever does. There are plenty of autistic adults who have to be given general anesthesia to have their teeth worked on. They've never gotten over the terror.

—Temple Grandin and Catherine Johnson, *Animals in Translation: Using the Mysteries of Autism to Decode Animal Behavior*

---

occupational therapist has worked only with teens on one end of the spectrum, she may not be as effective with those on the other end.

OCCUPATIONAL THERAPY

Depending on the age, ability, and need of the individual, occupational therapists can provide a variety of services. Their aim is to help the person meet goals in areas of everyday life that are important to them, such as self-care, work, and leisure. Assessments are carried out initially to discover the needs of the individual and provide support to learn skills in those areas. They can help with "motor clumsiness," and fine and gross motor skills. Some therapists are specifically trained in sensory integration (see below).

American Occupational Therapy Association
4720 Montgomery Lane, P.O. Box 31220, Bethesda, MD
    20824-1220
Tel.: 301-652-2682
TDD: 800-377-8555
Fax: 301-652-7711
Website: www.aota.org

SENSORY INTEGRATION (SI) THERAPY

This is practiced by specially trained occupational therapists, who believe that many behaviors exhibited by individuals with autism are an attempt to avoid certain types of sensations or to seek preferred stimuli, in order to balance out their nervous system. There are different strategies that are used. Occupational therapists who are well trained in sensory integration have designed individual programs that have led to improvements in behavior and skills by assisting individuals with ASDs to process and use sensory information. Data from patient records show these improvements. SI can be a valuable intervention, integrated into a teen's program, depending on the person's sensory issues.

With tweens and teens, the emphasis should be on teaching them to recognize when they are becoming overloaded and how to "self-regulate" and use sensory techniques on themselves to calm down.

Sensory Integration International
P.O. Box 5339, Torrance, CA 90510-5339
Tel.: 310-787-8805
Fax: 310-787-8130
Email: info@sensoryint.com
Website: www.home.earthlink.net/~sensoryint/

See also the Alert Program—this is a program for teaching teens to self-regulate (www.alertprogram.com/), and *How Does Your Engine Run?* (pamphlet) and *How Does Your Engine Run? Leader's Guide to the Alert Program for Self-Regulation,* both by Mary S. Williams.

HANDLE—HOLISTIC APPROACH TO NEURO-DEVELOPMENT AND LEARNING EFFICIENCY

HANDLE incorporates research and techniques from many disciplines and is not ASD specific. It includes principles and perspectives from medicine, rehabilitation, psychology, education, and nutrition. It is founded on an interactive, developmental model of human functioning and is practiced on individuals of all ages. After observational assessment and interviewing caregivers, individualized programs of activities and nutritional guidance are designed for each person. HANDLE treatment for autism spectrum disorders usually involves initial activities to increase the range of bodily movement incorporating specific tactile and vestibular activities, and other activities, selected in a developmentally sound sequence. There is no research on this method in regard to autism, but some parents have reported it to be beneficial for their child.

The HANDLE Institute
1300 Dexter Avenue North, 110 The Casey Family Building,
    Seattle, WA 98109

Tel.: 206-204-6000
Fax: 206-860-3505
Website: www.handle.org

INTERACTIVE METRONOME

The Interactive Metronome is a brain-based treatment program designed to promote and enhance brain performance and recovery through neurosensory and neuromotor exercises. The IM program provides a structured, goal-oriented process that requires the patient to synchronize a range of hand and foot exercises to a precise computer-generated reference tone heard through headphones. The patient attempts to match the rhythmic beat with repetitive motor actions. Over the course of the treatment, patients learn to focus and attend for longer periods of time, increase physical endurance and stamina, filter out internal and external distractions, improve ability to monitor mental and physical actions as they are occurring, and progressively improve performance. Research done with special education children and children with ADHD has shown positive results. Parents and professionals of children on the spectrum have reported some improvements in sequencing and motor planning.

Interactive Metronome
2500 Weston Road, Suite 403, Weston, FL 33331
Toll-Free: 877-994-6776
Tel.: 954-385-4660
Fax: 954-385-4674
Email: info@interactivemetronome.com

AUDITORY INTEGRATION TRAINING (AIT)

These methods were developed by Dr. Guy Berard and Dr. Alfred Tomatis and are based on the theory that some people have a hypersensitivity toward certain sound frequencies, making some common sounds painful to hear. In AIT, individuals wear headphones and listen to modulated sounds and music with certain frequencies filtered out. This is done over a period of time. It is not known exactly how it works physiologically speaking; however, individuals have reported benefits from these listening methods. Other listening programs have been developed that can be used at home without any special equipment.

The Society for Auditory Intervention Techniques is a great resource for information on various types of auditory therapies. A review of twenty-eight reports of studies between January 1993 and May 2001 on AIT, as developed by Dr. Berard, was undertaken by Dr. Edelson and Dr. Rimland. They concluded that "The balance of the evidence clearly favors AIT as a useful intervention, especially in autism." However, the Tomatis method does not appear to be supported by any published research studies at time of writing.

Society for Auditory Intervention Techniques
P.O. Box 4538, Salem, OR 97302
Email: info@sait.org
Website: www.sait.org

For more information, see *The Sound of a Miracle*, by Annabel Stehli (about her daughter's recovery from autism through AIT).

There are also programs that have been developed for home and school use. For more information, read more about the different types of programs and ask professionals and parents who have used them about the benefits and drawbacks of each of the different methods.

For more information, see *SAMONAS Sound Therapy: The Way to Health Through Sound,* by Ingo Steinbach.

Samonas Auditory Intervention
Website: www.samonas.com
Tel.: 800-699-6618
Email:poaUS@samonas.com

The Listening Program
Website: www.advancedbrain.com/autism
Tel.: 888-228-1798
Fax: 801-627-4505
Email: info@advancedbrain.com

VISION THERAPY

Eyesight has to do with the sharpness of the image seen by the eye, while vision is the ability to focus on and comprehend what the eye is seeing. Vision plays a major role in sensory integration as well as language and social-emotional development. Optometric vision therapy can be described as physical therapy for the eyes and brain, consisting of a series of exercises to improve the specific visual skills and perceptual abilities underlying the learning process. These activities involve the use of lenses and or prisms and other prescribed activities to improve the visual system's organization, integration, and efficiency. Vision therapy is not ASD specific, but may be helpful in some cases. If you decide to consult an optometrist about vision therapy, make sure he is a certified member of the College of Optometrists in Vision Development (COVD).

College of Optometrists in Vision Development
243 N. Lindbergh Blvd., Ste #310
St. Louis, MO 63141
Tel.: 314-991-4007 or 888-268-3770
Fax: 314-991-1167
Website: www.vision3d.com
www.covd.org

IRLEN LENSES

These were developed by Helen Irlen for individuals with a sensory perceptual problem known as Irlen Syndrome. Irlen's theory is that people with reading problems and perceptual difficulties are very sensitive to white-light spectrum wavelengths, which overstimulate certain cells in the retina, resulting in incorrect signals being sent to the brain. She found that by placing different-colored overlays on printed pages, light sensitivity and perceptual distortions were reduced. These colors were then applied as a tint on glasses. There is no strong empirical research to support the use of Irlen lenses as an autism-specific therapy; however, colored overlays on printed matter and tinted glasses have been shown to be helpful for a number of students. There is anecdotal evidence that some people with ASDs have light sensitivity, and they have reported a major difference in their sensory processing when wearing tinted glasses.

For more information, see *Reading by the Colors,* by Helen Irlen, and visit www.irlen.com.

A good resource for books and information on sensory issues and holistic approaches to health is Developmental Delay Resources, 5801 Beacon Street, Pittsburgh, PA 15217, *www.devdelay.org.* Developmental Delay Resources is a nonprofit organization dedicated to meeting the needs of those working with children who have developmental delays, including an autism spectrum disorder, in sensory motor, language, social, and emotional areas.

To Teach Skills and Appropriate Behaviors

Listed here are treatments that look at what the person is able to do and work on specific skills to improve their level of functioning, so that they can function in society and continue to develop and learn.

APPLIED BEHAVIOR ANALYSIS (ABA)

This has been proven to be the most effective way to teach young children with ASDs. Specific skills are taught by breaking them into small steps, each one building on the previous one. Different methods are used to help the child learn, such as prompting (helping the child by guiding him through the desired response), shaping, and rewarding (for correct responses). ABA has been used for many years to successfully teach individuals of varying abilities and can be used to teach in all skill areas, including academic, self-help, speech and language, and socially appropriate behavior. For older children and teenagers, it is often used for teaching specific skills necessary to independence as well as appropriate behaviors.

Some of the terms used in ABA include:

Task Analysis: This consists of analyzing a skill or task that needs to be taught, by identifying each step of the skill and which steps the person needs to learn. For example, if teaching someone at home how to set the table, you would analyze the whole sequence, from walking to the cupboard, opening the cupboard with the right hand, picking up a plate with the left hand, closing the cupboard with the right hand, walking to the table, and so on. This is very useful for figuring out which steps in a task are problematic for the child or teen learning a skill or task.

Discrete Trial Teaching (DTT): This is a method of teaching that is very systematic and consists of the teacher's presentation or request, the child's response, and the consequence to that response (that is, a reward if correct), a short pause, and then the next trial. Each trial is "discrete"—that is, separate, so it is clear what is being requested of the child and what is being rewarded.

Errorless Learning (no-mistake learning): When a new behavior is taught it is important for the student to be successful from the beginning. Thus, teachers *prompt* a successful behavior, hand over hand, if necessary. The prompts are gradually removed so that the behavior will eventually occur simply to a request or some other appropriate cue.

Care should be taken when choosing an ABA specialist to supervise a behavioral program. For more information on board-certified providers, go to www.bacb.com. A competent professional will most certainly be a member of the Association for Behavior Analysis, www.abainternational.org. Bear in mind that some ABA providers only work on intensive programs with young children. It is important to ask any professional if they have experience with adolescents.

For more information, see *Steps to Independence,* by Bruce Baker and Alan J. Brightman. There are many good books available about ABA programs for early intervention, but this is a good book for using ABA strategies at home to teach everyday skills. It is an easy-to-understand, practical book for parents, with ideas on what and how to teach at home, and is useful with older children and teenagers.

RAPID PROMPTING METHOD (RPM)

RPM is a method used for teaching academics by eliciting responses through intensive verbal, auditory, visual, and/or tactile prompts. RPM presumes to increase students' interest, confidence, and self-esteem. Prompting is intended to keep students focused while allowing them to be successful. This is a very low-tech method requiring only paper and pencil. A lesson might begin with a teacher's simple statement, followed by a question about what was just said. Next, the teacher writes possible answers and spells the choices aloud. Students learn to select answers by picking up choices and eventually pointing to letters on an alphabet chart or keyboard to spell answers. RPM was developed by India native Soma Mukhopadhyay. Originally Mukhopadhyay taught her son, and then tried her method, improving and adapting it to different learning styles (such as auditory or visual; left brain/right brain) in a classroom of severely autistic children in Los Angeles for two years. Mukhopadhyay has since used RPM with more than 200 individuals with an ASD, some of them teenagers and adults.

More empirical study is needed, but anecdotal evidence from parents and professionals indicates that RPM is a viable means for improving communication and academic success for some persons with autism. This method appears to be most helpful for those who are nonverbal or lacking in conversational skills. A basic RPM manual is soon to be published written by Mukhopadhyay and Portia Iversen, cofounder of the Cure Autism Now Foundation.

Helping Autism through Learning and Outreach (HALO)
P.O. Box 303399, Austin, TX 78703
Tel.: 512-327-4250
Fax: 512-327-4495
Website: www.halo-soma.org
Email: information@halo-soma.org

TEACCH

The Treatment and Education of Autistic and Related Communication Handicapped Children was developed by Eric Schopler at the University of North Carolina at Chapel Hill in the early 1970s. TEACCH started out as a parent and child psychoanalysis group and quickly became a skill-based approach dependent on a strong parent-professional collaboration. It focuses on teaching functional skills while modifying the environment to facilitate the needs of the individual. Structured teaching and the use of visual materials and schedules are used to enhance the acquisition of skills by providing a stress-free environment. Vocational preparation is a strong component of this program. The effectiveness of individual components of TEACCH has been validated in a number of studies. However, there appears to be a lack of research in terms of individual gains. Adapting the environment for the person does make it easier for them, but in doing so it may remove some of the natural "stresses" that create opportunities for learning. Sometimes classrooms based solely on TEACCH principles appear to be about making the class easier for the teacher to handle, and appear to lack social interaction and social skills development, which many individuals with autism need.

Individual components of the TEACCH method can be useful strategies to use with teenagers who are visual learners. For auditory learners, an auditory component will probably need to be added.

Division TEACCH Administration and Research
CB# 7180, 310 Medical School Wing E, The University of North
    Carolina at Chapel Hill, Chapel Hill, NC 27599-7180, USA
Tel.: 919-966-5156
Fax: 919-966-4003
Website: http://www.teacch.com/

For Building Relationship Skills

THE DEVELOPMENTAL, INDIVIDUAL-DIFFERENCES, RELATIONSHIP-BASED (DIR) MODEL

This was developed by Dr. Stanley I. Greenspan. Parents and floortime therapists help children master the emotional milestones needed to develop a foundation for learning. The approach is based on his belief that emotions give meaning to our experiences as well as a direction to our actions. Parents and therapists work on four goals: encouraging attention and intimacy, two-way communication, encouraging the expression and use of ideas and feelings, and logical thought. Case studies of adolescents with moderate- to high-functioning autism receiving DIR therapy document that the teens showed improvement in their ability to relate, socialize, use language, and regulate emotions over time.

Stanley I. Greenspan, M.D.
4938 Hampden Lane, Ste. 229, Bethesda, MD 20814
Tel.: 301-657-2348
Conference-Training Course Tel.: 301-320-6360
Website: www.stanleygreenspan.com

For more information, see the following:

The Child With Special Needs: Encouraging Intellectual and Emotional Growth, by Stanley I. Greenspan, M.D., and Serena Wieder

The Boy Who Loved Windows: Opening the Heart and Mind of a Child Threatened with Autism, by Patricia Stacey

RELATIONSHIP DEVELOPMENT INTERVENTION (RDI)

Developed by Dr. Steven Gutstein, the primary goal of the RDI program is to systematically teach the motivation for and skills of experience sharing interaction. It is a parent-based clinical treatment and begins at each child's level and teaches skills to the next level. Dr. Gutstein has identified six different abilities that are essential for success in dynamic systems: Emotional Referencing, Social Coordination, Declarative Language, Flexible Thinking, Relational Information Processing, and Foresight and Hindsight.

Connections Center
4120 Bellaire Boulevard, Houston, TX 77025
Tel.: 713-838-1362
Fax: 713-838-1447
Website: www.connectionscenter.com
Email: administrator@connectionscenter.com

For more information, see *Relationship Development Intervention with Young Children: Social and Emotional Development Activities for Asperger Syndrome, Autism, PDD and NLD,* by Steven E. Gutstein, Rachelle K. Sheely

COGNITIVE BEHAVIOR THERAPY

Cognitive behavior therapy combines cognitive therapy and behavior therapy. It has been proven effective in the neurotypical population in helping a person change the way he thinks about and responds to feelings such as anxiety, anger, and sadness. Using cognitive behavior therapy with children and adults on the more able end of the spectrum is a more recent development that appears to be effective.

For more information, see *Exploring Feelings: Cognitive Behaviour Therapy to Manage Anxiety* and *Exploring Feelings: Cognitive Behaviour Therapy to Manage Anger*, by Dr. Tony Attwood.

Communication

By the time they have reached the teen years, most children with autism will have developed or learned a communication system. However, some of the less functionally able may still be having difficulties in this area, even just for asking for what they want or need. Some children may use a few different methods of communication.

PICTURE EXCHANGE COMMUNICATION SYSTEM (PECS)

This is a practical communication system that allows a person to express his needs and desires without being prompted by another person, by using pictures or a series of pictures to form a sentence. PECS has been used successfully with some older individuals with autism who are nonverbal. The person first learns to communicate by handing someone a picture of the object he wants, then sentence strips, and so on. Not only does this facilitate communication, it motivates the person to interact with others. PECS is easy to incorporate into any existing program and does not require expensive materials. Behaviorally based instructional techniques are used to implement the program (such as prompting, shaping, fading, etc.). Basic concepts can be taught using PECS, and the picture icons can be used for visual schedules to help the person. Codeveloped by Andy Bondy and Lori Frost, this method helps relieve the frustration of those unable to speak.

Pyramid Educational Consultants
226 West Park Place, Suite 1, Newark, DE 19711
Tel.: 888-PECS-INC (888-732-7462)

Fax: 302-368-2516
Email: pyramid@pecs.com
Website: www.pecs.com

For more information, see *A Picture's Worth: PECS and Other Visual Communication Strategies in Autism,* by Andy Bondy and Lori Frost.

RAPID PROMPTING METHOD (RPM)

As described earlier in this chapter, RPM is a method used for teaching academics by eliciting responses through intensive verbal, auditory, visual, and/or tactile prompts. Students learn eventually to point to letters on an alphabet chart or keyboard to spell answers and to communicate. This method was developed by India native Soma Mukhopadhyay.

Helping Autism through Learning and Outreach (HALO)
P.O. Box 303399, Austin, TX 78703
Tel.: 512-327-4250
Fax: 512-327-4495
Website: www.halo-soma.org
Email: information@halo-soma.org

AUGMENTATIVE DEVICES

For teens who are nonverbal, augmentative communication devices may be a good choice. These devices help individuals in producing and or understanding speech and can be as low-tech as a board with pictures to sophisticated electronic speech synthesizers. For more information, ask your school district assistive technology expert who should be able to assess your teen, his needs as well as abilities, and then try different communicative devices with him. Listed here are just a few devices and companies that make them.

Dynavox Systems, Inc.
2100 Wharton Street, Pittsburgh, PA 15203
Tel.: 888-697-7332
Website: www.dynavoxsys.com

Ablenet, Inc.
1081 Tenth Avenue S.E., Minneapolis, MN 55414-1312
Tel.: 800-322-0956
Fax: 612-379-9143
Website: www.ablenetinc.com

Enabling Devices—Toys for Special Children, Inc.
385 Warburton Avenue, Hastings-on-Hudson, NY 10706
Tel.: 914-478-0960
Fax: 914-478-7030

To Teach Social Skills and Social Communication

For many tweens and teens, social skills training is a particularly important area of focus. Social skills are a difficult area and need to be taught for those with an ASD. Research has shown that many people with autism have "mind blindness." That is, they do not understand that people think differently from how they do, have their own plans and points of reference. This may be why they are often unable to anticipate what others may say or do, which creates problems in social behavior and communication. For many tweens and teens, social skills training is a particularly important area of focus. There are different methods of teaching social skills and social communication. Some strategies are discussed in more detail in chapter 4 in regard to school, while others are listed here.

Social Stories: This method promotes desired social behavior by describing (through the written word) social situations and appropriate social responses. Developed by Carol Gray, social stories may be applied to a wide variety of social situations and are created with the learner, who takes an active role in developing the story.

Social stories usually have descriptive sentences about the setting, characters, and their feelings and thoughts, and give direction in regard to the appropriate responses and behaviors. Comic strip conversations are illustrations of conversations that show what people say and do as well as emphasize what people may be thinking. Social stories and comic strip conversations can be adapted to many functioning levels and situations, and anyone can learn to create them. They are particularly useful for learning how to deal with unstructured time such as recess and lunchtime.

For more information, see *Comic Strip Conversations: Colorful, Illustrated Interactions with Students with Autism and Related Disorders, The New Social Story Book,* and *The Original Social Story Book,* all by Carol Gray.

Social Skills Groups: These teach specific social skills by breaking them down and providing practice in a "safe" environment. Depending on the age or grade level, different social skills are emphasized, including making conversation, turn taking, joining a group, dealing with bullying, friendship, and understanding facial expressions. Social skills training usually takes place in groups of four to six children and is usually beneficial for the more able person with an ASD. Social skill development is one of the biggest challenges children with ASDs face, and a well-structured social skills group can be beneficial.

For more information, see www.udel.edu/bkirby/asperger/social. html.

Circle of Friends: The object of a Circle of Friends is to make sure the child is included in activities and feels a part of the group. A social "map" that lists the child's social contacts is prepared, with his help. Then, classmates are identified who would like to help the child and be placed on the "map." A facilitator helps with the circle of friends, and the volunteers act as mentors to the child in teaching appropriate social skills in social situations such as greeting the child, walking to class with him, and being helpful and friendly in other ways. In 1997, the Leicestershire Autism Outreach Team in the UK established seven such circles. The results were very promising. Not only did the child with an ASD show benefits, but so did the six to eight children who volunteered to form each circle. The benefits also extended beyond the immediate circle. For more information, read the article on the OASIS website: www.udel.edu/bkirby/asperger/social.html.

For more information, see "Common Sense Tools: MAPS and Circles for Inclusive Education," by Marsha Forest and Jack Pearpoint

There are many other books and strategies out there to help teach social skills and social communication. Each one has merits, and choosing the right method will depend on the needs and strengths of the particular teen or tween. You may wish to investigate some of these:

The Unwritten Rules of Social Relationships by Temple Grandin and Sean Barron.

Social Skills Training for Adolescents with General Moderate Learning Difficulties, by Ursula Cornish and Fiona Ross.

Incorporating Social Goals in the Classroom: A Guide for Teachers and Parents of Children with High-Functioning Autism and Asperger Syndrome, by Rebecca A. Moyes.

The Social Skills Picture Book, by Jed E. Baker.

Social Skills Training for Children and Adolescents with Asperger Syndrome and Social-Communications Problems, by Jed E. Baker.

Do-Watch-Listen-Say: Social and Communication Intervention for Children with Autism, by Kathleen Ann Quill.

Thinking About You, Thinking About Me, by Michelle Garcia Winner.

Inside Out, by Michelle Garcia Winner.

S.O.S. Social Skills in Our Schools, by Michelle A. Dunn.

Teaching Children with Autism to Mind-Read: A Practical Guide for Teachers and Parents, by Patricia Howlin and Simon Baron-Cohen.

Autism: A Social Skills Approach for Children and Adolescents, by Maureen Aarons and Tessa Gittens.

The Parent Coach: A New Approach to Parenting in Today's Society, by Steven Richfield, Psy.D., with Carol Bochert.

Parent Coaching Cards: Social and Emotional Tools for Children, by Steven Richfield, Psy.D., with Carol Bochert.

OASIS: Online Asperger Syndrome Information and Support has a section on Social Implications and Strategies that has useful websites and books (www.udel.edu.bkirby/asperger/social).

Music Therapy

Most people respond favorably to music, including people with ASDs. Music can be immensely motivating and enjoyable. In music therapy, goals are tailored to the needs of each individual and may include increasing nonverbal interaction such as turn taking and eye contact, exploring and expressing feelings, and being creative and spontaneous. Some parents have reported that their children began to learn to speak as a result of being taught nursery rhymes and other songs. Research shows that there are indeed some favorable benefits to music therapy.

American Music Therapy Association:
8455 Colesville Road, Ste. 1000, Silver Spring, MD 20910
Tel.: 301-589-3300
Fax: 301-589-5175

Email: info@musictherapy.org
Website:www.musictherapy.org

Assistive Technology and Computer Programs

Broadly speaking, assistive technology means any item, piece of equipment, or product system that is used to increase, maintain, or improve the functional capabilities of a person. It can be a high-technology item such as a LightWRITER to help someone type what they cannot say verbally. Or it can be low technology such as picture icons used to communicate something a person wants, or larger letters on keyboard keys. Check with knowledgeable speech therapists and your school's assistive technology expert to see what items they have found useful for teens such as yours, as well as with the latest research and computer specialists to see what is new.

Some children with autism can easily use computer programs, and learn well by using them. Others struggle with the sensory issues of too much to look at and too much to listen to. Some programs have been designed for students with autism in mind. This area is in constant evolution as advances in technology continue to develop. Although not all of the following are ASD specific, here are some good places to get information:

Autism and ICT: A Guide for Teachers and Parents (ICT stands for Information and Communications Technology), by Colin Hardy, Jan Ogden, Julie Newman, and Sally Cooper.

Alliance for Technology Access (ATA) is a network of community-based centers, vendors, and professionals. Website: www.ataccess. org/, address: 1304 Southpoint Blvd., Suite 240, Petaluma, CA 94954, tel.: 707-778-3011, TTY:707-778-3015, fax: 707-765-2080.

Techable provides individuals with disabilities, their families, and support professionals, information and access to assistive technology devices. Website:www.techable.org, email: techweb @techable.org, address: 1114 Brett Drive, Suite. 100, Conyers, GA 30094, tel.: 770-922-6768, fax: 770-922-6769.

Inclusive Technology: The Special Needs People. This website has a comprehensive list of different types of programs for people with special needs and is updated regularly. Website: www.inclusive. co.uk.

FOOD FOR THOUGHT
Biomedical Interventions

When my son Jeremy, now sixteen, was little, the DAN! protocol did not exist and biomedical interventions where not as evolved as they are now. While living in the UK, Jeremy did go on the Hunter/Gatherer Diet, had hair samples examined, and took magnesium, B_6, and DMG. Back then, this was all considered a bit weird, like visiting the witch doctor and practicing voodoo. We never told our stateside friends about it; it was bad enough we lived in Europe!

Fast-forward about twelve years, and we see that science and research is showing that for at least part of the population, biomedical interventions, whether swallowed, injected, or merely rubbed on the skin, are helping some children improve or even recover from autism. Anecdotal evidence, data from client records, and before and after videotapes, are showing these changes. Some recent studies are providing links to understanding why these interventions are helping some children.

Meanwhile, armed with my hard-earned money and some knowledge as to how these interventions might help my son, I took Jeremy to see a DAN!-trained doctor. The first step was giving my credit card number. The second was agreeing to doing all these analyses on Jeremy, involving five different blood kits from three different labs, one urine kit, one hair analysis kit, and four stool samples to be collected four days in a row.

A few thousands of dollars lighter but burdened by boxes of collection kits, as well as a thick file of papers, I arrive home feeling totally overwhelmed. Reading over the papers that explain how and what to do, and where to send which analysis kit and which papers to send to my medical insurer if I am even thinking about attempting a partial refund, I wonder how I am going to manage to do all of this. I am not a lady of leisure. The doorbell rings twice; more collection kits arrive via UPS—how am I going to keep this all straight? Perhaps the reason these treatments are recommended for younger children is that the parents are also younger. They have not yet had as many years getting beat up by the system as we older parents have, and they still have some energy in reserve.

Like any neurotypical person, I put the collection kits and paperwork in a corner of the dining room, where they will sit until I get the time, courage, and energy to figure it all out. It's not so difficult, but it's time-consuming. And meanwhile, I have to get back to work to pay off that credit card bill that will be arriving any day now.

CLOSING COMMENTS

I am imagining a future of people who work.
A future of orange and mauve.
People who are not my family who like to spend time with me,
happy to be my friends.
People like Monique, Allan, and Maureen:
people who respect my intelligence without wasting my time.
I am not stupid and I have feelings.
California and France are for me good places to live because
I like the beach and the city.

JEREMY SICILE-KIRA, 16 YEARS OLD

WHEN I was given my son Jeremy's official diagnosis by a specialist, I went into shock. I couldn't breathe, I couldn't move, I felt a sharp pain in my heart, even though I had already known he was not developing normally. I pulled myself together and decided I'd better write down everything the specialist was saying, because I knew I wouldn't remember later, when the emotions would hit me even harder. As I hunted for a pen in my bag, the specialist handed me a pencil and said cheerfully, "Here, use one of these. If you're lucky, you will find a good institution for Jeremy and he will learn to package pencils like this one into boxes. That's where this one came from."

Unfortunately, this kind of story is all too familiar to many of the parents reading this book. When I try to analyze the factors that have made such a difference in Jeremy's prognosis, I attribute it to a few different ones, the first one being sheer stubbornness—sheer stubbornness on my part to refuse to accept that my son cannot learn, that he is not capable of learning. The second factor is knowledge. I learn everything I can about autism, about Jeremy, about teaching methods, about the different therapies and biomedical interventions and traditional medications about the research and science behind it all. I try the ones that make sense and that address the challenges he faces.

The third factor is surrounding Jeremy with people who believe in him and respect him, who teach him as best they can what he needs to know for today, and who will work with me in preparing him and creating what is necessary for his future life as an adult (including activities that are simply for fun and relaxation). Because, at the end of the day, we parents cannot do it on our own; we need a community of people who believe that our teenager can make progress, who believe that the teenager has the right to a good life and the right to the pursuit of happiness.

Most parents of teenagers on the autism spectrum are acutely aware that their child is no longer little, that their child is too old for early intervention. They fear that the "window of opportunity" for learning appears to be closing a bit more every day. In reality, the window of opportunity for learning *never* closes. There are now many strategies out there to help teenagers on the spectrum learn and grow and become more independent. As well, there are biomedical interventions and traditional medications that will be helpful for some. The focus of how and what they learn may change, but they can still reach their potential in terms of independence and life skills, and even have some teenage fun along the way.

There is the realization that, except for a few rare individuals, our children will always face challenges. For some of us parents, it will be necessary to revisit our own attitudes about disability and mental health. This can create yet even more discord between parents and partners, adding more stress to a family life that for many is precarious at best.

Some able people on the spectrum live independently, earn a living by doing something they are interested in, and are successful. They feel their life has worth. However, most adults on the spectrum today are unemployed or underemployed, and many suffer depression or unhappiness. This is because we—parents, educators and other professionals—are still depending on systems that obviously are not working to prepare our teenagers for their future as adults.

The good news is that we are living in an era where possibilities abound thanks to the philosophy of self-determination that our society has embraced. Although currently there are not enough appropriate adult services available there are new funding models for obtaining or creating appropriate housing and employment opportunities. Parents and professionals and people on the spectrum can create different possibilities based on each person's wants and needs. It is actually an exciting and hopeful time, with many opportunities available for translating your teenager's dreams into realities. For that to happen, we all need to start thinking outside the box and work together. By joining together, creating future possibilities for employment and living, and preparing our teenagers in high school, we can create more choices for our loved ones on the spectrum. It is up to us to be the change we want to see.

The teenage years can be confusing, challenging, maddening, exciting, and life changing—for both teens and parents. One thing is certain: tweens and teens on the autism spectrum *can* learn and thrive, and with the help of parents and other concerned adults, they can lead productive and happy lives.

Meanwhile, we must remember to take time and enjoy fun moments with our children. After all, they are still only teenagers, for now.

BIBLIOGRAPHY

Aarons, M., and T. Gittens. *An Integrated Approach to Social Communication Problems.*

Aarons, M., and T. Gittens. 2001. *Autism: A Social Skills Approach for Children and Adolescents.* Speechmark Publishing.

American Psychiatric Association. 1994. "Disorders Diagnosed in Childhood: Autism Disorder—DSM-IV Criteria." Psychologynet website: www.psychologynet.org/autism.html (28 January 2002).

Anderson, W., S. Chitwood, and D. Hayden. 1997. *Negotiating the Special Education Maze: A Guide for Parents and Teachers.* Bethesda, MD: Woodbine House.

Association of Regional Center Agencies. 2005. *A New Day: Alternatives to Traditional Support.* Sacramento, CA: ARCA.

Attwood, T. 1998. *Asperger's Syndrome: A Guide for Parents and Professionals.* London: Jessica Kingsley Publishers Ltd.

Attwood, T. 2002. *Why Does Chris Do That?* London: The National Autistic Society.

Attwood, T. 2004. *Exploring Feelings: Cognitive Behaviour Therapy to Manage Anger.* Arlington, TX: Future Horizons.

Attwood, T. 2004. *Exploring Feelings: Cognitive Behaviour Therapy to Manage Anxiety.* Arlington, TX: Future Horizons.

Autism One Conference. May 2005. *A Conference for Parents and Practitioners for the Care, Treatment, and Recovery of Children with Autism.* Chicago. Website: www.autismone.org.

Autism Research Institute. "Autism Research Review International." Bernard Rimland, editor. Vol. 14, no. 3. San Diego, CA: Autism Research Institute.

Autism Research Institute. May 2001. "Mercury Detoxification Consensus Group Position Paper." Autism Research Institute website: www.autism.com/ari/mercury/consensus.html (14 January 2003).

Autism Society of America. 2004. "Life After High School." Autism Society of America website: www.autism-society.org.

Autism Society of America. 2004. "Safety in the Home." Autism Society of America website: www.autism-society.org.

Baker, B., and A. Brightman. 1997. *Steps to Independence: Teaching Everyday Skills to Children with Special Needs.* Baltimore, MD: Paul H. Brookes Publishing.

Baker, J.E. 2001. *The Social Skills Picture Book: Teaching Play, Emotion, and Communication to Children with Autism.* Arlington, TX: Future Horizons.

Baker, J.E. 2003. *Social Skills Training for Children and Adolescents with Asperger Syndrome and Social-Communication Problems.* Shawnee Mission, KS: Autism Asperger Publishing.

Barber, A. 1999. *Vision and Sensory Integration.* Santa Ana, CA: Optometric Extension Program.

Barnhill, G.P. 2002. *Right Address . . . Wrong Planet: Children with Asperger Syndrome Becoming Adults.* Shawnee Mission, KS: Autism Asperger Publishing.

Baron-Cohen, S. 1995. *Mindblindness.* Cambridge, MA: MIT Press.

Bashe, P.R., and B.L. Kirby. 2001. *The OASIS Guide to Asperger Syndrome: Advice, Support, Insight, and Inspiration.* New York: Crown Publishers.

Bateman, B.D. "Legal Requirements for Transition Components of the IEP." Wrightslaw website: www.wrightslaw.com/info/trans.legal.bateman.htm (25 March 2005).

Becker, W.C. 1971. *Parents Are Teachers: A Child Management Program.* Champaign, IL: Research Press.

Behavioral Intervention Association. "Exploring Treatment Options." Behavioral Intervention Association website: bia4autism.org/ques3.php (7 December 2002).

Behavioral Intervention Association. "Family Questions." Behavioral Intervention Association website: www.bia4autism.org/ques2.php (7 December 2002).

Behavioral Intervention Association. "Questions to Ask Providers." Behavioral Intervention Association website: www.bia4autism.org/ques6.php (7 December 2002).

Bellini, S., and C. Pratt. 2003. Indiana Parent/Family 2003 Needs Assessment Survey, Bloomington IN: Indiana Resource Center for Autism and Indiana Institute on Disability and Community Productivity in Core Functions Areas.

Bicknell, A. 1999. *Independent Living for Adults with Autism and Asperger Syndrome: A Guide for Families of People with Autistic Spectrum Disorders.* London: The National Autistic Society.

Bleach, F. 2001. *Everybody Is Different: A Book for Young People Who Have Brothers or Sisters with Autism.* London: The National Autistic Society.

Bolick, T. 2001. *Asperger Syndrome and Adolescence.* Gloucester, MA: Fair Winds Press.

Bolton, P., M. McGuire, and S. Whitehead. 2001. *A Life in the Community . . . Supporting Adults with Autism and Other Developmental Disorders Whose Needs are Challenging.* Cambridge, UK: University of Cambridge.

Bondy, A., Frost, L. 2002. *A Picture's Worth: PECS and Other Visual Communication Strategies in Autism.* Bethesda, MD: Woodbine House.

Boyd, B. 2003. *Parenting a Child with Asperger Syndrome.* London: Jessica Kingsley Publishers.

Bundy, J. February 2004. "University Program Helps Autistic Students." The Associated Press.

Buron, K. D., and M. Curtis. 2003. *The Incredible 5-Point Scale.* Shawnee Mission, KS: Autism Asperger Publishing.

Carlson, E., L. Chen, K. Schroll, and S. Klein. 2003. "SPeNSE: Study of Personnel Needs in Special Education." U.S. Department of Education Office of Special Education, WESTAT.

Chassman, M. 1999. *One-on-One: Working with Low-Functioning Children with Autism and Other Developmental Disabilities.* Verona, WI: IEP Resources Publication.

Child First. 2005. *Chores: Volume 3.* The Able Individual Video Learning Series.

Child First. 2005. *Dressing: Volume 2.* The Able Individual Video Learning Series.

Collier, V. 2002. "Raising Teenagers with Autism." *Advocate* 35: 18–24.

Communication (the magazine of the National Autistic Society). Autumn 2002, 36:3.

Community Alliance for Special Education, and Protection and Advocacy. 2004. *Special Education Rights and Responsibilities.*

Community Services for Autistic Adults and Children. 2004. "CSAAC's Vocational Program." CSAAC website: *www.csaac.org/voc.htm.*

Cornish, U., and F. Ross. 2004. *Social Skills Training for Adolescents with General Moderate Learning Difficulties.* London: Jessica Kingsley Publishers.

Coulter, D. 2001. *Asperger Syndrome: Transition to College and Work*. Website: www.coultervideo.com.

Crane, K., M. Gramlich, and K. Peterson. 2004. "Putting Interagency Agreements into Action." National Center on Secondary Education and Transition website: *www.ncset.org/publications/printresource.asp?id=1689* (March 25, 2005).

Crook, W. 1986. *The Yeast Connection*. New York: Vintage Books.

Davies, J. *Able Autistic Children: Children with Asperger's Syndrome: A Booklet for Brothers and Sisters*. Child Development Research Unit, University of Nottingham.

Davis, J. *Children with Autism: A Booklet for Brothers and Sisters*. Child Development Research Unit, University of Nottingham.

Davis, B. 2001. *Breaking Autism's Barriers: A Father's Story*. London: Jessica Kingsley Publishers. Reproduced with the permission of Jessica Kingsley Publishers.

Davis, B., and W. Goldband Schunick. 2002. *Dangerous Encounters: Avoiding Perilous Situations with Autism*. London: Jessica Kingsley Publishers.

Delmolino, L., and S. L. Harris. 2004. *Incentives for Change: Motivating People with Autism Spectrum Disorders to Learn and Gain Independence*. Bethesda, MD: Woodbine House.

Department for Education and Skills: Autism Working Group (2002), Autism Spectrum Disabilities Newsletter. 2001. "Supporting Adults with Autism in the Community." Paul Brookes Publishing website: http://www.pbrookes.com.

Edelson, M. 23 March 2003. "Theory of Mind." Center for the Study of Autism. Salem, OR. Website: www.autism.org/mind.html.

Edelson, S., and B. Rimland. *The Efficacy of Auditory Integration Training: Summaries and Critiques of 28 Reports*. (January 1993–May 2001). San Diego: Autism Research Institute.

Edgar, J. 1999. *Love, Hope and Autism*. London: The National Autistic Society.

Exceptional Children. 2004. "Finding Effective Intervention and Personnel Preparation Practices for Students With Autism Spectrum Disorders." Yellobrix website: www.infobrix.yellowbrix.com.

Falvey, M. A. 1989. *Community-Based Curriculum: Instructional Strategies for Students with Severe Handicaps*. Baltimore, MD: Paul H. Brookes Publishing.

Fast, Y., et al. 2004. *Employment for Individuals with Asperger Syndrome or Non-Verbal Learning Disability*. London: Jessica Kingsley Publishers.

Federal Funding for the IDEA. Alexandria, Virginia: National Association of State Directors of Special Education.

Field, S., and A. Hoffman. 2002. "Preparing Youth to Exercise Self-Determination" *Journal of Disability Policy Studies.*

Fleisher, M. 2003. *Making Sense of the Unfeasible.* London: Jessica Kingsley Publishers.

Fombonne, E. 2003. "The Prevalence of Autism." *JAMA,* 289: 87–89.

Friend, M. 1997. "Educational Partnerships through Effective Communication: Workshop for North County CAC, March 10."

Garcia Winner, M. 2000. *Inside Out: What Makes the Person with Social Cognitive Deficits Tick?* San Jose, CA: Michelle G. Winner, SLP.

Garcia Winner, M. 2002. *Thinking About You, Thinking About Me.* San Jose, CA: Michelle G. Winner, SLP.

Getman, G. N. 1993. *How to Develop Your Child's Intelligence.* Santa Ana, CA: Optometric Extension Program.

Goldblatt, E., and D. Mentink. 2004. "18 Tips For Getting Quality Special Education Services For Your Child." Oakland, CA: Protection and Advocacy.

Gottschall, E. 2004. *Breaking the Vicious Cycle: Intestinal Health Through Diet.* Baltimore, ON: Kirkton Press.

Grandin, T. 1995. *Thinking in Pictures and Other Reports from My Life with Autism.* New York: Doubleday.

Grandin, T. 1996. "Making the Transition from the World of School into the World of Work." Center for the Study of Autism website: www.autism.org/temple/transition.html (10 February 2003).

Grandin, T. 1998. "An Inside View of Autism." Center for the Study of Autism website: www.autism.org/temple/inside.html (14 November 2002).

Grandin, T. 1998. "Evaluating the Effects of Medication." Center for the Study of Autism website: www.autism.org/temple/meds.html (13 February 2003).

Grandin, T. 2000. "My Experiences with Visual Thinking Sensory Problems and Communication Difficulties." Center for the Study of Autism website: www.autism.org/temple/visual.html (14 November 2002).

Grandin, T. 2002. "Teaching Tips for Children and Adults with Autism." Center for the Study of Autism website: www.autism.org/temple/tips.html (10 February 2003).

Grandin, T., and K. Duffy. 2004. *Developing Talents: Careers for Individuals with Asperger Syndrome and High-Functioning Autism.* Shawnee Mission, KS: Autism Asperger Publishing.

Grandin, T., and C. Johnson. 2004. *Animals in Translation: Using the Mysteries of Autism to Decode Animal Behavior.* New York, NY: Scribner.

Grandin, T., and M. M. Scariano. 1986. *Emergence: Labeled Autistic.* Novato, CA: Arena Press.

Gray, C. 1993. *The Original Social Story Book*. Arlington, TX: Future Horizons.

Gray, C. 1994. *Comic Strip Conversations: Colorful, Illustrated Interactions with Students with Autism and Related Disorders*. Arlington, TX: Future Horizons.

Gray, C. 1994. *The New Social Story Book: Illustrated Edition*. Jenison, MI: Jenison High School.

Greenspan, S. I., and S. Wieder. 1998. *The Child with Special Needs: Encouraging Intellectual and Emotional Growth*. Reading, MA: Perseus Books.

Griffen, C., and D. Hammis. 2003. *Making Self-Employment Work for People with Disabilities*, Baltimore MD: Brookes.

Gutstein, S. E. 2001. *Autism Aspergers: Solving the Relationship Puzzle*. Arlington, TX: Future Horizons.

Hall, K. 1988. *Asperger's Syndrome: The Universe and Everything*. London: Jessica Kingsley Publishers.

Hammer, E. 1996. "Anticipatory Guidance for Parents of Children with Disabilities: What Happens to Families When a Child Has Chronic Problems?" Website: www.winfssi.com/Anticipatory.html (8 September 2002).

Harpur, J., M. Lawlor, and M. Fitzgerald. 2004. *Succeeding in College with Asperger Syndrome*, London: Jessica Kingsley Publishers.

Harris, S. L. 1994. *Topics in Autism: Siblings of Children with Autism. A Guide for Families*. Bethesda, MD: Woodbine House.

Hart, D., K. Zimbrich, and T. Whelley. 2002. "Challenges in Coordinating and Managing Services and Supports in Secondary and Postsecondary Options." National Center on Secondary Education and Transition website: www.ncset.org/publications/printresource.asp?id=719 (March 25, 2005).

Hawkins, G. 2004. *How to Find Work for People with Asperger Syndrome*. London: Jessica Kingsley Publishers.

Heinrichs, R. 2003. *Perfect Targets: Asperger Syndrome and Bullying*. Shawnee Mission, KS: Autism Asperger Publishing.

Hénault, Isabelle. 2005. *Asperger's Syndrome and Sexuality: from Adolescence through Adulthood*, London, UK: Jessica Kingsley Publishers.

Hersey, J. 1998. *Why Can't My Child Behave? Why Can't She Cope? Why Can't He Learn?* Alexandria, VA: Pear Tree Press.

Hesmondhalgh, M., and C. Breakey. 2001. *Access and Inclusion for Children with Autistic Spectrum Disorders: Let Me In*. London: Jessica Kingsley Publishers.

Holmes, A. 2000. "Autism Treatment: Chelation of Mercury for the Treatment of Autism." Healing Arts website: www.healing-arts.org/children/holmes.html (22 January 2003).

Howlin, P. 1997. *Autism: Preparing for Adulthood.* London: Routledge.

Howlin, P., and S. Baron-Cohen. 1998. *Teaching Children with Autism to Mind-Read: A Practical Guide for Teachers and Parents.* London: John Wiley and Sons.

Hughes, C., and E. W. Carter. 2000. *The Transition Handbook. Strategies High School Teachers Use That Work!* Baltimore, MD: Paul H. Brookes Publishing.

"IDEA 2004: Transition Services for Education, Work, Independent Living." Wrightslaw website: www.wrightslaw.com/idea/art/defs.transition.htm (March 25, 2005).

"IEP & Transition Planning: Frequently Asked Questions." Wrightslaw website: www.wrightslaw.com/info;/trans.faqs.htm (March 25, 2005).

Ives, M. 1999. *What Is Asperger Syndrome, and How Will It Affect Me? A Guide for Young People.* London: The National Autistic Society.

Jackson, J. 2004. *Multicoloured Mayhem.* London: Jessica Kingsley Publishers.

Jackson, L. 2001. *A User Guide to the GF/CF Diet for Autism, Asperger Syndrome and AD/HD.* London: Jessica Kingsley Publishers.

Jackson, L. 2002. *Freaks, Geeks & Asperger Syndrome: A User Guide to Adolescence.* London: Jessica Kingsley Publishers. Reproduced with the permission of Jessica Kingsley Publishers.

Kaplan, L. P., and J. D. Burstein. 2005. *Diagnosis Autism: Now What? 10 Steps to Improve Treatment Outcomes: A Parent-Physician Team Approach.* Draper, UT: Etham Press.

Klein, F. 2001. "Autistic Advocacy." Frank Klein website: home.att.net/~ascaris 1/index.html (8 September 2002).

Kranowitz, C. S. 1998. *The Out-of-Sync Child: Recognizing and Coping with Sensory Integration Dysfunction.* New York: Perigee.

LaSalle, B. 2003. *Finding Ben: A Mother's Journey Through the Maze of Asperger's.* New York: McGraw-Hill.

Lawson, W. 2003. *Build Your Own Life.* London: Jessica Kingsley Publishers.

Lawson, W. 2005. *Sex, Sexuality and the Autism Spectrum.* London: Jessica Kingsley Publishers.

Ledgin, Norm. 2002. *Asperger's and Self-Esteem: Insight and Hope Through Famous Role Models,* Houston TX: Future Horizons.

Lewis, L. 1998. *Special Diets for Special Kids.* Arlington, TX: Future Horizons.

Lord, C., and J. McGee, 2001. "Educating Children with Autism." Washington, DC: National Research Council, National Academy Press.

Lovaas, O. I. 1981. *Teaching Developmentally Disabled Children: The ME Book.* Austin, TX: Pro-ed.

Markova, D., and A. Powell. 1992. *How Your Child Is Smart: A Life-Changing Approach to Learning.* Berkeley, CA: Conari Press.

Marquette, J. 2005. *Becoming Remarkably Able: Walking the Path to Independence and Beyond.* Louisville, KY: Jackie Marquette.

McAfee, J. 2002. *Navigating the Social World: A Curriculum for Individuals with Asperger's Syndrome, High-Functioning Autism and Related Disorders.* Arlington, TX: Future Horizons.

McCandless, J. 2003. *Children with Starving Brains: A Medical Treatment Guide for Autism Spectrum Disorder.* Thousand Oaks, CA: Bramble Books.

Melberg Schwier, K., and D. Hingsburger. 2000. *Sexuality: Your Sons and Daughters with Intellectual Disabilities.* Baltimore, MD: Paul H. Brookes Publishing.

Mesibov, G. "What is TEACCH?" TEACCH website: www.teacch.com/aboutus.html (14 November 2002).

Meyer, D. 1997. *Views from Our Shoes: Growing Up with a Brother or Sister with Special Needs.* Bethesda, MD: Woodbine House.

Meyer, R. N. 2001. *Asperger Syndrome Employment Workbook: An Employment Workbook for Adults with Asperger Syndrome.* London: Jessica Kingsley Publishers.

Mockler Casper, C., K. Timmons, and B. Wagner Brust. 2001. *Emotional Intelligence Leader's Guide.* Carlsbad, CA: CRM Learning.

Mukhopadhyay, T. R. 2003. *The Mind Tree.* New York: Arcade Publishing.

Muller, E., A. Schuler, B. Burton, and G. Yates. (2003). "Meeting the Vocational Support Needs of Individuals with Asperger Syndrome and Other Autism Spectrum Disabilities," *Journal of Vocational Rehabilitation,* 18 (3), 163–176.

————. (2004) Autism: Challenges Relating to Secondary Transition, Alexandria, VA: Project Forum at NASDSE with the US Department of Education's Office of Special Education Programs (OSEP).

Myer, V. 1994. *SibShops: Workshops for Siblings of Children with Special Needs.*

Nally, B. 2000. *Experiences of the Whole Family.* London: The National Autistic Society.

Nally, B., and E. V. Bliss. 2000. *Recognizing and Coping with Stress.* London: The National Autistic Society.

Naseef, R. A. 2001. *Special Children, Challenged Parents: The Struggles and Rewards of Raising a Child with a Disability.* Baltimore, MD: Paul H. Brookes Publishing.

The National Autistic Society. 1991. *Approaches to Autism: An Easy-to-Use Guide to Many and Varied Approaches to Autism.* London: The National Autistic Society.

The National Autistic Society. 1999. *Words Will Really Hurt Me: How to Protect Your Child from Bullying; A Guide for Parents and Carers.* London: The National Autistic Society.

The National Autistic Society. 2002. *The Autism Handbook.* London: The National Autistic Society.

National Center on Secondary Education and Transition. January 2004. "Current Challenges Facing the Future of Secondary Education and Transition Services for Youth with Disabilities in the United States."

National Information Center for Children and Youth with Disabilities. 1999. "Helping Students with Cognitive Disabilities Find and Keep a Job." Technical assistance guide. Volume 3, April 1999.

National Research Council. 2001. *Educating Children with Autism.* Washington, DC: National Academy Press.

Newport, J. 2001. *Your Life Is Not a Label.* Arlington, TX: Future Horizons.

Newport, J., and M. Newport. 2002. *Autism-Asperger's & Sexuality: Puberty and Beyond.* Arlington, TX: Future Horizons.

Notbohm, E., and V. Zysk. 2004. *1001 Great Ideas for Teaching and Raising Children with Autism Spectrum Disorders.* Arlington, TX: Future Horizons.

Nuehring, M. L., and P. L. Sitlington. 2003. "Transition as a Vehicle: Moving from High School to an Adult Vocational Service Provider." *Journal of Disability Policy Studies,* (14)1:23–25.

OASIS Online Asperger Syndrome Information and Support. 2004. "Adult Issues, Resources and Contributions from and for Individuals with AS and Autism." Website: www.udel.edu/bkirby/asperger/personswith.html.

Office of Special Education and Rehabilitative Services in the US Department of Education (2005), Statue Changes in IDEISA'04, Individual Education Program (IEP), www.directionservice.org/cadre/stat_index_ideia.cfm.

O'Neill, J. L. 1999. *Through the Eyes of Aliens: A Book About Autistic People.* London: Jessica Kingsley Publishers.

Oregon Optometric Physicians Association. 1986. *The Effects of Vision on Learning and School Performance.* Milwaukie, OR: Oregon Optometric Physicians Association.

Ozonoff, S., G. Dawson, and J. McPartland. 2002. *A Parent's Guide to Asperger Syndrome & High-Functioning Autism.* New York: The Guilford Press.

Paige, R. 2003. "Principles in Reauthorizing IDEA." Wrightslaw website: wrightslaw.com/news/2003.

Pangborn, J., and S. MacDonald Baker. 2005. *Autism: Effective Biomedical Treatments—Have We Done Everything We Can for This Child? Individuality in an Epidemic.* Boston: DAN!

Paradiz, V. 2002. *Elijah's Cup: A Family's Journey into the Community and Culture of High-Functioning Autism and Asperger's Syndrome.* New York, NY: The Free Press.

Patterson, G. R. 1971. *Families: Applications of Social Learning to Family Life.* Champaign, IL: Research Press.

Peirangelo, R., and R. Crane. 1997. *The Complete Guide to Special Education Services: Ready-to-Use Help and Materials for Successful Transitions from School to Adulthood,* Des Moines, IA: Center for Applied Research in Education, Simon & Schuster.

Peirangelo, R., Guiliani. 2004. *Transition Services in Special Education: A Practical Approach,* Upper Saddle New Jersey: Allyn & Bacon.

Perner, L. "Even if The Emperor *Does* Wear Clothes, Should it Be Everyone's Goal to See This? Planning for a Fulfilling Life." University of California, Riverside.

Perner, L. 2002. "Preparing to Be Nerdy Where Nerdy Can Be Cool: College Planning for the High Functioning Student with Autism." www.professorsadvice.com.

Pollack, A. 2004. "Trials End Parents' Hopes for Autism Drug Secretin." *New York Times* website: www.nytimes.com/2004/01/06/health/06AUTI.html?pagewanted-1.

Powell, A. 2002. *Taking Responsibility: Good Practice Guidelines For Services—Adults with Asperger Syndrome.* London: The National Autistic Society.

Prince-Hughes, D. 2002. *Aquamarine Blue 5.* Athens, OH: Ohio University Press.

———. 2002. *Aquamarine 5: Personal Stories of College Students with Autism,* Athens, Ohio: Swallows Press/ Ohio University Press.

Prince-Hughes, D. 2003. "Understanding College Students with Autism." Washington, DC: The George Washington University HEATH Resource Center.

Protection & Advocacy. 2005. "Special Education Rights and Responsibilities." Protection & Advocacy website: www.pai-ca.org/ (7 June 2005).

Rapp, D. 1996. *Is This Your Child's World? How You Can Fix the Schools and Homes That Are Making Your Child Sick.* New York: Bantam Books.

Richfield, S., with C. Borchert. 2003. *The Parent Coach: A New Approach to Parenting in Today's Society.* Longmont, CO: Sopris West.

Rimland, B. 1964. *Infantile Autism: The Syndrome and Its Implications for a Neural Theory of Behavior.* Prentice Hall.

Rimland, B. 2000. "The Most Airtight Study in Psychiatry? Vitamin B_6 in Autism." *Autism Research Review International* 14: 3–5.

Rosenberg, M. S. 2000. *Everything You Need to Know: When a Brother or Sister is Autistic.* New York: The Rosen Publishing Group.

Rosimos, D. S., and D. L. Wilson. "It's Not About Jobs, It's About Income." Income Links.

Sacks, O. 1995. *An Anthropologist on Mars: Seven Paradoxical Tales.* New York: Alfred A. Knopf.

Sainsbury, C. 2000. *Martian in the Playground.* London: Lucky Duck Publishing.

Segar, M. 1997. "A Survival Guide for People with Asperger Syndrome." Autism and Computing Organization website: www.autismandcomputing.org.uk/marc2.html (18 January 2003).

Semon, B., and L. Kornblum. 2002. *Feast Without Yeast.* Wisconsin: Wisconsin Institute of Nutrition.

Seroussi, K. 2002. *Unraveling the Mystery of Autism and Pervasive Developmental Disorder.* New York: Broadway Books.

Shattock, P., P. Whiteley, and D. Savery. 2002. *Autism as a Metabolic Disorder: Guidelines for Gluten- and Casein-free Dietary Intervention.* Autism Research Unit. University of Sunderland.

Shaw, W. 2002. *Biological Treatment for Autism and PDD.* Website: www.noamalgam.com/biologicaltreatments.html (18 January 2002).

Shellenberger, S., and M. Williams 1992. *An Introduction to "How Does Your Engine Run": The Alert Program and Self-Regulation.* Albuquerque, NM: Therapy Works.

Sherman, D. 2003. "Autism—Your Child's Legal Rights to a Special Education." About Autism Law website: www.aboutautismlaw.com.

Shore, S. "Survival In the Workplace." www.udel.edu/bkirby/asperger/survival_shore.html.

Shore, S. 2001. *Beyond the Wall: Personal Experiences with Autism and Asperger Syndrome.* Shawnee Mission, KS: Autism Asperger Publishing.

Shore, S. 2002. "Dating, Marriage and Autism." *Advocate* 35: 24–28.

Shore, S. M., et al. 2004. *Ask and Tell: Self-Advocacy and Disclosure for People on the Autism Spectrum.* Shawnee Mission, KS: Autism Asperger Publishing.

Sicile-Kira, C. 2004. *Autism Spectrum Disorders: The Complete Guide to Understanding Autism, Asperger's Syndrome, Pervasive Development Disorder, and Other ASDs.* New York: Perigee.

Slater-Walker, G., and C. Slater-Walker. 1988. *An Asperger Marriage.* London: Jessica Kingsley Publishers.

Small, M., and L. Kontente. 2003. *Everyday Solutions: A Practical Guide for*

Families of Children with Autism Spectrum Disorders. Shawnee Mission, KS: Autism Asperger Publishing.

Smith Myles, B., and D. Adreon. 2001. *Asperger Syndrome and Adolescence: Practical Solutions for School Success*. Shawnee Mission, KS: Autism Asperger Publishing.

Smith Myles, B., M. L. Trautman, and R. L. Schelvan. 2004. *The Hidden Curriculum: Practical Solutions for Understanding Unstated Rules in Social Situations*. Shawnee Mission, KS: Autism Asperger Publishing.

Sohn, A., and C. Grayson. 2005. *Parenting Your Asperger Child: Individualized Solutions for Teaching Your Child Practical Skills*. New York: Perigee.

Stanberry, K. 2004. "The Individual Transition Plan—An Overview." Schwab Learning website: www.SchwabLearning.org.

Stehli, A. 1991. *The Sound of a Miracle*. New York: Avon Books.

Stengle, L. J. 1996. *Laying Community Foundations for Your Child with a Disability: How to Establish Relationships That Will Support Your Child after You're Gone*. Bethesda, MD: Woodbine House.

Strohm, K. 2002. *Being the Other One: Growing Up with a Brother or Sister Who Has Special Needs*. Boston, MA: Shambhala Publications.

Sullivan, R. 2001. "Position Paper on the National Crisis in Adult Services for Individuals with Autism: A Call to Action." San Diego, CA: Autism Society of America.

Sullivan R. C. 2004. "Lifetime Services for Individuals with Autism: A Working, Community-Integrated Model." Trainland website: trainland.tripod.com/ruthchrist.htm.

Tantam, D., and S. Prestwood. 1999. *A Mind of One's Own: A Guide to the Special Difficulties and Needs of the More Able Person with Autism or Asperger Syndrome*. London: The National Autistic Society.

Timetable for Autism: An Overview of Educating Children and Young People with Autistic Spectrum Disorders. 1999. London: The National Autistic Society.

"Transition." Wrightslaw website: wrightslaw.com/info/trans.index.htm (25 March 2005).

Twachtman-Cullen, D., and J. Twachtman-Reilly. 2002. *How Well Does Your IEP Measure Up? Quality Indicators for Effective Service Delivery*. Higganum, CT: Starfish Speciality Press.

U.S. Department of Education. 2002. *Executive Summary—Twenty-fourth Annual Report to Congress on the Implementation of the Individuals with Disabilities Education Act*. Ed.gov website:www.ed.gov.

Vatter, G. "Group Homes and Other Alternatives." Website: www.geocities.com/Heartland/Woods2869/alternatives.html.

Vermeulen, P. 2000. *I Am Special: Introducing Children and Young People to Their Autism Spectrum Disorder*. London: Jessica Kingsley Publishers.

Wallace, T. 2003. "Paraprofessionals." Florida: University of Florida, Center on Personnel Studies in Special Education.

Wehman, P. 2001. *Life Beyond the Classroom: Transition Strategies for Young People with Disabilities*. Baltimore, MD: Paul H. Brookes Publishing.

Weider, S., and S. Greenspan. 2003. "Climbing the Symbolic Ladder in the DIR Model Through Floor Time/Interactive Play" Sage Publications and the National Autistic Society.

Welton, J. 2004. *What Did You Say? What Did You Mean? An Illustrated Guide to Understanding Metaphors*. London: Jessica Kingsley Publishers.

Wheeler, M. 2004. *Toilet Training for Individuals with Autism & Related Disorders: A Comprehensive Guide for Parents & Teachers*. Arlington, TX: Future Horizons.

Wilens, T. E. 2004. *Straight Talk About Psychiatric Medications for Kids*. New York: The Guildford Press.

Willey, L. H. 1999. *Pretending to be Normal: Living with Asperger's Syndrome*. London: Jessica Kingsley Publishers. Reproduced with the permission of Jessica Kingsley Publishers.

Willey, L. H. 2003. *Asperger Syndrome in Adolescence: Living with the Ups, the Downs and Things in Between*. London: Jessica Kingsley Publishers.

Willey, L. H. 2001. *Asperger Syndrome in the Family: Redefining Normal*. London: Jessica Kingsley Publishers.

Williams, D. 1988. *Autism: An Inside-Out Approach*. London: Jessica Kingsley Publishers.

Williams, D. 1992. *Nobody Nowhere*. New York: Times Books.

Williams, D. 1994 *Somebody Somewhere*. London: Transworld Publishers.

Williams, D. 2004. *Everyday Heaven*. London: Jessica Kingsley Publishers.

Wing, L. 1981. "Asperger Syndrome: A Clinical Account." London: The National Autistic Society.

Wing, L. 2001., *The Autistic Spectrum*. London: Ulysses Press.

Wright, P. W .D., and P. D. Wright. 2002. "Wrightslaw: Special Education Law." Hartfield, VA: Harbor House Law Press.

Wright, P. W. D. "Wrightslaw: Alert! Proposed IDEA 2004 regulations Available Now!" *The Special Ed Advocate Newsletter,* 12 June 2005. website: www.Wrightslaw.com/idea/law.htm (11 June 2005).

Wrobel, M. 2003. *Taking Care of Myself: A Hygiene, Puberty and Personal Curriculum for Young People with Autism*. Arlington, TX: Future Horizons.

Permissions Information for *Adolsecents on the Autism Spectrum*

INDEX

Epic Photojournalism

Chantal Sicile-Kira is a national speaker and advocate who has been involved with autism spectrum disorders for nearly twenty years as both a parent and a professional. Her first book, *Autism Spectrum Disorders,* was the recipient of the 2005 Autism Society of America's Outstanding Literary Work of the Year Award. A former researcher on BBC documentaries and a line producer for a TV series in Paris, France, she currently hosts a weekly radio show "The Real World of Autism" on Autism One Radio (www.autism one.org), and writes for various publications. She sits on the advisory board or board of directors of various non-profits, and is the founder of Autism: Making a Difference. With the help of her son, she continues to train future autism professionals. For more information visit www.chantal sicile-kira.com.